Staging the Other in Nineteenth-Century British Drama

Writing and Culture in the Long Nineteenth Century

Edited by J.B. Bullen and Isobel Armstrong

PETER LANG
Oxford • Bern • Berlin • Bruxelles • Frankfurt am Main • New York • Wien

Staging the Other in Nineteenth-Century British Drama

Tiziana Morosetti (ed.)

PETER LANG
Oxford • Bern • Berlin • Bruxelles • Frankfurt am Main • New York • Wien

Bibliographic information published by Die Deutsche Nationalbibliothek.
Die Deutsche Nationalbibliothek lists this publication in the Deutsche Nationalbibliografie; detailed bibliographic data is available on the Internet at http://dnb.d-nb.de.

A catalogue record for this book is available from the British Library.

Library of Congress Control Number: 2015952197

Cover image: Detail from a hand-coloured lithograph from the title page of *The Will and The Way*, Purkess's Penny Pictorial Plays, no.21. Courtesy of the Special Collections and Archives, Templeman Library, University of Kent, Canterbury, UK.

ISSN 2235-2287
ISBN 978-3-0343-1928-7 (print)
ISBN 978-3-0353-0777-1 (eBook)

Hochfeldstrasse 32, CH-3012 Bern, Switzerland
info@peterlang.com, www.peterlang.com, www.peterlang.net

This publication has been peer reviewed.

Printed in Germany

Contents

Figures

TIZIANA MOROSETTI

Introduction

This volume is the outcome of the international conference *The 'Exotic' Body in Nineteenth-century British Drama* (Oxford, 25–6 September 2014), itself one of the dissemination activities of a two-year project on the same topic I undertook as a Marie Curie Research Fellow at Oxford between 2012 and 2014. The conference provided a true testing ground for that project, the main goal of which – an exhaustive bibliography of all plays featuring 'exotic' characters, settings, and themes on the nineteenth-century British stage – demanded clarification first of all regarding that very term, 'exotic'. Inverted commas abounded in my notes, and the conference seemed somewhat bound to confirm the caution of my approach, if only because 'exotic' is a term that still awaits full canonization within studies of Empire and its cultural background, its employment, especially since the publication of Graham Huggan's ground-breaking study,[1] mainly established within the postcolonial context. Had not delegates accepted the challenge implied by the call for papers, then, and proposed their own definitions of 'exotic', I would have most certainly ended up overlooking its possibilities as a critical term, and for this, I remain deeply thankful for a conference that was as varied as it was rich.

After all, it is only in a second definition of the word that 'exotic' may mean 'Outlandish, barbarous, strange, uncouth. Also, having the attraction of the strange or foreign, glamorous' (OED) – all adjectives that sit particularly well within a theatrical context in which cultural and ethnic difference, often elaborated through the lenses of Empire, held great fascination for audiences. In the main definition of the word, however, that is, 'Belonging to another

1 Graham Huggan, *The Postcolonial Exotic: Marketing the Margins* (London and New York: Routledge, 2001).

country, foreign, alien', or, in a narrower sense, 'Introduced from abroad, not indigenous' (OED), 'exotic' is still largely under-used to describe 'otherness' in nineteenth-century British culture. Yet, it is this technical acceptation that best describes a case such as that of the Māoris on the London stage of the 1860s, or that of the increasingly popular human zoos, in which actual 'savages' were displayed and performed – whereas other terms, such as 'picturesque', often recurrent in relation to the often fascinating features of Georgian and Victorian theatre, remain as vague as they are informed by negative connotations.

What the conference achieved was in particular to highlight how 'exotic' as a critical term can complement and complicate visions of the Other. While, as Toni Wein points out in the essay that opens this collection, 'it is the very physicality of the marker that distinguishes the exotic body as different from any other Other', in nineteenth-century drama such physicality worked towards hierarchies in the way people of non-British origin especially were portrayed on stage. As we shall see in the latter part of this introduction, and as pointed out by many of the contributions gathered in this volume, these *degrees of exoticism* often went in parallel with the degree of realism employed on stage. The 'exotic' body came to represent a particular type of Other, a spatial or geographical variation of 'otherness', as Zara Barlas suggests, with specific visual connotations that rendered non-European bodies in particular immediately recognizable on stage. Yet, interpreted as basically an 'unusual corporeal body', as Arthur W. Bloom has it, the 'exotic' also applies to a number of less obvious examples than the Māori or the Zulu, such as the sailor – the press-ganged sailor in particular, 'often conceived as a primitive being dwelling on the margins of civilization', as Sara Malton explains – thus embracing virtually each and every character, each and every costume. In fact, if we accept Jonathan Arac and Harriet Rivo's definition of 'exoticism' as 'the aestheticizing means by which the pain of [imperial] expansion is converted to spectacle, to culture in the service of empire',[2] it is

2 Jonathan Arac and Harriet Rivo, eds, *Macropolitics of Nineteenth-Century Literature: Nationalism, Exoticism, Imperialism* (Philadelphia: University of Pennsylvania Press, 1991), 3.

the entire theatrical process that came to be 'exotic' in nineteenth-century Britain. The spectacular nature, as well as the consistent exaggeration of genres like the pantomime, the extravaganza or the melodrama tended to reverberate on all characters and settings involved, so that theatre 'rendered people, objects and places strange even as it domesticated them',[3] as Graham Huggan has it. In this light, even Britain and the British could be portrayed in a very 'exotic' light.

Staging the Other in Nineteenth-Century British Drama includes a selection of the papers presented at the conference (plus three contributions – mine, Schultz's, and Yeandle's[4] – that were not in the programme), and while it sets out to expand on the issues delineated above, it also proposes a specific focus on the body and the bodily – be it the fictional body of characters as they walk through the copious examples of 'exotic', imperial-themed, foreign-oriented drama, and/or the actual body of the actors/actresses that impersonated them. 'Complicit in colonial and imperial methods of domination' (Toni Wein) as they were, 'exotic' bodies 'served to enforce colonial ideologies and help generate support for British foreign policy' (Peter Yeandle), but they also exposed the 'topsy-turvydom', in Serena Guarracino's term, that often accompanied the process of othering on the Georgian and Victorian stages.

Not limited to an analysis of costumes and staging techniques, this collection involves a discussion of all things visual, from make-up to settings, without forgetting, however, that in many cases it is still *texts* that we are confronted by – both printed plays and the texts (reviews, contemporary criticism, etc.) – through which many of these performances have survived down to us. Although it is physical bodies that represent diversity on stage, 'When a character is offered or received as exotic, ethnically different, or ethnically typical in some way, these qualities derive from cultural texts in circulation, rather than from physical bodies' themselves, as Michael Bradshaw points out. This is particularly true for nineteenth-century British theatre, the recurrent intertextuality of which, born out of a general trend to

3 Huggan, *The Postcolonial Exotic*, 13.

4 Peter Yeandle was a keynote speaker at the conference, but spoke on a different topic.

borrow from a variety of sources, was enhanced by a competition between venues so fierce that plays and performances were consistently recycled in a self-nurturing struggle for survival.

However, while drama, not theatre,[5] is the main focus or starting point for most contributions in this collection, it is important to stress that any understanding of 'drama' as a 'script for theatrical performance'[6] does *not* necessarily imply an accordingly hierarchical understanding of authorship. In a context in which 'virtually anybody could write a play – and virtually everybody did',[7] as Frank Rahill has it, playwrights were also often performers and/or managers at once, so that authorship became intangible and virtually inseparable from production – what Jacky Bratton has termed the *intertheatricality*,[8] and Jane Moody the *ventriloquism*[9] of nineteenth-century British drama.

Nor does the investigation of 'drama' in this volume rule out an examination of popular entertainment as well, the contamination between the two – a relevant reason for the nineteenth century being long regarded as 'the nadir of the English drama, the decades when [...] dogs sometimes

5 See the distinction drawn by Keir Elam, according to which 'theatre' is 'the complex of phenomena associated with the performer-audience transaction: that is, with the production and communication of meaning in the performance itself and with the systems underlying it', while 'drama' is 'the mode of fiction designed for stage representation and constructed according to particular ("dramatic") conventions'. Keir Elam, *The Semiotics of Theatre and Drama* (London and New York: Routledge, 2002), 2.

6 Simon Shepherd and Mick Wallis, *Drama/Theatre/Performance* (London and New York: Routledge, 2004), 163.

7 Frank Rahill, *The World of Melodrama* (University Park and London: The Pennsylvania State University Press, 1967), 173.

8 Jacky Bratton, 'Jane Scott the Writer-Manager', in Tracy C. Davis and Ellen Donkin, eds, *Women and Playwriting in Nineteenth-century Britain* (Cambridge: Cambridge University Press, 1999), 77–98, 77.

9 Jane Moody, 'Illusions of Authorship', in Tracy C. Davis and Ellen Donkin, eds, *Women and Playwriting in Nineteenth-century Britain* (Cambridge: Cambridge University Press, 1999), 99–124, 107.

had more lines to deliver than great tragedians'[10] – remaining a key feature of Georgian and Victorian theatre. When lamenting the lack of 'works of a truly permanent value',[11] it is their uneasiness at this hybridity that critics have often expressed, above all when trying to establish sure criteria of 'merit' or hierarchies within the intricate world of nineteenth-century performing arts. This is the case with an essay published in 1980, Anthony Coxe's 'Equestrian drama and the Circus', the interest of which lies in its attempt to draw a clear line between *fiction* and *reality*. Equestrian drama, one of the most popular genres of the century, is by the author defined thus:

> A bastard entertainment, the result of a misalliance between the theatre and the circus. The spectacle is seen against a representational background. In the traditional theatre the audience is confronted with make-believe on the stage. Go backstage and the illusion is lost [...]. In the circus there is no scenery, no backstage; the spectacle can be seen from all sides, like sculpture. Because the audience holds the spectacle in its midst, there are eyes all round to see that there is no make-believe.[12]

To see the theatre as 'interpretative', and therefore an art, and the circus as 'demonstrative', and therefore 'simply a craft', just because, as the author goes on, 'after all, jugglers *actually do* keep six clubs turning in mid-air',[13] seems to ignore that there are, without saying, a number of other tricks in the circus for which some suspension of disbelief *is* in fact required (unless one wishes to believe that a woman can be seriously split in six, or that a fire-eater will actually eat fire).

Beside the theoretical objections that one may have against Coxe's argument, however,[14] what matters here is that his interpretation does not

10 Elaine Hadley, *Melodramatic Tactics: Theatricalized Dissent in the English Marketplace, 1800–1885* (Stanford University Press, 1995), 2.

11 Allardyce Nicoll, *A History of English Drama* (Cambridge: Cambridge University Press, 1952–59), vol. IV, 1800–1850, 59.

12 Antony D. Hippisley Coxe, 'Equestrian Drama and the Circus', in David Bradby, Louis James, Bernard Sharratt, eds, *Performance and Politics in Popular Drama* (Cambridge: Cambridge University Press, 1980), 109–18, 109.

13 Ibid.

14 On the one hand, it may be pointed out that the circus has its own narrative, as the ability of a juggler is not independent of how it is presented to the audience, nor is the

do any justice to the specific notion of circus (or theatre, for that matter) in the nineteenth century. In the frenzy for novelty that was characteristic of the whole century, and laid the train for much of the 'exotic' on stage, reality and fiction did often overlap – both on stage and in the ring – to present audiences with pieces of 'realism' or 'truth' that were, however, all invariably subject to illusion. This is a point 'Lord' George Sanger (1825–1911), himself a liminal figure between the circus and the theatre, stresses beautifully in several passages of his *Seventy Years a Showman*. Audience expectations were central in defining what a show *should have been* about, so that when, later in the century, as a renowned and wealthy manager, Sanger decided to put a white elephant on show, although he could have acquired a proper one, he only exhibited one that had been whitewashed. The actual, sacred 'white' elephant was in fact not properly white, and therefore unfit for business, while 'the people wanted a white elephant, so [...], assisting nature with art, gave them what they desired – a handsome creature white as driven snow'.[15]

The point is of central relevance to the topic of this collection, as issues of 'authenticity' are as problematic as they are unavoidable in examining representations of the Other on the nineteenth-century British stage. Whatever degree of 'exoticness' was presented to the audience, it had

---

audience's enjoyment of that ability neutral or insensitive to the liminal, provisional, and, indeed, *fictional* space provided by the circus. On the other, theatre must also be said to have its good share of 'reality'. Because, of course, Coxe is right in seeing equestrian drama as a cross-over between theatre and the circus: as in the theatre, the plot, the characters, the scenery are fictional; as in the circus, the horses on stage are real, the rider is an actual rider, and the skills a rider needs are also real, as they stay with him or her when the show is over. But what about an actor that only *pretends* to be a rider (or a juggler)? After all, the *body* of the actor/actress, like the body of the rider, is all we have both on and off stage; it is the same body (however different its function) as it steps in and out of fiction; it is a real body, that no fiction can prevent from accidentally falling off a stage (or off a horse); and the skills an actor needs to make a convincing rider or juggler on stage will also stay with them when their performance is over. Even a fictional juggler may have to be able to actually keep six clubs turning in mid-air.

15 'Lord' George Sanger, *Seventy Years a Showman* (London and Toronto: J.M. Dent and Sons Ltd, 1926), 271.

to respond to specific expectations, so that, in the case of the American actor Edwin Forrest, for instance, 'his acting style and the original plays in which he performed were designed to create an American persona and to reinforce both English and American assumptions about what that persona would be', as Arthur W. Bloom reminds us. Similarly, as I show in my own essay, theatrical constructions of the Zulus and their counterpart in human zoos were centred on what the Zulus, the 'Kaffirs' more generally, were assumed to be by British audiences. Whether it was actual 'savages' that were displayed on stage or their blackface impersonations made little difference as for their presumed 'authenticity'. 'Real savages' also had to impersonate themselves, as they were to embody in their performances what was expected of them in terms of savagery, dangerousness, and striking appearance. Ira Aldridge's 'self-staging as an exotic African prince', as Sophie Duncan shows in her essay, is yet another example of this process.

Presented as 'authentic', not all landscapes and/or costumes resembled a verisimilitude to the original, the degree of realism employed on stage betraying in many ways the degree of exoticism attached to any given production. On the one hand, the overlapping of 'real' and fictional elements was partly due to historical circumstances; in the case of colonial melodrama, for instance, as argued by Heidi Holder, its origins 'in the traditions of equestrian, military and aquatic melodrama [...] ensured a persistent emphasis on physical realism and historical accuracy'[16] but also meant the permanence of a 'fantasy element' that was kept 'alive and present on the stage'.[17] On the other hand, however, different political and cultural perceptions of the Other also contributed to its diversification on stage, stressing 'fact' and fiction differently according to who or what was being portrayed. Whereas, for example, 'spectacle and authenticity went hand in hand in the

16 Heidi J. Holder, 'Melodrama, Realism and Empire on the British Stage', in J.S. Bratton, Richard Allen Cave, Breandan Gregory, Heidi J. Holder and Michael Pickering, eds, *Acts of Supremacy: The British Empire and the Stage, 1790–1930* (Manchester and New York: Manchester University Press, 1991), 129–49, 132.

17 Ibid.

recreation of the Ancient World',[18] although ancient Egypt in particular certainly 'appealed to the cult of the picturesque',[19] other 'exotic' productions such as those dealing with the war of Crimea showed, as observed by Jacky Bratton, 'little regard for actual events'.[20] In a production of *The Passage of the Deserts*, a play set in Egypt during the Napoleon Campaigns, a llama and a wild zebra were introduced, and yet another zebra crossed Tartary in a production of *Mazeppa*, Andrew Ducrow not seeming to care much 'for correctness of local colouring' if he could 'produce an effect by disregarding it', as A.H. Saxon has it.[21]

The 'effect' at which most productions were aimed in nineteenth-century Britain should not, however, lead us to false conclusions about audiences. As Jim Davis and Victor Emeljanow have argued in their seminal *Reflecting the Audience*, audiences have also been constructed as credulous, illiterate, coarse and aggressive in the overall 'mythologized picture'[22] of nineteenth-century theatre, with East End theatres in particular being portrayed by West End critics as 'something remote and "other"'.[23] We may be tempted today to dismiss the audiences' reactions to 'exotic' performances as exploitative and racist, or to see these audiences as fundamentally *unaware* of the propaganda that was poured on them, but, as I will argue further in my conclusion, audiences may well also have been *made* aware, if not of the political message, of the tricks that such message conveyed. While it is in fact undeniable that performances such as the pantomime 'operated as a cultural site for the dissemination of imperial ideology' (Yeandle), given that it is first and utmost to 'illegitimate' genres, as convincingly argued

18 Jeffrey Richards, *The Ancient World on the Victorian and Edwardian Stage* (Basingstoke: Palgrave Macmillan, 2009), 23.

19 Richards, *The Ancient World*, 17.

20 J.S. Bratton, 'Theatre of War: The Crimea on the London Stage 1854–5', in David Bradby, Louis James, Bernard Sharratt, eds, *Performance and Politics in Popular Dram* (Cambridge: Cambridge University Press, 1980), 119–37, 121.

21 A.H. Saxon, *Enter Foot and Horse: A History of Hippodrama in England and France* (New Haven and London: Yale University Press, 1968), 187.

22 Jim Davis and Victor Emeljanow, *Reflecting the Audience: London Theatregoing 1840–1880* (Iowa City: University of Iowa Press, 2001), 97.

23 Davis and Emeljanow, *Reflecting the Audience*, 46.

by Jane Moody, that we have to turn to understand 'how British imperialism was being transformed into dramatic spectacle',[24] the ambiguity of a theatrical culture that at the same time hid and highlighted the artificiality of such propaganda must yet also be kept in mind.

This is a particularly interesting point made by the opening essay, Toni Wein's '"By a Nose" or "By a Hair": Bearding the Jew on the Georgian Stage', which, analysing the beard as a signifier of Jewish 'exoticness', stresses how 'The more the beard becomes a metonymic displacement for the Jew, the more its function as a reality effect calls attention to itself, forcing the thing to simultaneously avow and disavow its own status'. In marking the difference between Edmund Kean's and Charles Macklin's interpretation of Shylock, the beard more generally became, on the Georgian stage, a 'detachable, reproduceable, and hence convertible meme for Jewishness' – but as such, also an obvious, hyper-visible mark of difference.

A counterpoint to Wein's analysis is Michael Bradshaw's 'The Jew on Stage and on the Page: Intertextual Exotic', which takes into account two plays in particular, Henry Hart Milman's *Fazio* (1815), and Thomas Wade's *The Jew of Arragon; or, the Hebrew Queen* (1830), the former employing in his central character a 'disguised deployment of some of the distinctive features of Jewish caricature', so that, although it does not openly feature any Jewish character, the play nonetheless contributed to a stereotype that was mainly the result of intertextuality. Both Wein and Bradshaw also aptly show how the Jewish stereotype tended to incorporate characteristics that were common to other 'Oriental' types, such as circumcision, equally 'a marker for Islam, especially in the form of the threatening power of the Ottoman Empire', as Bradshaw has it.

As Arthur W. Bloom reminds us in his 'Edwin Forrest: The Exotic American Body on the Nineteenth-Century English Stage', however, the 'exotic' body on the nineteenth-century stage need not be associated necessarily with the features, as mysterious as they are often vague, of any 'Oriental' type, nor with those, even more alien, of the black African, as

24 Jane Moody, *Illegitimate Theatre in London, 1770–1840* (Cambridge: Cambridge University Press, 2000), 7.

'[d]uring 1836, 1837, 1845 and 1846 the exotic body on the English stage was male, white, muscular and American'. In impersonating the protagonists of John Augustus Stone's *Metamora; or, the Last of the Wampanoags* and Robert Montgomery Bird's *The Gladiator*, Forrest 'appeared to embody American freedom while simultaneously foretelling the tragic fate of the Indian and the slave'.

But readers will not fail to note interesting similarities between the masculinity displayed by Forrest, and that of two undeniably 'exotic' and 'picturesque' groups: the Zulus and the Māori. In my contribution, I juxtapose two famous exhibitions of Zulus, Charles Caldecott's 'Zulu Kaffirs' (1853) and Farini's 'Friendly Zulus' (1879) with their theatrical counterpart, in particular Edward Fitzball's *Amakosa; or, Kaffir Warfare* (1853) and *The Grand Equestrian Spectacle of the War in Zululand* (1879). In constructing the body of the Zulu so as to highlight the valour of British troops on the South African fronts, these performances built on ideas about the 'African' body that reveal mixed, diversified, and often contradictory attitudes towards the 'dark' continent.

The sensation pursued by these performances was also at the core of productions featuring real Māori actors: *Wahena; or The Maori Queen* (Princess's Theatre, Edinburgh, 1863) and J.B. Johnstone's *The Emigrant's Trial; or, Life in New Zealand* (Marylebone Theatre, London, 1864). As in the case of the Zulus, the Māori are also perceived as a 'superior class of men and women', and as such distinct from the 'lower' savages of other areas of the Empire. But the interest in Marianne Schultz's essay, which presents rarely investigated materials, lies also in that it highlights how Māori on stage – be it in theatrical performances or in more scientific-oriented displays such as that of fourteen 'New Zealand Native Chiefs' assembled at the Alhambra Palace Theatre, Leicester Square, in 1863 – were not just presenting themselves, but more often *performing* themselves to the delight of British audiences.

The 'enacted' body of the Other, as Peter Yeandle shows in his 'Performing the Other on the Popular London Stage: Exotic People and Places in Victorian Pantomime', is employed in constant juxtaposition to that, both political and actual, of the British, so that 'the contrast of "home" and "foreign" bodies' in Victorian pantomime actively contributed 'to collective identity formation'. Employing significant quantitative analysis, and investigating two main areas – pantomimic responses to the Indian Rebellion of 1857 and the evolution of the *Jack and the Beanstalk* story in the second part of the century – this essay also explores the relation between bodies and landscapes, as it is the place that first 'positioned the "other" beyond civilization itself', so that it is the overall visual concept of pantomime that must be examined so as to best appreciate its political impact.

While nineteenth-century theatre was, as mentioned above, highly intertextual in its approach, Sara Malton's 'Impressment, Exoticism and Enslavement: Revisiting the Theatre of War through Thomas Hardy's *The Trumpet-Major* (1880)' is an important contribution regarding that other main area of exchange: that between theatre and the novel. In this essay, however, it is not the way theatre responded to the publication of relevant novels that is investigated, but rather the way in which the novel, and one author in particular, Thomas Hardy, responded to the stimuli of the theatrical experience. Through a discussion of a specific but wide-impacting phenomenon, impressment or coerced naval service, Malton investigates the way 'historical novels often notably revisit and revise earlier dramatic forms in order to foreground the pressed sailor's plight, exoticism, and [...] his connection to slavery', focusing in particular on how *The Trumpet Major* was informed by pantomime.

A thorough examination of a telling case of 'exotic' body, that of the nautch girl, is instead at the core of Zara Barlas's 'Transcultural Operatics: India on the British Stage in *The Nautch Girl, or, The Rajah of Chutneypore*', in which Edward Solomon's 1891 operetta and the visual features of its early twentieth-century productions are in particular explored, as 'Musical entertainments set in "exotic" locations often relied on visual hints and pointers to locate the work in a specific regional and cultural setting'. While '*authenticity* was an inherent aspect of this artwork', changes in costumes and settings reveal evolving attitudes towards India and nautch girls specifically, but also, as the essay argues, the limits of a genre, comic operetta, the main intention of which 'was to provide light entertainment'.

The last two contributions in this collection, Serena Guarracino's 'Singing the Exotic Body across the Atlantic: From *The Mikado* to the *Swing Mikado* and Beyond' and Sophie Duncan's 'A Progressive *Othello*:

Modern Blackness in Chakrabarti's *Red Velvet* (2012)', move steadily to the twentieth and twenty-first centuries to investigate the legacy of nineteenth-century British drama and, in particular, that of its 'exotic' portraits. Also a contribution on musical theatre, Guarracino's focuses on the fortune of Gilbert and Sullivan's *The Mikado* 'not as a vehicle for staging the Other but as an exotic body *per se*, whose permanence in contemporary theatres allows for a continuous redefinition of what stands as Other'. A production in particular, the all-black *Swing Mikado*, staged in Chicago in 1939, is examined here to show how the 'Japan of pure invention' that emerged from *The Mikado* found inspiring and unexpected re-interpretations in the contemporary Anglophone world, amongst which a 2011 Opera Australia production in which 'the Victorian and Japanese exotic are so intertwined as to become practically indistinguishable'.

Last but not least, Sophie Duncan's essay invites us to follow Adrian Lester as Ira Aldridge on the stage of Lolita Chakrabarti's recent *Red Velvet* to consider the way this 'speculative restaging of Aldridge's *Othello* associates nineteenth-century blackness not merely with the "exotic", but also emphatically with the modern and progressive'. Chakrabarti's 'redeployment of historical material' – if at times loosely interpreted, as shown by Duncan through a punctual and painstaking reconstruction of contexts and sources – supports a view of Aldridge's diversity as aligned to 'multiple progressive figures marginalized by their radical identities and networks'.

The political connotation of contemporary readings of nineteenth-century drama further adds to a theatrical landscape already ripe with cultural and social implications. Far from representing only a (considerable) portion of Georgian and Victorian entertainment, 'exotic' performances are particularly endowed to shed light on the complex mechanisms underlying the relation between theatre and the Empire. Never as straightforward and hierarchical as the renowned educational role of Victorian entertainment may lead us to believe, this relation is further complicated by the employment of staging devices that, as mentioned earlier, are presented as 'authentic' but are obviously the result of artefact. This inherent ambiguity is also what should alert us to the possibility that audiences may have been fully aware of the propaganda machine that nineteenth-century drama could be.

In commenting on two of his shows in particular, 'Shoal of Trained Fish in their Exhibition of a Naval Engagement' and 'The Wonderful Performing Fish and a Tame Oyster that sits by the fire and smokes his yard of clay', 'Lord' George Sanger again explains that the public craved 'novelty' so much that it was no problem, really, should the novelty disappoint, because 'they liked to see others gulled as well as themselves, so the *game* went merrily on'.[25] Earlier on in the century, when Sanger was still working with his father on the peepshow, having candles at night was once more not a problem, because 'No doubt the candles, placed as they were, detracted from the effect of the pictures, but people in those days were not so particular as they are now, and as long as they had plenty of colour in the backgrounds were perfectly satisfied'.[26] Although these comments may today sound very derogatory, they nonetheless suggest that audiences may have not been completely oblivious of the *game*, as Sanger himself calls it, that bringing novelty to them implied. This does not rule out complicity. But it allows us for more nuanced, intriguing readings of the nineteenth-century theatrical landscape, the contradictions of which mirrors those of an extraordinary century.

Acknowledgements

The research leading to this publication received funding from the People Programme (Marie Curie Actions) of the European Union's Seventh Framework Programme (FP7/2007–2013) under REA grant agreement n° 299000. I am also indebted to staff at the University of Kent Special Collections, the British Library, the National Fairground Archive at the University of Sheffield and the Harvard Theatre Collection for their support. This volume would have not been possible without the enthusiasm

25 'Lord' Sanger, *Seventy Years a Showman*, 56. Emphasis added.
26 Ibid.

and competence of Laurel Plapp at Peter Lang, to whom I am grateful for hosting this publication. But my warmest thanks go to all delegates and keynote speakers at the conference, for an inspiring debate and for their encouragement, as well as to Kirsten Shepherd-Barr for her consistent support and feedback on my project. The Faculty of English at Oxford, in the persons of Elleke Boehmer, Sos Eltis, Sally Shuttleworth, Michèle Mendelssohn, and Michelle Kelly in particular, made me feel very welcome, and was an excellent host for the conference. The stimulating discussions provided by the Postcolonial Seminar, the Victorian Literature Seminar and the Race and Resistance Network also helped clarify many issues concerning the 'exotic' and its interpretation. Last but not least, my thanks go to Luke, as always, for his feedback and love – and for Noemi Rose.

Bibliography

Arac, Jonathan, and Harriet Rivo, eds, *Macropolitics of Nineteenth-Century Literature: Nationalism, Exoticism, Imperialism* (Philadelphia: University of Pennsylvania Press, 1991).

Bratton, J.S., 'Theatre of War: the Crimea on the London Stage 1854–5', in David Bradby, Louis James, Bernard Sharratt, eds, *Performance and Politics in Popular Drama* (Cambridge: Cambridge University Press 1980), 119–37.

——, 'Jane Scott the Writer-Manager', in Tracy C. Davis and Ellen Donkin, eds, *Women and Playwriting in Nineteenth-century Britain* (Cambridge: Cambridge University Press, 1999), 77–98.

Coxe, Antony D. Hippisley, 'Equestrian Drama and the Circus', in David Bradby, Louis James, Bernard Sharratt, eds, *Performance and Politics in Popular Drama* (Cambridge: Cambridge University Press, 1980), 109–18.

Davis, Jim, and Victor Emeljanow, *Reflecting the Audience: London Theatregoing 1840–1880* (Iowa City: University of Iowa Press, 2001).

Elam, Keir D., *The Semiotics of Theatre and Drama* (London and New York: Routledge, 2002).

Hadley, Elaine, *Melodramatic Tactics: Theatricalized Dissent in the English Marketplace, 1800–1885* (Stanford: Stanford University Press, 1995).

Holder, Heidi J. 'Melodrama, Realism and Empire on the British Stage', in J.S. Bratton, Richard Allen Cave, Breandan Gregory, Heidi J. Holder and Michael Pickering, eds, *Acts of Supremacy: The British Empire and the Stage, 1790–1930* (Manchester and New York: Manchester University Press, 1991), 129–49.

Huggan, Graham, *The Postcolonial Exotic: Marketing the Margins* (London and New York: Routledge, 2001).

Moody, Jane, 'Illusions of authorship', in Tracy C. Davis and Ellen Donkin, eds, *Women and Playwriting in Nineteenth-century Britain* (Cambridge: Cambridge University Press, 1999), 99–124.

——, *Illegitimate Theatre in London, 1770–1840* (Cambridge: Cambridge University Press, 2000).

Nicoll, Allardyce, *A History of English Drama* (Cambridge: Cambridge University Press, 1952–59), vol. IV, 1800–1850.

Rahill, Frank, *The World of Melodrama* (University Park and London: The Pennsylvania State University Press, 1967).

Richards, Jeffrey, *The Ancient World on the Victorian and Edwardian Stage* (Basingstoke: Palgrave Macmillan, 2009).

Sanger, 'Lord' George, *Seventy Years a Showman* (London and Toronto: J.M. Dent and Sons Ltd, 1926).

Saxon, A.H., *Enter Foot and Horse: A History of Hippodrama in England and France* (New Haven and London: Yale University Press, 1968).

Shepherd, Simon, and Mick Wallis, *Drama/Theatre/Performance* (London and New York: Routledge, 2004).

TONI WEIN

'By a Nose' or 'By a Hair': Bearding the Jew on the Georgian Stage

ABSTRACT

As long ago as 1990, Roy Porter and G.S. Rousseau called for Jews to be considered under the sign of exotica. Like nabobs and other colonial figures, Jews straddled the divide between alien and native, outsiders and in. This talk maps the evolution of physical markers for the stage Jew that take hold toward the end of the eighteenth century.

As farces of the period increasingly target anxieties about Jewish assimilation, Jewish characters cease being represented as clean-shaven and accoutred like, nay sharing the very clothes of, the Christian British gentry, in all the current fashion. Instead, they begin wearing beards as their ethnic stamp. I compare 1780's *A Specimen of Jewish Education* and its companion, *A Specimen of Jewish Courtship* (1787), whose characters share the bare faces of current fashion, with two watershed plays a few years later: Kemble's 1790 licensing for Drury Lane of a farce originally titled *The Jew's Beard* but presented as *Mordecai's Beard*, and Richard Cumberland's *The Jew*, which describes its title character Sheva as 'naturally' bearded. Beards become identified with other stereotypic traits assigned the Jews, such as effeminacy, limping, and disease, and form a line separating them forever from acceptance. Not until the belligerent climate of the build-up to the Crimean War did changing notions of masculinity provoke a 'Beard Movement'.

The Jew's beard shows us that the exotic body is composed of fragmentary parts that reduce to things. Both the fact and the sign of an objectified position, the beard fits the 'special, sharp case of commodities' identified by Arjun Appadurai as 'commodities by diversion, objects placed into a commodity state though originally specifically protected from it' (*The Social Life of Things: Commodities in cultural perspective*, 1986, p. 16). The more the beard becomes a metonymic displacement for the Jew, the more its function as a reality effect calls attention to itself, forcing the thing to simultaneously avow and disavow its own status. Ultimately, things that attach to a human type dehumanize as they reconfigure, not least because they make the person anomalous and isolated.

***

I want to thank the staff of the Huntington Library for their support and assistance, especially for the opportunity to spend a summer with the Larpent collection. This essay would not be possible without them.

I begin with portraits of perhaps the most famous Jew in the Georgian period: William Shakespeare's Shylock as performed by Charles Macklin. Beginning in 1741 and continuing for the next forty years, Macklin revolutionized the role by playing the character as malevolent instead of as the comic bumbler he had become. As Alexander Pope famously declared, 'This is the Jew that Shakespeare drew' (see Figure 1).[1] Over a half century later, when Edmund Kean essayed the role to acclaim, he built on Macklin's interpretation but gave Shylock greater pathos. However, for my purposes, a signal difference divides the two presentations, one fully visible on Edmund Kean's chin (see Figure 2).

In this essay, I will argue that the appearance of Kean's beard constitutes a 'discursive formation' wherein we can read the production of

1 Pope may have believed in the authority of Macklin's imagination, but artists who drew Macklin as Shylock lacked a singular vision. Instead, the presence or absence of a beard becomes a vexed question. For instance, Zoffany paints Macklin in the role with a beard. The beard style itself is a stiletto beard, a fashion popular in the seventeenth century but obsolete by 1680. See Elliot Horowitz, 'The Early Eighteenth Century Confronts the Beard: Kabbalah and Jewish Self-Fashioning', *Jewish History* 8 [1994]: 95–115, 98. Because Zoffany worked in the mid-1760s and 1770s, contemporary with Macklin at the height of his powers, his work might seem authoritative. But Zoffany reworked portraits and sometimes added topical details to enhance consumer appeal; such is certainly the case with *Charles Macklin as Shylock* where the stiletto beard appears, and where he inserted the faces of two judges who had presided over a trial in which Macklin had prevailed. <http://www.tate.org.uk/art/artworks/zoffany-charles-macklin-as-shylock-n06005/text-summary>. Accessed March 23, 2015. This habit of revision complicates the dating of his works. Even in other portraits that show Macklin as lightly bearded, with the most vestigial of shadows ringing his neck, such as the one owned by the University of Michigan, the impression given is that of a clean-shaven face, with a wisp perhaps marring that visage slightly. These images belie descriptions of Macklin's costume as containing 'a red hat [...] piqued beard, loose black gown'. Philip H. Highfill, Jr, 'Performers and Performing', in Robert Hume, ed., *The London Theatre World, 1660–1800* (Carbondale: Southern Illinois University Press, 1980), 143–80, 165.

Figure 1: Portrait of Macklin, author unknown. © National Portrait Gallery, London.

knowledge and discern the shaping of social and cultural relations.[2] I trace the changing face of the stage Jew in a rather literal fashion, as he ceases to resemble other men of the earlier eighteenth century in his clean-shaven

2 The phrase comes from Marcia Pointon, *Hanging the Head: Portraiture and Social formation in Eighteenth-Century England* (New Haven: Yale University Press, 1993), 112.

Figure 2: Portrait of Kean, by Henry Meyer, published by R. Barnard, after Walter Henry Watts. Mezzotint, published 2 May 1814 (March 1814). © National Portrait Gallery, London.

appearance and acquires a beard as the symbol of Jewish essence.[3] More than just a fashion change, Shylock's beard represents the stage birth of the modern exotic Jewish body, a transformation driven by social anxieties and population pressures.[4]

The exotic

Though at times the exotic can seem like a fairly shaggy category, post-colonial theorists have long understood it as complicit in colonial and imperial methods of domination.[5] Slotting native peoples or objects under

3 Previous work on the stage representation of the Jew has broadly painted the frequent use of dialect, specific linguistic blunders, and body parts such as nose and beard, without analysing the stages through which these markers pass. See, for instance, Frank Felsenstein, *Anti-semitic Stereotypes: A Paradigm of Otherness in English Popular Culture, 1660–1830* (Baltimore: Johns Hopkins University Press, 1995); Michael Ragussis, *Theatrical Nation: Jews and Other Outlandish Englishmen in Georgian Britain* (Philadelphia: University of Pennsylvania Press, 2010).

4 The beard was not always the exclusive province of the Jew; for much of the eighteenth century, it belonged to the Turk, on stage and in portraits. The quintessential bearded Turk is Colman's *Bluebeard*, produced at Drury Lane in 1798, after a 1791 pantomime version played at Covent Garden. I would argue that the translation of the beard from the face of the Turk to the face of the Jew witnesses to intensified anxieties as a result of increased immigration.

5 Roy Porter and G.S. Rousseau refer to the exotic as 'a code-word for modes of belief and behavior that transgressed the norms of Christian, civilized, rational Europe' as well as conveying ideas of 'some inner, secret strangenesses, far transcending superficial diversities of costume and custom, icons and idols, and defying assimilation, even understanding'. *Exoticism in the Enlightenment* (Manchester: Manchester University Press, 1990), 5. Edward Ziter uses the term at times as a synonym for people of foreign geographic or racial extraction; alternatively, he reduces it to an externalized gesture rendered visually. See, e.g., page 76, where he opines, 'the exotic was delivered in architectural details that had already become associated with fancy and

that rubric permitted them to be viewed appreciatively, with a pseudo-sympathy for cultural difference that disguised its appropriative force. The very fact that objects and people are so designated speaks to its artificiality. Graham Huggan denies that the exotic can be found in nature, deeming it rather a 'particular mode of aesthetic *perception*' that manufactures in place of discovering the strange and mysterious.[6] The resultant production of exoticism does more than just 'mask[s] the inequality of the power relations without which the discourse could not function'; it converts the exotic from an exercise of power politics into a culturally consumed spectacle.[7]

A 1790s playbill for a private exhibit in the Strand gives us a taste of such spectacles.[8] It trumpets the appearance of the 'Newly-Discovered Animal, The BONASSUS, From the Appalachian Mountains of North America'. From the first paragraph, we see the emphasis on the widespread appeal of the attraction, and on the imprimatur of royal approval, validating the motive and method of viewing:

> This huge, terrific, and unparalleled animal has met with the unqualified praise of our illustrious and honoured Royal Family; having been noticed by their Royal Highnesses the Dukes of Sussex and Cambridge, the late revered duke of Kent's Consort and Family, the Duke of Clarence and Family, Duke of Gloucester and Military suite, his

---

light entertainment'. *The Orient on the Victorian Stage* (Cambridge University Press, 2003), 76. For postcolonial theories, see, for instance, Chris Bongie, *Exotic Memories: Literature, Colonialism, and the Fin De Siècle* (Stanford: Stanford University Press, 1991); Peter Mason, *Infelicities: Representations of the Exotic* (Philadelphia: Johns Hopkins University Press, 1998); and the essays in Sue Thomas, ed., *Victorian Traffic: Identity, Exchange, Performance* (Newcastle: Cambridge Scholars Publishing, 2009).

6 *The Postcolonial Exotic: Marketing the Margins* (London: Routledge, 2001), 13–14.

7 Jonathan Arac and Harriet Ritvo. *Macropolitics of Nineteenth-Century Literature: Nationalism, Exoticism, Imperialism* (Philadelphia: University of Pennsylvania Press, 1995), 3.

8 From theatrical clipping boxes at the Huntington Library. Since this particular playbill is hammocked in between a clipping recounting the RH visit to two 'fairies' dwarves in 1791, and a clipping about the spotted Jamaican boy dated June 13, 1795, I assume it occurred somewhere in there.

> Highness the Prince of Saxe Cobourg and Aide-de camps; nearly the whole of the peerage, the Foreign Ambassadors, and their numerous suites, the Chief Ministers of State, the heads of the Church, the Army and Navy, including those illustrious chiefs, the DUKE OF WELLINGTON and LORD EXMOUTH, together with the whole of the Cognoscenti and Literati of the age.

Rarity, extremes of emotion, and the register of the sublime all contribute to the initial abstract description of the creature. Moreover, in characteristic Romantic fashion, the advertisement levels peers and poets, entertainment and instruction. The nobility may have 'noticed' the exhibit, but the Bonassus has enlightened 'the Man of Science, the Historian, the Naturalist, and the Traveller' in a manner that bids fair, the advertisement suggests, to outlast royal attention.

Once the advertisement moves from the abstract to the particular, the description takes on a sympathetic tone, accomplished by blurring the distinction between animal and human: 'His fascinating powers are most wonderful. He has now been fourteen months at 287, Strand, solely dependant on himself', as though he were Master Betty or any juvenile performer in grosso, instead of a large animal with a trainer. Physically, he is said to combine the attributes of predators and prey in both the animal and human kingdoms, making him simultaneously threatening and familiarly endearing: 'He has the horns of the Antelope, the head of an Elephant, a long beard descending to his knees, the hind part of a Lion, an immense bunch of hair, like a tiara, upon his head,– his eye is placed upon the cheek-bone, and he has an ear like the human species'. Composed of discrete, disjunct parts, the Bonassus nonetheless forms an exotic whole that embodies future imperial aspirations in the form of a lost colonial remnant 'from the Appalachian Mountains of North America', a symbolic function stamped by the engraving that follows immediately, a depiction by S. Davenport of three animals: a camel, an Indian water buffalo, and a bison or bonassus.

The advertisement for the Bonassus confirms the verdict of Porter and Rousseau that, as spectacle, exotic productions simultaneously display and suppress the very cultural differences they are designed to mark, generating in the process a fetishistic relationship that ensnares the spectator in a double movement of attraction and repulsion (4–5). Nonetheless, despite Porter and Rousseau's longstanding call for Jews to be considered under the sign of exotica, the spectacle of the stage Jew complicates the rather tidy agreement that has pooled around definitions of the exotic, both in terms of the factors contributing to its emergence and in terms of the mechanisms by which it takes shape. Scholars hold it crucial that the Other who inhabits the category of exotic remain distant or distanced. However, Jewish migration into England at the end of the eighteenth century and throughout the nineteenth, especially from Eastern European countries, increasingly challenged British ability to keep their exotic force at bay.[9] Driven more by the need to fix and define the Other at home than in service of a futurist fantasy of bloodless conquest, the process of exoticizing the stage Jew takes a different course from that employed for colonial or imperial possessions. Whereas the Bonassus wears a 'long beard descending to his knees', like a religious Jew, the beard forms but one of the symbols of his strangeness. Its exotic body is composed of parts that form a whole. The Jew's beard, in contrast, shows us how a normal body becomes exotic.[10]

9 While numbers are extremely unreliable, we can sketch out parameters. At the end of the period running from 1750 to 1815, historians reckon the total population of London at roughly 900,000. Of those, Jews add anywhere from 17,000 to 22,000. The majority of those would have been predominantly poor Ashkenazim with no fixed trades and few skills, 12–15,000, up from under a thousand at the start of the previous century; roughly 5,000 Sephardim had long been resident in the country. See Todd Endelman, *The Jews of Britain 1656–2000* (Berkeley: University of California Press, 2002), 48. Endelman claims 8–10,000 Ashkenazi Jews arrived over the entire course of the French revolutionary war period. By 1830, Francis Goldschmid would place the number of Jews living in Great Britain and Ireland at 30,000. *Remarks on the Civil Disabilities of British Jews* (London: Henry Colburn and Richard Bentley, 1830).

10 A similar process occurs in the medieval period. Sara Lipton has catalogued the birth of the medieval Jewish body and identifies three tropes: the hat, the nose, and the beard. She attributes the motives for such representational strategies to a need to give the 'innovative artworks in which Hebrews appeared an aura of sacred antiquity', to protect them from accusations of novelty in a change-fearing society. 'For the same reason, the prophets wear beards, symbols of maturity, wisdom, and dignity. (As with the hats, the beards have little to do with actual Jewish appearances

Pageant of types

The stereotype dominating the earlier eighteenth century associated the Jew with old Spanish wealth, ushered into the kingdom by special invitation under Cromwell. This type moved along public courts and halls, engaging in lotteries and on the change. We see this type represented in the second plate of the famous Hogarth series 'The Harlot's Progress', and in the satirical cartoon 'Devotion at Duke's Place', set at the Sephardic synagogue. Macklin preserved this type not only when creating Shylock but also in his *Love A-La Mode*, the first play of the eighteenth century to contain a Jewish character, produced on December 12, 1752, as well as in his *The Man of the World* of 1779, the play Dougald MacMillan called 'one of the more aggravated instances of governmental interference with the stage'.[11]

The figure of the Jew in *The Man of the World* circulates as a verbal portrait, exchanged as part of her entry fee into society by Rodolpha upon her arrival. Rodolpha enumerates the members of what she calls the 'cabinet council', a mixture of 'oddities' combined into the 'perfect gallimaufry': a 'duke and a haberdasher, a red-hoit patriot and a sneering courtier, a discarded statesman and his scribbling chaplain, with a busy, bawling, muckle-headed prerogative lawyer; all of whom were ready every minute to gang together by the luggs, about the in and the out meenistry'. The Jew shares company with a host of mid-eighteenth century types, ridiculed for behavioral actions but not condemned for physical attributes. She continues:

---

or religious practices. Jewish men were by no means uniformly bearded at this time)'. 'The Invention of the Jewish Nose', *The New York Review of Books* (14 November 2014).

11 'The Censorship in the Case of Macklin's A Man of the World', *The Huntington Library Bulletin* 10 (1936), 79–101, 79. Michael Ragussis reminds us that Jewish characters appeared early in the century in dances and song. *Theatrical Nation: Jews and Other Outlandish Englishmen in Georgian Britain*, 29.

> Then, Sir Pertinax, in a retired part of the room, in a by-corner, snug, we had a Jew and a bishop.
>
> SIR PERTINAX: A Jew and a bishop! Ha, ha! A devilish guid connection that: and pray, my lady, what were they about?
>
> LADY R: Why, sir, the bishop was striving to convert the Jew; while the Jew, by intervals, was slyly picking up intelligence fra the bishop, about the change in the meenistry, in hopes of making a stroke in the stocks.
>
> OMNES: Ha, ha, ha!

Like members of the relatively small Sephardic community, this Jew betrays no distinctions of social class or race. In a dog-eat-dog world, he is merely one more canine.[12]

However, Macklin's text does betray a proleptic insecurity when Sir Pertinax continues in praise of the Jew: 'Ha, ha, ha! Admirable! Admirable! I honour the smouse! Ha! It was devilish clever of him, my lord devilish clever! The Jew distilling the bishop's brains'.[13] The word 'Smouse' refers to the German or Ashkenazic Jews, distinct from the Sephardic community and just beginning to be present in England. With the tide of German Jewish immigration towards the end of the eighteenth century, though, 'smouse' becomes a derogatory epithet signaling racial and religious identity, swallowing Sephardi and Ashkenazi without regard, just as the beard will encroach on the face of Judaism.

12 As Nicholas Hudson argues, 'the *continental* division of humanity [...] restrained authors from identifying certain groups, such as Anglo-Saxons, "Aryans", or Jews, as distinct "races"'. While scientists like Blumenbach noticed physical variations from European Christians, they believed that each continent held a single race. Accordingly, 'Jews remained only a "nation", physically influenced by their Middle-Eastern heritage, their distinct customs, and their harsh life in European ghettos'. 'From "Nation" to "Race": The Origin of Racial Classification in Eighteenth-Century Thought', *Eighteenth-Century Studies* 29/3 (1996), 247–64.

13 Act II, sc. 1. In *The Select London Stage: A Collection of the Most Reputed Tragedies, Comedies, Operas, Melodramas, Farces, and Interludes* (London: G. Balne, 1827), 7.

Unlike the process driven by gender anxieties and fashion during the mid-Victorian period, though, when beards exploded onto all registers of the social scene, the beard as a physical marker for the stage Jew takes time to catch hold. As late as the 1780s, characters share the bare faces of current fashion.[14] This is true in 1780's *A Specimen of Jewish Education*, entered for licensing by Sheridan, and its companion, *A Specimen of Jewish Courtship* (1787), both of which plays present us with 'men of business', even when that business happens to be usury. Jews in these plays take advantage of the law, mingle with Christians in the parks and attend fashionable retreats.

Nevertheless, beards form a part of the conversation between father Moses and son Shadrac in *Jewish Education*, the first play. Catechizing his son about the business, ethical, and moral practices of the Jew, Moses trumpets the benefits of a protean appearance. When Shadrac worries that swearing false witness will lead to the stockade, his father minimizes the consequences: Christians suffer shame and disgrace; but a Jew can always alter his appearance, either by shaving, growing, or buying a beard, and thus escape permanent detection.

The sequel, *Specimen of Jewish Courtship*, even more insistently thematizes appearance and its ability to deceive.[15] The main characters Shadrac and Leah model the fruits of their parents' peddling literally and figuratively, trying on for one another different costumes and bits of finery that have been pawned by customers. They select their outfits more from a materialistic than an aesthetic point of view. Shadrac calculates how the richness of Leah's appearance in a brocade dress will enhance his reputation and thus increase his business potential: 'I may get a Guinea or two

14 *Moses and Shedrach; or, a Specimen of Jewish Education*. Application 13 April 1780, Richard Brinsley Sheridan for DL; produced April 17. John Genest speculates that the play was written by Baddeley, who specialized in roles as Jews; he played the first Moses in *The School for Scandal*. See *Some Account of the English Stage: From the Restoration in 1660 to 1830*. In ten volumes. Vol. 7. (Bath: Printed by H.E. Carrington; London: Sold by Thomas Rood, Great Newport Street, 1832), 193–4.

15 This short piece is denominated a 'Prelude to *The Mistake of a Minute*', a one-act 'entertainment'.

to be bail for somebody before I go out of the Gardens'. Rather than taking offense, Leah conspires with him: 'Oh if dat is de caishe I can give you more credit, for I will take out dese two Diamond Rings which my Papa has in pawn [...] and mit a bit of sewing silk tie dem to mine ears for a pair of earrings [...]'. Her provisional ownership, signaled by the tenuous thread connecting the earrings to her person, underscores the artificiality of Jewish appearance.[16]

Thematically, the farce echoes numerous criticisms of the credit-financed cult of appearances that surface, for example, in the novels of Frances Burney. We soon learn that the dresses Leah wears have come into her father's possession because their owners, Alderman Squander's wife and Lady Betty Flippant, have ruined themselves through fashion. Perversely, the Jews plan to feed off of Christian pain by converting a loss through fashion into profit, tying in with notions of Jews as scavenging on 'legitimate' businesses. The meta-theatrical dimensions of the scene make the Jew the ultimate actor: their process of 'trying on' elaborately playacts at identity, signaling at once its performative dimension and its need for audience. But it also implicitly absolves any hint of English pretense, making such underhanded behavior the province solely of Jews.

Symbolically, *Specimen of Courtship* marks the moment of separation: although characters in this play may be objects of satire and scorn, they remain visually familiar. Characters are not only clean-shaven and accoutered like the Christian British gentry, they share their actual clothes. As later plays increasingly target anxieties about Jewish immigration and assimilation; Jewish characters cease being represented in all the current fashion. Instead, they begin wearing beards as their ethnic stamp and the Jew acquires an exotic body.

16 Just as Zoffany, when he chooses to paint in the beard on Macklin, depicts it as artificially attached by a highly visible cord, rather than making the beard an organic part of the character. In general, at this point we might say the beard is no more firmly attached to the representation of the stage Jew than it is to Macklin's face.

The beard as signifier

Modern history varies sharply from ancient in the esteem with which facial hair is held. As Christopher Oldstone-Moore reports, beards have experienced sporadic popularity: briefly during the late sixteenth and early seventeenth centuries, and again in the mid-Victorian period. A few years later, beards marked you as affiliated with radical politics, like socialism or Chartism, and were generally unfashionable.[17] French revolutionary officers sported moustaches, which created a fad among the English in the 1820s and 1830s. Not until the belligerent climate of the build-up to the Crimean War did changing notions of masculinity provoke a 'Beard Movement'.[18] A youth-dominated culture in the second generation of the Romantic era preferred bare skin; even the Devil, depicted in a 1797 print, has a five o'clock shadow instead of a beard.

Assimilating Jews shaved, signifying aspirations to transform either religiously or socially, just as the more wealthy Sephardim followed continental practice and maintained smooth skins. Ritually Orthodox Eastern European Jewry, and especially Kabbalists, though, viewed beards as a pious necessity. In consequence, as Dominic Green and Marsha Schuchard argue, 'a beard became the marker of Levantine and Eastern Jewishness'.[19] Connecting the beard to the newest immigrant population into England, the one still struggling towards self-sufficiency, made it socially undesirable; suggesting that it form an adequate disguise to evade the law in *Specimen of Jewish Education* makes it morally and ethically undesirable as well.

17 'The Beard Movement in Victorian Britain', *Victorian Studies* 48/1 (2005), 7–34.

18 Although he approaches the topic from Biblical history, Meir Soloveichik's argument that the Torah privileges beards because 'pagans' such as the Egyptians shaved shows that even the most ancient valuations depend upon context and culture. 'Why Beards?' *Commentary* (Feb. 2008) <https://www.commentarymagazine.com/article/why-beards/> accessed 31 August, 2013.

19 '"Our Protestant Rabbin": A Dialogue on the Conversion/Apostasy of Lord George Gordon', *Common Knowledge* 19/2 (2013), 283–314.

As a secondary sexual characteristic, beards have played a disproportionate role in determining character. Barbara Stafford muses, 'We might think of beards as "the equivocal ornamental grotesque", redolent of the rococo and "he uncontrolled imagination"'.[20] Londa Schiebinger notes that ethnologists 'made its presence or absence an important marker of race'.[21] Racial logic influenced gender logic: women were deemed inferior creatures because they, too, lacked beards (Schiebinger 124–5). With a beard as the boundary line for polite society, it seems less surprising that the bearded Jew should become the dominant image on stage and page.[22] Etching categorical limits onto the face of those deemed outside those limits, the beard simultaneously naturalizes the reason for those limits and proposes them as self-evident.

Two watershed productions at the end of the eighteenth century perform just that work of naturalization: a Drury Lane farce in 1790 originally titled *The Jew's Beard* but presented as *Mordecai's Beard*, mounted by John Philip Kemble; and Richard Cumberland's 1794 full-length piece *The Jew* at Covent Garden, which describes its title character, Sheva, as 'naturally' bearded. Physically and characterologically, these two plays build on the notion of Jews as 'Specimens' articulated in the earlier titles, further eradicating the vision of them as members of society portrayed in Macklin's comedies.

20 *Body Criticism. Imagining the Unseen in Enlightenment Art and Medicine* (Cambridge, MA: The MIT Press, 1991), 29.

21 *Nature's Body. Gender in the Making of Modern Science* (Boston: Beacon Press, 1993), 116–17; see also 122.

22 Did earlier beard lovers find a difficulty staring them in the face, so to speak, when confronted by the equally ubiquitous stereotype of the bearded Jew? Once the tide had turned in favour of beards, the new advocates promoted a link between facial hair and good health, with beards supposedly lending protection against disease. This emphasis on eugenics reverses the links between beards, Jews, and disease. According to Susan Walton, a shaved face then gets linked with an effeminate body, whereas just the opposite had been true in the stereotype of the Jew. Susan Walton, 'From Squalid Impropriety to Manly Respectability: The Revival of Beards, Moustaches and Martial Values in 1850s in England', *Nineteenth-Century Contexts* (2008), 229–46.

The Jew's Beard opens in the apartment of an Irish chairman. As he sits to his dinner, the sounds of a Jewish pedlar float in through the window, calling for any 'Old Cloaths'. The Irishman beckons him to enter and tempts him with promises of 'a good bargain'. Then he turns his head and addresses the audience directly in a long aside, meditating on how he plans to cheat the Jew. Thus, before the Jew appears on stage, the audience has been primed to side with the Irish Chairman. The opening scene in the Irish apartment, the conspiratorial relationship established by the direct address: these help foster the sense of audience identification. Moreover, the Jew addresses the Irishman by name, Mr Donavon O'Strap, whereas the Jew remains nameless until his song, halfway through, where he mispronounces his own name by rhyming Mordecai with play. Having established a sense of identification between the audience and O'Strap, the play proceeds to reinforce that identification by assigning the rejected exotic Other, in this case the Jew, a defining physical feature.

And it is the very physicality of the marker that distinguishes the exotic body as different from any other Other. Whereas the Jew attacks O' Strap's *behavior*, such as his willingness to sell his testimony for any party, bearding the Jew locates the social problem in *essence*, as an intrinsic property. O'Strap takes Jewish refusal to eat pork as evidence that Jews lack souls. O'Strap threatens to make 'a good Christian' of him by forcing pork upon him. When the Jew persists in his refusal, O'Strap says, 'if I can't convert your whole Body, I will at least Christen your Beard my Jewell so here goes'. Reverence for the beard was reported to be part of Middle Eastern Muslim culture. According to Elliot Horowitz, kissing the beard was a common act of love and respect, and spitting on the beard constituted the ultimate affront. One can easily see the similarity between the idea of spitting on and of smearing the beard, as in *The Jew's Beard*. Synedochal exchange guarantees the beard as the detachable, reproduceable, and hence convertible meme for Jewishness. It also positions the beard as the gateway, the vulnerable point of access to the Jew's defenses against assimilation. Sure enough, Mordecai capitulates. Internal conviction melts at the aroma of pig fat; Mordecai can barely restrain himself from sucking every vestige of evidence from his beard. The beard becomes the mark identifying the Jew as weak, avaricious, and hypocritical.

By the time Richard Cumberland opened his new five-act play of *The Jew* on 8 May 1794, Sheva's beard was neither remarkable nor a plot device. Abba Rubin may have enthused that the 'times were ripe for a new Jewish literary image [...]. The old irrational fears were generally dispelled, and ignorance and prejudice were replaced by the beginnings of knowledge and experiences'.[23] But the 'new literary image' consolidates the trend I have been describing, and cements the beard as the hallmark of the Jew.[24] Even though the play ostensibly presents Sheva as a man of integrity, his beard marks him as weak and feminized.[25] Text underscores image: even the friendlier Christians refer to him as a *thing* or shudder at the thought of having dealings with him.[26]

Productions such as *Mordecai's Beard* and *The Jew* demonstrate another eccentric feature of the Jew's beard: it becomes identified with the stereotype of the Jew by moving *up* through the generic ranks. In the process, it reveals a cross-fertilization that occurs despite the supposed rigidity of genre.[27] For example, early nineteenth-century critics of theatre assessed the different kinds, Comedy, Tragedy, and Farce, as performing different work:

23 Abba Rubin, *Images in Transition: The English Jew in English Literature, 1660–1830* (Westport, CN and London: Greenwood Press 1984), 130.

24 This reification into a 'malevolent, Thing-like category' offers a mechanism to displace fear into disdain. See Susan Zickmund, 'Approaching the Radical Other: The Discursive Culture of Cyberhate' in Jones, S.G., ed., *Virtual Culture: Identity and Communication in Cybersociety* (London: Sage, 1997), 185–205.

25 Complicating the portrait even more, the stage lingo that has by this time substituted itself for the actual speech of men matches Sheva to all the other Yiddish-speaking villains, making class and character distinctions difficult. On the Jewish stage dialect, see M.J. Landa, *The Jew in Drama* (London: P.S. King and Son Ltd., 1926), 120.

26 'Frederick: That fellow would not let his shadow fall upon the earth, if he could help it. Charles: You are too hard upon him. The thing is courteous' (Act I, scene 1, 11). See also 15. 'Eliza Ratcliff does the shivering. Nor does Sheva shrink from objectifying himself. In the stage business, Sir Stephen grabs Sheva's lapels to shake him menacingly at this point. Sheva shows the slightest hint of anger when he admonishes Sir Stephen: "Take your hand from ma coat! ma coat and I are very old, and pretty well worn out together"'.

27 Technically, 'A Specimen of Jewish Education' is a 'petit piece' to Sheridan; 'A Specimen of Jewish Courtship' is a prelude to 'The Mistake of a Minute'; and 'Jew's Beard' is an interlude.

> A FARCE, properly so called, is a short dramatic piece of broad humour and bustle, in which an author is not restricted by the rules and decorum of legitimate Comedy. It seems to be tacked to our plays, as a sort of composition with the galleries, whose tenants, as the existing theatrical laws do not permit their betters and them to seek amusement in distinct theatres adapted to their several tastes, claim the privilege of an hour's coarse and uncontrolled mirth, after having endured five acts of pathos, or of refined wit.[28]

Deeming farce a sop to the vulgar, the author reduces it to a crude bodily discharge. His dismissive attitude unfortunately resembles contemporary opinion about the significance of farce among scholars of nationalism. In their eyes, farce lacks benevolence and eccentricity replaces representativeness, fatal flaws for nation-building.[29] 'Fantastical' though the performance of character and situation may be, that alone does not preclude any audience identification. Identification gets forged when shared witnessing *fixes* by the placement of the beard an exotic Other too close for comfort; identification provides cohesion and a sense of community. As Paula Backscheider noted long ago, a process of evolution is required for drama to acquire hegemonic force:

> The authors' imaginations, the orchestrated languages available, and the demands and expectations of all those involved in the creation, production, and reception of the work refine and fix the basic pattern and its elements. It then has created its own world, and the audience becomes familiar with it through repetition. At this point, the pattern is available not only for confirmation and reassurance but also for

28 *The Modern British Drama*. In Five Volumes. Volume Fifth. Operas and Farces (London: Printed for William Miller, Albemarle Street, by William Savage, Bedford Bury, 1811), v. He even distinguishes between farces and after-pieces, comparing the latter to more legitimate comedies, from which they differ only in point of length. See also the Preface by the unnamed editor of *The British Drama; Comprehending the Best Plays in the English Language. Operas and Farces* (London: Published by William Miller, Old Bond-Street. Printed by James Ballantyne, Edinburgh, 1804).

29 See, e.g., Mita Choudhury, 'Gazing at His Seraglio: Late Eighteenth-Century Women Playwrights as Orientalists', *Theatre Journal* 47/4, Eighteenth-Century Representations (Dec., 1995), 481–502; and Barbara Freedman, *Staging the Gaze: Postmodernism, Psychoanalysis, and Shakespearean Comedy* (Ithaca: Cornell University Press, 1991).

> allowing a testing of the boundary between the permitted and the forbidden, the temporary and the impossible. The reactions shared by people in a group become collective consciousness, which reaffirms borders and limits. It finally delivers the predictable and reassures about communal norms, socials relations, and natural and political order.[30]

Such a 'collective consciousness' arises from theatre's 'consistent necessity for repetition and reenactment in public venues' and it produces a 'non-negotiable legitimacy'.[31] The very ability of the beard to migrate indicates its acceptance as a popular culture trope, while the migration of the image through the generic levels of theatrical respectability, from farce to the main bill of the patent theatres and beyond, ensures that it simultaneously acquires a natural authority.

This naturalization plays against the danger that the very repetition of the image signals its artificiality. At the same time that theatrical display conjures up a secure and fixed, knowable identity for the Other, it undermines that claim by revealing the performative nature of identity. Nevertheless, this is not quite the same as saying that the theater's very formulaic repetitiveness indicates a *desire* to call such fictionalized interiority and essence into question.[32] Admittedly, during the initial phases of a stereotype or exoticization, theatre performs a double and contradictory dance. Beards become a costume for the face: they can be put on and off at ease, as testified by the audience at the Old Price riots in 1809. But the fact that they get donned for very particular reasons, most frequently to identify 'the Jew' and to associate that Jew with the cunning mendacity hinted by Moses that keeps him an abjected, objectified alien in society, means that the image ultimately acquires a specific gravity that stabilizes its meaning.

Whatever its status as reality effect or as guarantor of authenticity, the beard ultimately proves more reliable than skin colour in determining the way minorities in London get racialized in my period. This is true

30 Paula R. Backscheider, *Spectacular Politics: Theatrical Power and Mass Culture in Early Modern England* (Baltimore: Johns Hopkins, 1993), 238.

31 Ibid.

32 Lisa A. Freeman, *Character's Theater: Genre and Identity on the Eighteenth-Century English Stage* (Philadelphia: University of Pennsylvania Press, 2002), 27.

because, as David Worrall notes, 'Facial colour was often simply a question of the degree of intensity to which normal stage makeup was deployed'.[33] Beyond that, though, colour assignments themselves were unstable. Take, for instance, the designation 'sooty', an adjective opening up a palimpsest of worlds. Sootiness marks profession (chimney sweep); morality (associated with foul sin since the seventeenth century); tainted grain; and colour. Yet in terms of stage convention with make-up, the designation and the colour shift throughout the eighteenth century from a descriptor and colour used earlier in the period for Jews to a designation and colour reserved solely for Africans by the end of the eighteenth century.[34]

Ironically, in the case of the Jew's beard, theatre helps construct a cultural memory that colludes to rewrite the very history it had recorded. The success of *The Jew* may help explain why, in 1796, the engraver C. Woodward joined with Allen and West, 15 Paternoster Row, to publish a new print of 'The Jew and the Bishop', drawn from Macklin's comedy, with Cruikshank supplying the artwork.[35] The Jew is seated lower and on a plainer chair than the bishop, placed on the right side of print in full profile. Unlike his appearance in the original stage performance, he has large hook nose, long flowing goatee, large eyeballs, and a hairdo resembling a Puritan pageboy. Still associated with the Stock Exchange, as testified by the document he balances on his knees, with the words *Lloyd's Evening* and *'Stock'* the only two legible, he now more clearly resembles Shylock in his Middle European garb.[36] The interest in the story behind *Mordecai's Beard* likewise displays a curious time-lag and synchronicity. It was originally reported in

33 David Worrall, *Harlequin Empire: Race, Ethnicity and the Drama of the Popular Enlightenment* (London: Pickering and Chatto, 2007), 40 passim.

34 For a full discussion, see Worrall.

35 Bodleian library, Prints and Scraps box 2, Plate 65, Oct. 8, 1796.

36 Max Silverman and Nira Yuval-Davis think that Britain is now seeing that the colonialist paradigm doesn't account for racism and especially with respect to the case of Jews. But the idea of race has given way to the idea of racialization (8). 'This is a broader definition of the essentialist construction of groups, which accepts that this can be produced through the discourse of cultural absolutism as well as that of biological determinism'. 'Jews, Arabs and the theorisation of racism in Britain and France', *Explorations in Sociology* 52 (1999), 25–48, 42.

the *Gentleman's Magazine* for Tuesday, April 9, 1776: 'A woman who keeps a public house was tried, at the quarter-sessions, held at Westminster, for assaulting and greasing the chin of a Jew with pork. The jury gave a verdict for the plaintiff, with £10 damages'.[37] Its production in 1790 coincides with as it helps foster the bearding of the Jew.

A fragmentary part that reduces to a thing, the beard takes on meanings as it acquires purchase in the cultural imagination. Ultimately, things that attach to a human type dehumanize as they reconfigure, not least because they make the person anomalous and isolated. Both the fact and the sign of an objectified position, the beard fits the 'special, sharp case of commodities' identified by Arjun Appadurai as 'commodities by diversion, objects placed into a commodity state though originally specifically protected from it'.[38] Beards fulfil the same function as the Turk's turban, the corncob pipe and shillelagh of the Irish. Just as the stage Irishman sounds out his identity with musical vowels, so the stage Jew grows a beard. In particular, the image of the Jew with a beard stuck hard in one place: the face of Shylock.[39]

Bibliography

Appadurai, Arjun, ed., *The Social Life of Things: Commodities in Cultural Perspective* (Cambridge: Cambridge University Press, 1986).

Arac, Jonathan and Harriet Ritvo, eds, *Macropolitics of Nineteenth-Century Literature: Nationalism, Exoticism, Imperialism* (Philadelphia: University of Pennsylvania Press, 1991).

37 *Gentleman's Magazine* XLVI, 189. See Irma Lustig, 'Boswell and the Descendants of Venerable Abraham', *Studies in English Literature, 1500–1900*, 14. 3 [Summer], 1974: 435–48, n. 38, 447. EI: <http://links.jstor.org/sici?sici=0039-3657%28197422%2914%3A3%3C435%3ABATDOV%3E2.0.CO%3B2-N>.

38 Appadurai, ed., *The Social Life of Things: Commodities in Cultural Perspective* (Cambridge University Press, 1986), 16; see also Elaine Freedgood, *The Ideas in Things* (University of Chicago Press, 2006).

39 As a Google search of images will quickly show.

Backscheider, Paula R., *Spectacular Politics: Theatrical Power and Mass Culture in Early Modern England* (Baltimore: Johns Hopkins, 199).

Bongie, Chris, *Exotic Memories: Literature, Colonialism, and the Fin De Siècle* (Stanford: Stanford University Press, 1991).

Brah, Avtar, Mary J. Hickman, and Mairtin Mac an Ghaill, eds, *Thinking Identities: Ethnicity, Racism and Culture* (Houndsmills: Mac Millan, 1999).

The British Drama; Comprehending the Best Plays in the English Language: Operas and Farces (London: Published by William Miller, Old Bond-Street. Printed by James Ballantyne, Edinburgh, 1804).

Choudhury, Mita, 'Gazing at His Seraglio: Late Eighteenth-Century Women Playwrights as Orientalists', *Theatre Journal* 47/4, Eighteenth-Century Representations (1995), 481–502.

Cumberland, Richard, *The Jew* (London: J. Dicks, n.d.).

Endelman, Todd, *The Jews of Britain 1656–2000* (Berkeley: University of California Press, 2002).

Felsenstein, Frank, *Anti-semitic Stereotypes: A Paradigm of Otherness in English Popular Culture, 1660–1830* (Baltimore: Johns Hopkins University Press, 1995).

Freedgood, Elaine, *The Ideas in Things* (Chicago: University of Chicago Press, 2006).

Freedman, Barbara. *Staging the Gaze: Postmodernism, Psychoanalysis, and Shakespearean Comedy* (Ithaca: Cornell University Press, 1991).

Freeman, Lisa A., *Character's Theater: Genre and Identity on the Eighteenth-Century English Stage* (Philadelphia: University of Pennsylvania Press, 2002).

Genest, John, *Some Account of the English Stage: From the Restoration in 1660 to 1830.* In ten volumes. Vol. 7 (Bath: Printed by H.E. Carrington; London: Sold by Thomas Rood, Great Newport Street, 1832).

Goldschmid, Francis, *Remarks on the Civil Disabilities of British Jews* (London: Henry Colburn and Richard Bentley, 1830).

Green, Dominic, and Marsha Schuchard, '"Our Protestant Rabbin": A Dialogue on the Conversion/Apostasy of Lord George Gordon', *Common Knowledge* 19.2 (2013), 283–314.

Highfill, Philip H., Jr, 'Performers and Performing', in Robert Hume, ed., *The London Theatre World, 1660–1800* (Carbondale: Southern Illinois University Press, 1980), 143–80.

Horowitz, Elliot. 'The Early Eighteenth Century Confronts the Beard: Kabbalah and Jewish Self-Fashioning', *Jewish History* 8 [1994], 95–115.

Hudson, Nicholas, 'From "Nation" to "Race": The Origin of Racial Classification in Eighteenth-Century Thought', *Eighteenth-Century Studies* 29.3 (1996), 247–64.

Huggan, Graham. *The Postcolonial Exotic: Marketing the Margins* (London: Routledge, 2001).

Landa, M.J., *The Jew in Drama* (London: P.S. King and Son Ltd., 1926).
Lipton, Sara, 'The Invention of the Jewish Nose', *The New York Review of Books* (14 November, 2014).
Lustig, Irma S. 'Boswell and the Descendants of Venerable Abraham', *Studies in English Literature, 1500–1900*, 14. 3 (1974), 435–48.
MacMillan, Dougald, 'The Censorship in the Case of Macklin's A Man of the World', *The Huntington Library Bulletin* 10 (1936), 79–101.
Macklin, Charles, *The Way of the World*, in *The Select London Stage: A Collection of the Most Reputed Tragedies, Comedies, Operas, Melodramas, Farces, and Interludes* (London: G. Balne, 1827).
Mason, Peter, *Infelicities: Representations of the Exotic* (Baltimore: Johns Hopkins University Press, 1998).
The Modern British Drama. In Five Volumes. Volume Fifth. Operas and Farces (London: Printed for William Miller, Albemarle Street, by William Savage, Bedford Bury, 1811).
Moses and Shedrach; or, a Specimen of Jewish Education, 1780.
Oldstone-Moore, Christopher, 'The Beard Movement in Victorian Britain', *Victorian Studies* 48.1 (2005), 7–34.
Pointon, Marcia, *Hanging the Head: Portraiture and Social Formation in Eighteenth-Century England* (New Haven: Yale University Press, 1993).
Porter, Roy and G.S. Rousseau, *Exoticism in the Enlightenment* (Manchester, England: Manchester University Press, 1990).
Ragussis, Michael, *Theatrical Nation: Jews and Other Outlandish Englishmen in Georgian Britain* (Philadelphia, PA: University of Pennsylvania Press, 2010).
Rubin, Abba, *Images in Transition: The English Jew in English Literature, 1660–1830* (Westport, CN and London: Greenwood Press 1984.)
Schiebinger Londa, *Nature's Body: Gender in the Making of Modern Science* (Boston: Beacon Press, 1993).
Silverman, Max, and Nira Yuval-Davis, 'Jews, Arabs and the Theorisation of Racism in Britain and France', *Explorations in Sociology* 52 (1999), 25–48.
Soloveichik, Meir, 'Why Beards?' *Commentary* (Feb. 2008) <https://www.commentarymagazine.com/article/why-beards/> accessed 31 August 2013.
Stafford, Barbara, *Body Criticism: Imagining the Unseen in Enlightenment Art and Medicine* (Cambridge, MA: The MIT Press, 1991).
Thomas, Sue, ed., *Victorian Traffic: Identity, Exchange, Performance* (Cambridge Scholars Publishing, 2009).
Walton, Susan, 'From Squalid Impropriety to Manly Respectability: The Revival of Beards, Moustaches and Martial Values in 1850s in England', *Nineteenth-Century Contexts* 2008, 229–46.

Worrall, David, *Harlequin Empire: Race, Ethnicity and the Drama of the Popular Enlightenment* (London: Pickering and Chatto, 2007).

Zickmund, Susan, 'Approaching the Radical Other: The Discursive Culture of Cyberhate' in Jones, S.G., ed., *Virtual Culture: Identity and Communication in Cybersociety* (London: Sage, 1997), 185–205.

Ziter, Edward, *The Orient on the Victorian Stage* (Cambridge University Press, 2003).

MICHAEL BRADSHAW

The Jew on Stage and on the Page: Intertextual Exotic

ABSTRACT
This essay will examine two key texts in both performance and print contexts: Henry Hart Milman's *Fazio* (pub. 1815; Covent Garden 1818), and Thomas Wade's *The Jew of Arragon; or, the Hebrew Queen* (Covent Garden 1830; pub. 1830). In *The Jew of Arragon* Wade dramatizes the European Jew as a heroic outcast, resisting a legacy of oppression and exclusion; his campaigning play was greeted with open hostility at Covent Garden in 1830, not only for its sympathetic treatment of a Jewish character but for its implied support for emancipation. Milman, another historian of the Jewish people, had concentrated some of the anti-Semitic anxieties about usury and financial speculation in the alchemist villain of his tragedy *Fazio*. Both dramatists receive and challenge a cultural legacy from Shakespeare, and especially Marlowe, of the stage Jew as a rapacious figure, sexually as well as economically threatening, and defined by an exotic body whose distinctive marker – circumcision – was concealed but known to be present. Engaging and resisting the Renaissance intertexts of Barabas and Shylock, and also dramatizing the anxieties of the abstract money-markets of the nascent stock exchange, Wade and Milman make the exotic body of the Jew a site of negotiation between competing social impulses to include and to ostracize.

***

Dramatic bodies have intertexts, and are constructed through intertextual activity. Exotic others in literature and drama are always to some extent the product of textual practice and textual exchange. When a character is offered or received as exotic, ethnically different, or ethnically typical in some way, these qualities derive from cultural texts in circulation, rather than from physical bodies. In recent years there has been a growth in scholarly attention to the Jewish presence and the representation of Jews in the culture of the Romantic period and 'long nineteenth century.'

Romanticism's unacknowledged debt to a Jewish presence is a complex theme worthy of further debate; but a broad consensus has developed that the libertarian rhetoric of much Romantic writing is belied by the unresolved and often exploitative nature of its representation of Jewish people; Efraim Sicher, for example, argues: 'Romanticism has [...] tended to displace Jews into figures for conversion to a Christian eschatology while romanticizing the exiled state of wanderers from a destroyed Jerusalem'.[1] Judith Page also considers the subtlety of the Jew as other in British society, indicating how complex representing and reading a Jewish literary presence can become:

> Jews occupy a unique position because they were particularly difficult to pin down: they were mostly poor but they were also rich, they were foreign-looking but they also simulated British gentility, they spoke English but not always the king's English. Jews were difficult to categorize and to place within certain boundaries, unlike distant, colonized Others. If Romanticism tended to romanticize the outcast, Jews made the process more difficult because they were outcasts who were making inroads into the culture.[2]

There is a well-established case for the figure of 'the Jew' being a disruptive and interrogative presence in hegemonic western culture in the modern era, constituting a focus for anxiety and self-doubt in the majority Christian subject.[3] Throughout the Romantic and post-Romantic nineteenth century, Jewish characters continued to embody the self-other contradictions observed by Page above, and continued to be contested and disruptive figures, whose presence could be at once both indictment and incitement.

Seeking to investigate the 'intertextual exotic' in nineteenth-century writing, this chapter will examine two key dramatic texts in print and performance contexts: Henry Hart Milman's *Fazio* (1815) and Thomas Wade's *The Jew of Arragon* (1830). Milman's *Fazio* was published in 1815, and produced at Covent Garden in 1818; Wade's *The Jew of Arragon; or, the Hebrew Queen* was both produced at Covent Garden and published in book form in

1 Efraim Sicher, 'Imagining "the Jew": Dickens' Romantic Heritage', in Sheila A. Spector, ed., *British Romanticism and the Jews*, 139–55 (141). See also Galperin, 'Romanticism and/or Antisemitism'.

2 Judith W. Page, *Imperfect Sympathies: Jews and Judaism in British Romantic Literature and Culture* (Basingstoke: Palgrave Macmillan, 2004), 3–4.

3 See e.g.: Linda Nochlin and Tamar Garb, eds, *The Jew in the Text: Modernity and the Construction of Identity* (London: Thames and Hudson, 1995).

1830.[4] In *The Jew of Arragon* Wade dramatizes the European Jew as a heroic outcast, resisting a legacy of oppression and exclusion; Wade's campaigning play was greeted with open hostility at Covent Garden in 1830, not only for its sympathetic treatment of a Jewish character but specifically for its implied support for the cause of political emancipation. Milman, another historian of the Jewish people, had concentrated some of the antisemitic anxieties about usury and financial speculation in the alchemist villain of his tragedy *Fazio*. These dramatists receive and challenge a cultural legacy from Shakespeare, and especially Marlowe, of the stage Jew as a rapacious figure, sexually as well as economically threatening, and defined by an ambiguously exotic body. Both engaging and resisting the Renaissance intertexts of Barabas and Shylock, and also dramatizing the anxieties of the abstract money-markets of the nascent stock exchange, Milman and Wade make the exotic body of the Jew a site of negotiation between competing social impulses to include and to ostracize, to assimilate and to 'other'.

For Milman and Wade as dramatists committed to conventions of legitimacy in the theatre, the key reference points and standards of judgement were all to be found in the drama of their predecessors of the late sixteenth and early seventeenth centuries – Shakespeare and his contemporaries. A series of landmark publications kept the canonical plays of the Elizabethan period continually before audiences and readers in the early nineteenth century. Robert Dodsley's *A Select Collection of Old Plays*, in twelve volumes, was reprinted between 1825 and 1827. Elizabeth Inchbald's *The British Theatre* (1808) also made high-quality editions of old plays available to modern readers; its twenty-five volumes included works by Beaumont and Fletcher, Jonson, and Massinger. Authors whose works became available in dedicated collected editions included Massinger (1813), Jonson (1816), Marlowe (1826), Ford (1827), Webster (1830), and Middleton (1840). Elizabethan and Jacobean plays, and especially the tragedies, provided an almost unquestioned standard of excellence and

4 The play opened 20 October 1830, and was published in duodecimo format in the same year. See Allardyce Nicoll, *A History of English Drama, 1660–1900* (Cambridge: Cambridge University Press, 1955), IV, 415.

taste. This doctrine spawned a historically complicated genre of imitative drama, presented with a five-act structure and predominantly in blank verse, very often without the variation provided by prose speakers and prose scenes in the old plays; this sometimes dogmatic antiquarianism of form was however tempered by inventive strategies to reflect on modern preoccupations through character, plot, and imaginative theme. *Fazio* and *The Jew of Arragon*, like other plays of their time which adapt and hybridize the forms and conventions of Elizabethan theatre, rewrite the tragedy of chaotic rebellion against autocratic power as a struggle between the individual and a modern conception of the nation state. The Machiavellian power games of the Renaissance are further complicated by a sense of the abstraction of power in a financial modernity built upon speculations in imaginary gold.[5]

As well as Marlowe's tragic farce *The Jew of Malta* (c. 1592) and Shakespeare's 'problem comedy' *The Merchant of Venice* (c. 1597), a further significant intertext can be recognized in Edmund Kean's celebrated performance of Shylock at Drury Lane in 1814, lauded and interpreted by the critic William Hazlitt. Kean's style of performance was famously provocative, often dividing audiences along lines of economic and class identity, as Tracy Davis has argued.[6] In the case of Shylock, Kean had not only escaped from the constraining traditions of the stage Jew, the prosthetic nose conveying venality and concupiscence, the thick red wig with its symbolic association with Judas Iscariot; his performance was full of bold ambiguity and challenged audiences to reconsider the traditional version of the character. As Judith Page observes, 'Negative renditions of Shylock have followed Kean, but once the red beard and fake nose were no longer obligatory, interpretation of the role became an issue for discussion and

5 See also: Michael Bradshaw, 'Elizabethan Style in Drama', in Frederick Burwick, Nancy Moore Goslee and Diane Long Hoeveler, eds, *The Encyclopedia of Romantic Literature*, ed. 3, vols (Oxford: Blackwell, 2012), 415–21; and Frederick Burwick, 'The Romantic Drama', in Duncan Wu, ed., *A Companion to Romanticism* (Malden, MA and Oxford: Blackwell, 1999), 323–32.

6 See Tracy C. Davis, '"Reading Shakespeare by Flashes of Lightning": Challenging the Foundations of Romantic Acting Theory', *ELH* 62 (1995), 933–54.

debate'.[7] Page continues: 'Instead of playing Shylock safe as a villain, Kean dared his audience to think of Shylock as flawed but worthy of sympathy in his rage. Far from the sinister comic villain who could not fit into the world of romantic comedy, Kean's Shylock was a tragic figure, in Hazlitt's stunning echo of *King Lear*, a man more sinned against than sinning'.[8] The essayist Charles Lamb provides an apt contemporary comparison of Shakespeare's Shylock with Marlowe's Barabas, showing the game-changing impact that Kean had had: 'Shylock in the midst of his savage purpose is a man. His motives, feelings, resentments, have something human in them. "If you wrong us, shall we not revenge?" Barabas is a mere monster brought in with a large painted nose to please the rabble'.[9] As well as paying tribute to the magnetism and radical sympathy of Kean's performance, Hazlitt's essay ironically rethinks Shylock's relationship with his antagonists:

> He seems the depository of the vengeance of his race; and though the long habit of brooding over daily insults and injuries has crusted over his temper with inveterate misanthropy, and hardened him against the contempt of mankind, this adds but little to the triumphant pretensions of his enemies. There is a strong, quick, and deep sense of justice mixed up with the gall and bitterness of his resentment. The constant apprehension of being burnt alive, plundered, banished, reviled, and trampled on, might be supposed to sour the most forbearing nature, and to take something from that 'milk of human kindness', with which his persecutors contemplated his indignities.[10]

In Kean's performance and in Hazlitt's essay, Shylock is the same and not the same. He continues to embody the qualities of his former caricature self, such as resentment, bitterness, and misanthropy, but they now derive from his interaction with Christians, and from the Christians themselves. The stage Jew still has a function to perform, but less as the universal enemy of Christians than as the suffering embodiment and indictment of their

7 Page, *Imperfect Sympathies*, 54.
8 Page, *Imperfect Sympathies*, 56–7.
9 Quoted in Page, *Imperfect Sympathies*, 73.
10 William Hazlitt, 'The Merchant of Venice', in *The Characters of Shakespeare's Plays* (1817) <http://www.library.utoronto.ca/utel/criticism/hazlittw_charsp/charsp_ch23.html> accessed 5 May 2015, 1.

hypocrisy. The obsession with avarice has also begun to wane in Hazlitt's reading, and revenge blends uncomfortably with justice. This moment of transformation and emergence, when the rabble-pleasing Barabas, Marlowe's gleefully self-aware Machiavel, gives way to the defiantly, disturbingly human Shylock, is the intertextual context for the staging of Jews in the subsequent nineteenth century.

The historian, poet, and dramatist Henry Hart Milman was consistently drawn to Judaism in his writings, producing three notable works on related themes, *The Fall of Jerusalem* (1820), *Belshazzar* (1822), and *The History of the Jews* (1829). An Eton- and Oxford-educated Anglican priest and historian, Milman was very much an establishment figure among the poets and dramatists of his day; his writing was grudgingly admired by Byron, who nevertheless made his personal dislike very plain.[11]

Introducing Milman's 'closet drama' *The Fall of Jerusalem*, Donald Reiman identifies a dramatic contradiction that seems to have encumbered Milman's text and given rise to a strikingly retrograde view of its Jewish characters: 'To show that Jesus' weeping over evil Jerusalem was fulfilled in the Romans' destruction of the city, Milman must portray the Jewish defenders of the city as an evil people deserving of judgment. And since the cruelty of the Romans has no virtue in Milman's eyes, there are no characters (except the unbelievable Christian pair of Javan and Miriam) whose fate has any interest. The contest is between a Tamburlaine and a Bajazet, without Marlowe's belief in the heroism of conquest'.[12] Milman practically admits as much in his own introduction: 'The constant tradition of the Church has been, that no one professing that faith perished during all the havoc which attended on this most awful visitation. It has been my object also to show the full completion of prophecy in this great event'.[13] The text, which Milman describes as a 'dramatic fable',[14] conforms to the conversion narrative model identified by Michael Scrivener and Efraim

11 Henry Hart Milman, *The Fall of Jerusalem* [1820] *and Belshazzar* [1822], intro. Donald H. Reiman (New York and London: Garland, 1977), vi.

12 Milman, *The Fall of Jerusalem*, ix.

13 Milman, *The Fall of Jerusalem*, vi–vii.

14 Milman, *The Fall of Jerusalem*, vii.

Sicher. Proselyte Christians look on in awe, the only surviving refugees, as the ancient sacred city is destroyed by the scourge-like Roman army, a divine judgement dissolving the Old Covenant:

> But oh, Jerusalem! thy rescued children
> May not, retir'd within their secret joy,
> Shut out the mournful sight of thy calamities.
>   Oh, beauty of earth's cities! throned queen
> Of thy milk-flowing valleys! crown'd with glory!
> The envy of the nations! now no more
> A city—One by one thy palaces
> Sink into ashes [...][15]

By contrast, Milman's later work of historical scholarship *The History of the Jews* is notable for interpreting the Jewish nation as an Oriental tribe, alluding to the leaders, kings, and patriarchs of the Old Testament as 'sheikhs'. The text reviews specifically historical evidence, and generally excludes religious and spiritual discourse; Milman's work attracted hostility for this secularizing approach. The *History* will be considered in more detail below, as a bridge to the 'philosemitic' stance of Thomas Wade.

As a dramatist, Milman aspired and fully subscribed to the contemporary consensus on what constituted legitimate theatre, and was explicit about working with the finest literary traditions and pedigrees; in fact he is singled out by Allardyce Nicoll as an example of the self-appointed literary élite among dramatists of the time.[16] Nicoll's view of dramatic legitimacy in the early nineteenth century is pertinent to Milman: 'The trouble with the legitimate drama was not that it was legitimate but that it was too conscious and proud of its legitimacy'.[17] Nicoll goes on to discuss Milman's particular brand of legitimacy with regard to his one real attempt at a performable stage play, *Fazio*:

15 Milman, *The Fall of Jerusalem*, 156.

16 Nicoll, *A History of English Drama, 1660–1900*, IV, 155.

17 Nicoll, *A History of English Drama, 1660–1900*, IV, 155.

> Sheil, Maturin and Milman were the favourites of the literary critics of the earlier decades. [...] If Sheil and Maturin show the romantic tendency towards sensationalism, Henry Hart Milman displays the tendency towards Fletcherian fantastic 'tragedy.' Milman's work was not so definitely theatrical as that of his two companions. Not only was he more noted in another sphere of literary endeavour, but only one of his plays was written deliberately for the stage. This was *Fazio* (Surrey, Dec. 1816), originally performed at the Surrey as *The Italian Wife*, a drama which tells of the seizure of the dead Bartolo's gold by the hero Fazio, of his betrayal by his jealous wife, Bianca, and of her final repentance. The great merit of the play is the opportunity it gives for robust and full-blooded acting. Fazio is a good 'part' and there is ample opportunity for the display of talent in both Bianca and Arabella. Possibly this quality gave it its contemporary popularity.[18]

The eponymous antihero of *Fazio* is not explicitly identified as a Jewish character. Instead, Milman's original title foregrounds the Jacobean-style Italian setting, itself a form of scandalous exoticism, with the connotations of Catholicism and Machiavelli that appealed to contemporary Gothic novelists just as they had to Jacobean dramatists. However, I would argue that the play's central character is Milman's lightly disguised deployment of some of the distinctive features of Jewish caricature. The plot of *Fazio* is driven by financial greed; money is less a means of acquiring security, luxury, and power than a quasi-mystical fetish in the form of gold; his desire for and pursuit of gold does not make Fazio powerful, but depletes and corrupts him, alienating him from the state. The opening scene introduces Fazio and Bianca in an alchemical laboratory, an exotic setting with a heavy symbolic emphasis on avarice, and money as a transformative agent. The murdered Bartolo, whose wealth is stolen by the opportunist Fazio, has made himself fabulously rich through the trade of usury. In stealing Bartolo's gold, Fazio becomes polluted with the avaricious motives he had affected to despise, as Milman – displaying a cultured debt to Ben Jonson – degrades the vocation of alchemy from spiritual quest to the squalid indulgence of greed.[19]

18 Nicoll, *A History of English Drama, 1660–1900*, IV, 166–7.

19 Milman's choice of names for his characters is ostentatiously Jonsonian: Aldabella, Falsetto, Dandolo ('the King of Fashions'). Henry Hart Milman, *Fazio: A Tragedy* (London: J. Parker and J. Murray, 1816), 22.

But if Fazio recalls Jonson's Subtle and Volpone in his love of wealth, his smooth transition to stage villainy strongly resembles Marlowe's Jewish merchant Barabas. As he prepares to defile Bartolo's grave and rob his property, Fazio utters a soliloquy that appears to be modelled closely on Barabas's similar nocturnal speech in Act II of *The Jew of Malta*. Fazio, like Barabas, embraces the role of vengeful Machiavel, although unlike Barabas he can cite no outrages or provocations to rationalize his crimes, having decadently seduced himself.

> *Enter FAZIO, with a dark lantern.*[20]
> FAZIO. I, wont to rove like a household dog,
> Caress'd by every hand, and fearing none,
> Now prowl e'en like a gray and treasonous wolf.
> 'Tis a bad deed to rob, and I'll have none on't
> 'Tis a bad deed to rob – and whom! the dead?
> Ay, of their winding-sheets and coffin nails.[21]
> 'Tis but a quit-rent for the land I sold him,
> Almost two yards to house him and his worms;
> Somewhat usurious in the main, but what
> Is honest thrift to your keen usurer.
> Had he a kinsman, nay a friend, 'twere devilish.
> But now whom rob I? why, the state. In sooth,
> Marvellous little owe I this same state,
> That I should be so dainty of its welfare.
> Methinks our Duke hath pomp enough; our Senate,
> Sit in their scarlet robes and ermine tippets,
> And live in proud and pillar'd palaces,
> Where their Greek wines flow plentiful. Besides,
> To scatter it abroad amid so many,

20 In an early nineteenth-century context, Fazio's use of a 'dark lantern' in this scene has connotations not just of robbery, but specifically of grave-robbery.

21 This line appears to allude to the legal point that only such objects as shrouds could technically be stolen from a grave, since a human body could not be owned as a possession and therefore could not be stolen; consequently, grave-robbers were known to be fastidious in not removing any of the casket itself and leaving all clothing behind. See e.g. Ruth Richardson, *Death, Dissection and the Destitute* (London: Routledge, & Kegan Paul, 1987), 58–9.

It were to cut the sun out into spangles,
And mar its brilliance by dispersing it.
Away! away! His burying is my Rubicon!
Cæsar or nothing! Now, ye close-lock'd treasures,
Put on your gaudiest hues, outshine yourselves!
With a deliverer's, not a tyrant's hand,
Invade I thus your dull and peaceful slumbers,
And give you light and liberty. Ye shall not
Moulder and rust in pale and pitiful darkness,
But front the sun with light bright as his own.
[*Exit*]. (I, ii, 1–29)[22]

In Marlowe's scene and in Milman's, a dominant character newly committed to a path of villainy enters the stage at night bearing a torch. Barabas means to meet his daughter who has smuggled his wealth out of their house after his property was confiscated; Fazio is on the point of robbing a grave for a dead miser's riches. Both cast themselves as internal exiles reviled by society, choosing an animal with baleful associations to embody this newly adopted identity. Fazio displays a Marlovian will to power in wishing to make himself 'Cæsar or nothing'. And both scenes are based around the theme of excavating buried treasure – a furtive activity which can unlock and mobilize great wealth for someone who is bold enough to disregard the niceties of the law – and knows just where to dig:

Enter Barabas with a light.
BARABAS. Thus like the sad presaging raven that tolls
The sick man's passport in her hollow beak,
And in the shadow of the silent night
Doth shake contagion from her sable wings,
Vex'd and tormented runs poor Barabas
With fatal curses towards these Christians. (II, i, 1–6)[23]

22 Milman, *Fazio: A Tragedy* (London: J. Parker and J. Murray, 1816).

23 Christopher Marlowe, *The Complete Plays*, ed. Frank Romany and Robert Lindsey (London: Penguin, 2003). All quotations from Marlowe are from this edition.

As well as managing and adapting this source text in Marlowe's Jewish villain, Milman develops a number of complex visual ideas in Fazio's speech, such as the conflation of robbery with grave-robbery, and the conflation of the wealthy Bartolo's magnificent house with his little coffin buried in its little plot of ground; hence we have the merging of the body and its value with the gold and its value, and finally the merging of resurrection with burglary. Like many a cynically self-justifying thief, Fazio prefers to think in terms of *liberating* those commodities which he covets: 'ye close-lock'd treasures, [...]/With a deliverer's, not a tyrant's hand,/Invade I thus your dull and peaceful slumbers,/And give you light and liberty.' The speech imagines wealth not as the heavy clinking money bags loved by Barabas, but as the heat and brilliance of the sun, an abstraction of financial value in an age of virtual finance driven by speculation, confidence, and imagination.

In view of this strong consonance with the stage Jews of the Renaissance dramas which Milman knew well, one of the most significant features of *Fazio* is that the central character is not explicitly identified as Jewish at all: words like Jew and Hebrew are entirely absent from the text; the setting is an unspecified Italian state characterized by venality and corruption (a standard of Jacobean drama); however, it is made clear that Bartolo has gained his fortune not only through maritime trade, but also through usury. Milman thus re-attributes the received values of antisemitic prejudice as venal and hypocritical traits which are characteristic of Italian or Catholic or Christian or simply human society; the play is in this sense an exercise in de-semitizing the inheritance of Shylock and Barabas.

In alluding to and adapting Marlowe's stage Jew Barabas, Milman both practises and critiques the intertextual formation of an exotic Jewish other. Without explicitly naming Fazio as a Jewish character, Milman mobilizes so many of the key ingredients from the Marlovian example as well as from popular prejudice that, when combined with his established record of writing on themes and episodes from Jewish history, the intention seems highly likely. Fazio may not be named 'Jew', but he embodies for the audience and reader not only the moral and cultural qualities they associate with Jewish characters but also their collective guilt and complicity in a history of exploiting, ostracizing, and demonizing Jews. In his later work on the history of the Jewish nation, Milman analyses the self-justifying strategies of Christian capitalism in constructing the Jew as a subversive parasite; but in *Fazio* he gives this argument dramatic life and physical form.

It was however not this oblique dramatic unravelling of caricature stage Jewry, but Milman's work as a historian of the Jewish people which is a likely influence on the 'philosemitic' drama of Thomas Wade. In *The History of the Jews*, Milman had delivered a scathing verdict on antisemitic persecution in mediaeval and early modern England, in which successive monarchs raised punitive levies on London's exiled mercantile Jewish population. Milman's *The History of the Jews* was a successful and influential work; first published in 1829, running to a second edition the following year, and followed by a series of re-prints and abridgements (1843, 1863, 1874, 1876, 1909), it became the standard modern work on the theme, complementing the still-revered classical work by Flavius Josephus.[24] Milman's basically secular history nevertheless retains a sense of mission and destiny, responding to Jewish traditions of cyclical history: 'Scattered [...] over the face of the earth—hated, scorned, and oppressed, they subsist, a numerous and often thriving people; and in all these changes of manners and opinions retain their ancient institutions, their national character, and their indelible hope of restoration to grandeur and happiness in their native land'.[25] The narrative also uses Jewish experience as a universal focus to expose the shame of the modern European Christian states: 'Thus the history of this, perhaps the only unmingled, race, which can boast of high antiquity, leads us through every gradation of society, and brings us into contact with almost every nation which commands our interest in the ancient world; [...] it descends, at length, to all the changes in the social state of the modern European and Asiatic nations'.[26] Two chapters of Milman's *History* are

24 Josephus's *History* had been used as research material for the actor Charles Macklin as he prepared to perform Shylock at Drury lane in 1741: see Peter Thomson, 'Actors and acting from Garrick to Kean, in Jane Moody and Daniel O'Quinn, eds, *The Cambridge Companion to British Theatre, 1730–1830* (Cambridge: Cambridge University Press, 2007), 3–19, 5.

25 Henry Hart Milman, *The History of the Jews*, 2nd edn (London and New York: George Routledge and Sons, 1830), 1–2.

26 Milman, *The History of the Jews*, 2.

particularly relevant to Wade's drama, those dealing with the expulsion of the Jews from England and from Spain. Milman emphasizes that Jews in mediaeval Spain frequently occupied more socially elevated – even aristocratic – positions than in England: 'Prosperous and wealthy, they had not been generally reduced to the sordid occupations and debasing means of extorting riches, to which [...] they had sunk in other countries. They were likewise the most enlightened class in the kingdom—they were cultivators and possessors of the soil; they were still, not seldom, ministers of finance; their fame as physicians was generally acknowledged [...]'.[27] The narrative deals at length with enforced conversion, atrocity, and extermination. In his chapter of the expulsion of the Jews from England under Edward I in the late thirteenth century, Milman's writing is a study in learned understatement in anatomizing Christian hypocrisy:

> The Jews were pursued from the kingdom with every mark of popular triumph in their sufferings. [...] The number of exiles is variously estimated at 15,060 and 16,511; all their property, debts, obligations, mortgages escheated to the king. The convents made themselves masters of their valuable libraries, one at Stamford, another at Oxford, from which the celebrated Roger Bacon is said to have derived great information; and long after, the common people would dig in the places they had frequented, in hopes of finding buried treasures. Thus terminates the first period of the History of the Jews in England.[28]

Milman's analytical narrative observes how the Christian monarchy incorporated a performance of compassionate restraint into the act of expulsion, while also taking credit for stolen erudition; the symbolic theme of digging is here once again – digging for real gold, and perhaps for the metaphorical gold of learning.

Thomas Wade bases his tragedy *The Jew of Arragon* around just such a historical event; the setting may be Spanish, but Wade's cutting indictment of English historical guilt is clear enough. The play alludes a number of times to Shylock's speech on the common humanity of Christians and Jews in *The Merchant of Venice*. Xavier, the character played by Kemble,

27 Milman, *The History of the Jews*, 565.
28 Milman, *The History of the Jews*, 564.

recalls both Barabas and Shylock, not only in being an alien Jew in a venal and duplicitous Christian state, but also in becoming ruthless and vengeful through casual exploitation and persecution meted out by Christian society; unlike the grotesque comedy of Barabas or the righteous fury of Shylock, however, Xavier's response to provocation is pathetic, arousing sentimental morality in the implied spectator. Wade invokes the available Renaissance intertexts, and deliberately exceeds both of them with his protagonist, replacing the outsider individualism of Marlowe's and Shakespeare's characters with a modern theme of general emancipation.

Not a great deal is remembered about Thomas Wade: 'No author of his time has left less tangible biographic memorial. The only anecdote preserved is Fanny Kemble's testimony to the fortitude with which he bore the failure of his tragedy.[29] But Wade's *DNB* entry notes the spectacular failure of this play, in which he seems to have been emotionally very invested:

> 'The Jew of Arragon; or the Hebrew Queen', a tragedy (in five acts and in verse), produced at Covent Garden in October of that same year, though supported not only by Charles but by Fanny Kemble, was literally 'howled from the stage' on account of the partiality shown to the Jews. Wade, nothing daunted, published his play with a dedication to the Jews of England, and restored in capitals the passages deleted by the licenser on political grounds. (London, 12mo)[30]

Notwithstanding the polemic of the play, Michael Scrivener is sceptical about Wade's political sense, writing: 'As a play to promote the case for Jewish emancipation, *The Jew of Arragon* is a huge miscalculation, for it attacks the English investment in Jewish representation at a too radical level. [...] The Jewess in conversionist narratives is supposed to effect social harmony and mutual understanding, whereas Wade's Rachel provokes bloody war'.[31] The performance text of the play was crudely censored, and the public reaction hostile. In his indignation, Wade used his rapidly printed book version of

29 Richard Garnett, 'Thomas Wade (1805–75)', in *Dictionary of National Biography 1885–1900*, LVIII, 419–20 <http://en.wikisource.org/wiki/Wade,_Thomas_(1805-1875)_(DNB00)> accessed 23 May 2014.

30 Garnett, *Dictionary of National Biography 1885–1900*, LVIII, 419.

31 Scrivener, *After Shylock*, 136.

the play to launch a public retaliation: 'Thus much as to the subject of the tragedy. Its failure on the stage only renders its publication the more imperative. [...] Amid the general cry of condemnation (the invariable portion of ill-success, merited or unmerited) which has of late been rung so cheerily and continually in my ears ...'[32] But this is not merely injured literary vanity; in striking back against his critics, Wade has a mission, as he explains: 'To confirm the opinion of the two or three sensible people, that there is at least one superfluous office in the state, those words and sentences which were struck by the Deputy Play-Licenser from the manuscript copy of the tragedy submitted to him for his approval, I have caused to be printed in capitals; the liberal reader will smile in perusing them; and deign, perhaps, to anticipate with some pleasure the speedy abolition of a childish tribunal.'[33] In the footnote to the first such instance deleted by the censor, in which the hero Xavier projects a heavenly reward in the new Jerusalem to compensate for the years of persecution in the modern 'Babylon' (I, ii), Wade writes, 'In these amusing erasures, Mr Colman had evidently the fear of the Jews before his eyes.' With these capitalized passages and footnote retaliations Wade 'stages' his quarrel with the establishment in print: the text and its commentary enact a drama of persecution and resistance in the present moment of reading, which runs parallel to the historical action of the play. There are several more sarcastic comments at the foot of the page, such as 'Here again the licenser dazzles us' (III, iii). Wade reinforces his campaigning stance in one of the most striking dramatic prefaces or dedications of its time:

> Countrymen, the heroine of my tragedy, who once lived in the actual world, made a monarch captive to her dark-eyed beauty, and fell from that dangerous triumph to an early and bloody grave—was a Jewess; my hero, a personage altogether imaginary, and a creation (I would fain hope) not wholly unworthy of those glorious warriors, priests and kings of old from whom I have fabled him to be descended—is a Jew; my entire subject is Jewish; and the main object of my work has been to embody, in a dramatic form, the struggles, triumphs and sorrows (in some degree historical, but

32 Thomas Wade, 'Preface', in *The Jew of Arragon; or, The Hebrew Queen: a Tragedy in Five Acts* (London: Smith, Elder & Co., 1830), v–vi. All quotations from the play are from this edition.

33 Wade, 'Preface', in *The Jew of Arragon*, vii.

> for the most part fictitious) of a noble Hebrew and his daughter, amid the woes and oppressions of their once mighty race. To whom, then, could I dedicate my theme so fitly, as to you? And of what better occasion than the present could I avail myself, to add my weak and unknown voice to that gathering and all-prevailing power of opinion, which assents to and enforces your demand to be freed from those chains of exclusion with which you have so long, and so unjustly, been fettered by your Christian countrymen?[34]

Wade's preface indirectly references Shylock's speech on the common bodily humanity of Jewish people; and the author boldly asserts that his play is a polemic witnessing to the 'manifold persecutions' and 'many centuries of bigotry and darkness' suffered by British Jewry.[35]

The expository plot in Act I, scene 1 is basically that of *The Jew of Malta*: threatened once again by an Islamic enemy, the Christian state looks to its Jewish immigrant population to bail it out with emergency financial aid – compulsory levies or 'exactions', and punitive unsecured loans. In *The Jew of Arragon*, as in *The Jew of Malta*, the dramatic action centres on the unmarried daughter of a powerful yet ostracized Jew within a Christian state, and the erotic fascination she commands in Gentile men. Yet Wade's play proves to be an un-writing of Marlowe's, in that whereas Barabas conflates his daughter Abigail with his wealth, rejoicing in recovering both from the Christians in the euphoric 'my girl! my gold' speech (II, i, 45–53), Wade's Xavier exposes and shames the Christians' commodification of his daughter Rachel. The equivalence between the virginal female body and the potential of golden wealth is there in both texts, but it is owned by different characters.

> XAVIER. 'Tis fix'd! 'tis fix'd!—her aim shall be the crown—
> And may the Guide of Israel prosper us!
> Oh! well I know, she'll leap to my intent;
> For she hath dreams of glorious destiny—
> And I but hold a substance to her view,
> For their proud spirit to fill and animate:
> This deed's the child o'the time—and shall be done;
> A Hebrew Queen must rule in Arragon! [*Exit*]. (I, iii; 19)

34 Wade, 'Dedication', in *The Jew of Arragon*, ix–x.

35 Wade, 'Dedication', in *The Jew of Arragon*, x.

The solution proposed by Xavier to the Christian king's rapacious persecution of his community is his own daughter. Xavier refers to Rachel's ambition and desire for greatness, which he can use to his advantage, and it is a given that her exotic attractiveness will supplant the king's current fiancée Isabella. In making Xavier his vengeful and rebellious hero, therefore, Wade perpetuates something of what makes Marlowe's Barabas such a troubling anti-hero – the use of a female body as an object of financial and religious exchange, simultaneously bartered to resolve the imposed debt and contested in the struggle for conversion:

> My precious Rachel! I do glory in thee
> More than the Prophet in his Prophetess:
> Thou art design'd for work miraculous;
> And in thine inborn royalty of soul
> And outward-worn nobility, I read
> Annihilation of the King's decree,
> Glory and Power to Spanish Israel,
> And vengeance full for every Christian wrong
> Our patience hath bent us to. (II, i, 21)

Unlike her predecessor Abigail, Rachel does not provide a comforting example of conversion to Christianity, but remains proud in her Jewish identity until death, despite falling in love with the king Alphonso, whom she knows to be a tyrant who will steal the Jews' property and drive them out of Spain.

> RACHEL. Villains! I fear ye not: a desperation
> Makes me immortal! Sire, I drink to thee.
> [*Drinks the poison*].
> My dream! my dream!—Oh, speedy remedy!—
> I've dearly loved Alphonso, O, my father;
> And I do fear, with love that almost quench'd
> That higher love—my country; thine, my glory.
> We've reigned! 'tis something: all is over now.
> Thou see'st how calmly I do bear this torture—
> Thou'lt follow—Oh!—so; so; past suffering—
> My soul's asleep—the king— [*Dies*]. (V, iv; 79)

In sending her to her melodramatic death, Wade has Rachel declare that her love for her father and her nation is 'higher' than her rival erotic relationship with the Christian Alphonso. It is a measure of Wade's campaigning stance in this play that Rachel is briefly both a Jewess and queen of Aragon; Wade deliberately rejects the motif of the conversion of a Jewish daughter in his key intertext *The Jew of Malta*.

As a male Jew, Xavier is also identified by distinctive a marker – circumcision – which is concealed but known to be present; this contributes to his ambiguity and disruptive power in the Christian dramatic state. In discussing the sexual assertiveness of Wade's central character Xavier, Michael Scrivener cites a key semantic moment in the play: 'When Xavier gazes at Isabella in a sexually evaluative manner, the Christian Manrique protests: "Thy presence does inflict a circumcision". The encounters with Isabella and Manrique establish the dominant masculinity of Xavier, despite his age'.[36] But what does Manrique mean by this? This only direct mention of the key physical marker of Jewish identity may have an element of the erudite pun about it: by intruding on this Christian space and contaminating the chastity of a Christian woman, Xavier is cutting through or 'cutting around' that society; but is it he or Isabella who will be separated or isolated by the cut? An interesting feature of circumcision in early modern drama is that it is not unique to Judaism, but used equally as a marker for Islam, especially in the form of the threatening power of the Ottoman Empire; for example, Barabas attempts to bond with the Moslem slave Ithamore by observing that they are both circumcized, both villains, and both hate Christians.[37] As a signifier then, circumcision denotes the others of Christianity, as much as it denotes Judaism per se. With the offensive presence of his ostracized Jewish body, Xavier disrupts or 'cuts' the supposedly coherent community

36 Scrivener, *After Shylock*, 136.

37 Examples from Marlowe: 'You know our army is invincible;/As many circumcised Turks we have ...' (Bajazeth, 1 *Tamburlaine*, III, i, 7–8); 'In spite of these swine-eating Christians,—/Unchosen nation, never circumcis'd,/Such as (poor villains!) were ne'er thought upon/Till Titus and Vespasian conquered us,—/Am I become as wealthy as I was' (*The Jew of Malta*, II, iii, 17–21); 'Make account of me/As of thy fellow; we are villains both:/Both circumcised; we hate Christians both:/Be true and secret, thou shalt want no gold' (Barabas to Ithamore, *The Jew of Malta*, II, iii, 214–17).

or text of Aragon. A similarly crude kind of drama can be seen in Wade's use of the key word itself. The epithet 'Jew' is used frequently throughout *The Jew of Arragon*, not only as a term of abuse, but also as a blunt fact. 'Jew' is sometimes appended to a provocative or demeaning speech directed at Xavier, but it is also used as a quasi-statement, sometimes drawing the equally empty factual riposte 'Christian'. Jewish characters do not necessarily look different or sound different, or act differently or speak differently; but texts tell us emphatically, dogmatically, that they are and must be different. The proof is as uncertain and invisible as the presence of 'a circumcision', and as crude and obtuse as the repeated word 'Jew' itself. *The Jew of Arragon; or, the Hebrew Queen* is not a particularly fine or subtle play, but it effects a single-minded, systematic dismantling of the discourse of racial enmity. Did Thomas Wade think that London audiences were ready to applaud this drama, which cast them as complacent passive oppressors?

Literary intertextuality is an intrinsic part of the formation of an exotic body in the case of Jewish characters in nineteenth-century drama. The exotic male and female Jewish bodies in these plays by Milman and Wade are revisionist interventions, gathering and displacing the accumulated intertexts of prejudice. In addition to their intertextual formation, however, their exotic bodies are notable for their invocation of the increasingly abstract nature of financial value in the 1810s and '20s. Fazio and Xavier contribute to the accumulating cultural paradoxes of the Jew in the text or on the stage in British culture – the character who supposedly fetishizes gold, but is actually a focus for the anxious gold-obsession of society at large, a character supposedly consumed with venality and lust, whose power actually derives from the manipulation of appearances and beliefs, the abstract power of the imagination.

Bibliography

Bradshaw, Michael, 'Elizabethan Style in Drama', in Frederick Burwick, Nancy Moore Goslee and Diane Long Hoeveler, eds, *The Encyclopedia of Romantic Literature*, 3 vols (Oxford: Blackwell, 2012), 415–21.

Burwick, Frederick, 'The Romantic Drama', in Duncan Wu, ed., *A Companion to Romanticism* (Malden, MA and Oxford: Blackwell. 1999), 323–32.

Cheyette, Bryan, ed., *Between Race and Culture: Representations of 'the Jew' in English and American Literature* (Stanford: Stanford University Press, 1996).

——, ed., *Constructions of the 'the Jew' in English Literature and Society: Racial Representations, 1875–1945* (Cambridge: Cambridge University Press, 1993).

Davis, Tracy C., '"Reading Shakespeare by Flashes of Lightning": Challenging the Foundations of Romantic Acting Theory', *ELH* 62 (1995), 933–54.

Garnett, Richard, 'Thomas Wade (1805–75)', in *Dictionary of National Biography 1885–1900*, LVIII, 419 <http://en.wikisource.org/wiki/Wade,_Thomas_(1805–1875)_(DNB00)> accessed 23 April 2014.

Hazlitt, William, 'The Merchant of Venice', in *The Characters of Shakespeare's Plays* (1817) <http://www.library.utoronto.ca/utel/criticism/hazlittw_charsp/charsp_ch23.html> accessed 5 May 2015.

Marlowe, Christopher, *The Complete Plays*, ed. Frank Romany and Robert Lindsey (London: Penguin, 2003).

Milman, Henry Hart, *The Fall of Jerusalem* [1820] *and Belshazzar* [1822], intro. Donald H. Reiman (New York and London: Garland, 1977).

——, *Fazio: A Tragedy* (London: J. Parker and J. Murray, 1816).

——, *The History of the Jews*, 2nd edn (London and New York: George Routledge and Sons, 1830).

Moody, Jane and D. O'Quinn, eds, *The Cambridge Companion to British Theatre, 1730–1830* (Cambridge: Cambridge University Press, 2007).

Nicoll, Allardyce, *A History of English Drama, 1660–1900* (Cambridge: Cambridge University Press, 1955), vol. 4, *Early Nineteenth-Century Drama, 1800–1850*.

Nochlin, Linda and Tamar Garb, eds, *The Jew in the Text: Modernity and the Construction of Identity* (London: Thames and Hudson, 1995).

Page, Judith W., *Imperfect Sympathies: Jews and Judaism in British Romantic Literature and Culture* (Basingstoke: Palgrave Macmillan, 2004).

Richardson, Alan and Sonia Hofkosh, eds, *Romanticism, Race, and Imperial Culture, 1780–1834* (Bloomington and Indianapolis: Indiana University Press, 1996).

Ruth Richardson, *Death, Dissection and the Destitute* (London: Routledge & Kegan Paul, 1987).

Scrivener, Michael, *Jewish Representation in British Literature 1780–1840: After Shylock* (Basingstoke: Palgrave Macmillan, 2011).

Spector, Sheila A., ed., *British Romanticism and the Jews: History, Culture, Literature* (New York and Basingstoke: Palgrave Macmillan, 2002).

Wade, Thomas, *The Jew of Arragon; or, The Hebrew Queen: a tragedy in five acts* (London: Smith, Elder & Co., 1830).

ARTHUR W. BLOOM

Edwin Forrest: The Exotic American Body on the Nineteenth-Century English Stage

ABSTRACT

In 1836 the exotic body on the English stage was male, white, muscular and American. It belonged to the melodramatic tragedian Edwin Forrest who chose to introduce himself to English audiences as Spartacus the tragic hero of Robert Montgomery Bird's *The Gladiator*, a role that allowed him to appear in a topless tunic that emphasized his muscle builder physique. He was likened to the Farnese Hercules in stature, and English audiences and critics, accustomed to the refined characterizations of Kemble, Siddons and Macready saw in Forrest an American version of Edmund Kean. He seemed quintessentially American in his lack of subtlety, 'a savage newly caught from out of the American backwoods [...] replete with a rough music befitting one who in his youth has dwelt a free barbarian among the mountains'. Forrest was an American other, and his otherness was a complete fabrication. He was born and brought up in Philadelphia, one of the most genteel of American cities, had spent only four years in what was then the American west (Cincinnati, Louisville, New Orleans) and had become a theatrical sensation opening as Othello at the Bowery Theatre in New York on November 6, 1826. His acting style and the plays in which he performed were designed to create an American persona and to reinforce English assumptions about what that persona would be. Both as Spartacus and as the title character in John Augustus Stone's *Metamora; or the Last of the Wampanoags*, Forrest's personal physicality and what Walt Whitman called 'his loud-mouthed ranting style' appeared to embody American freedom while simultaneously foretelling the tragic fate of the slave and the Indian. His physical exoticism as Spartacus transported audiences to a world that had disappeared or, in the case of *Metamora*, was rapidly disappearing.

***

The currently fashionable term 'exotic body' refers to that which is foreign to or 'other' than that to which it is being compared. This essay employs the term both in that manner and in a more mundane sense of an unusual corporeal body. During 1836, 1837, 1845 and 1846 the exotic body on the English stage was male, white, muscular and American. It belonged to the melodramatic tragedian Edwin Forrest, who introduced himself to

English audiences as Spartacus, the tragic hero of Robert Montgomery Bird's *The Gladiator*, a role that allowed him to appear in a topless tunic that emphasized his muscle-builder physique. While a photograph from 1861 shows a frankly disappointing level of musculature, drawings from an earlier period (see Figures 1 and 2) indicate an audience perception that

Figure 1: Drawing of the youthful Edwin Forrest as Spartacus. University of Pennsylvania Library, Philadelphia, Pennsylvania.

Figure 2: Drawing of the youthful Edwin Forrest as Spartacus. Victoria and Albert Museum, London.

Forrest's body was 'exotic' in the sense of monumentally beyond the physical norm, particularly in costume accessories that pointed toward his groin.

Forrest spent his life working on his body. He walked on his hands and rubbed his body with rough towels until it gleamed. In 1872 he died of a stroke while lifting weights before breakfast. He was initially motivated by a fear of heredity. Born in 1806, Forrest lost his father to tuberculosis in 1819, and the boy's narrow chest suggested to those around him that might not reach manhood. He later remembered: 'I often heard [...] people say: "Ned is a weak child; we fear [his mother] shall never be able to raise him" [...]. Early in life I took a great deal of exercise and made myself what I am, a Hercules'.[1] The Scots actor John Coleman wrote: 'As the Gladiator [...] he was the Farnese Hercules in the flesh. It is true that his acting had nothing of psychological subtlety about it, but it was thorough, straight, manly, and convincing [...]. In Hamlet, when he exclaimed "My father's brother – but no more like my father than I to Hercules!" a Scotsman in the pit interjected: "Hoo awa', mon! Dinna talk damned nonsense! Ye are Hercules himself"!'[2] The critic for the London *Morning Herald* wrote: 'Mr Forrest is, in person, most remarkable for symmetrical but somewhat Herculean proportions. He might take the Farnese club and stand a perfect model to a painter or sculptor. His neck is also as a pillar of strength, and his head finely set on'.[3]

English audiences and critics, accustomed to the refined characterizations of John Philip Kemble, Sarah Siddons and William Charles Macready, saw in Forrest an American version of the passionate Romantic actor Edmund Kean. He seemed quintessentially American in his lack of subtlety, 'a savage newly caught from out of the American backwoods [...] replete with a rough music befitting one who in his youth has dwelt a free

1 William Moody, *Edwin Forrest: First Star of the American Stage* (New York: Alfred A. Knopf, 1960), 15.

2 John Coleman, *Fifty Years of an Actor's Life* (New York: James Pott & Co., 1904), 334–5.

3 *Public Ledger*, 25 November 1836.

barbarian among the mountains'.[4] Forrest was an American other, but his otherness was a complete fabrication. He was born and brought up in Philadelphia, one of the most genteel of American cities, had spent only four years in what was then the American West (Cincinnati, Louisville, New Orleans) and had become a theatrical sensation as Othello at the Bowery Theatre in New York in 1826, at the age of 20. His earliest biographers romanticized his boyhood adventures with dissolute sea captains, noble Indians and even the frontier hero Jim Bowie, but throughout his life Forrest preferred the company of upper-class, refined, cultured individuals. He seldom made friends with theatre people, seeking instead the companionship of newspaper men, writers, poets, lawyers and other professionals. But his acting style and the original plays in which he performed were designed to create an American persona and to reinforce both English and American assumptions about what that persona would be. As Theresa Saxon writes, 'For audiences associated with working-class venues [in a portion of New York City called the Bowery] Forrest was the exemplar of [...] an heroic style that suited their ideals of a democratic American nation'.[5]

In 1829 Forrest offered $500 for a tragedy in five acts in which the hero would be 'an aboriginal of this country'. The winner was John Augustus Stone's *Metamora; or the Last of the Wampanoags*. It set the pattern for Forrest's subsequent original characters, particularly Spartacus and Jack Cade. All are proponents of individual freedom against aristocratic tyranny, but, because Forrest saw himself as a tragedian, all had to perish in the cause of liberty. As both Metamora and Spartacus, Forrest's personal physicality and what Walt Whitman called 'his loud-mouthed ranting style' appeared to embody American freedom while simultaneously foretelling the tragic fate of the Indian and the slave. Joe Cowell, an Englishman working as an actor in early nineteenth-century America, saw in Forrest's lack of cultivation a reflection of the audiences that had proclaimed him a star:

4 *The Sun* (18 October 1836) quoted in Horatio Alger Jr and William Rounseville Alger, *Life of Edwin Forrest*, I (Philadelphia: J.B. Lippincott & Co., 1877), 303.

5 Theresa Saxon, *American Theatre History, Context, Form* (Edinburgh: Edinburgh University Press, 2011), 118.

> [Forrest as a young man] had had the advantage of some useful practice [...] in the South and West, to which almost 'undiscovered country' [...] but few foreigners had dared to venture. He possessed a fine, untaught face and good, manly figure and although unpolished in his deportment, his manners were frank and honest, and his uncultivated taste, speaking the language of truth and Nature would be readily understood [by] [...] the class of people among whom his fortunes had thrown him.[6]

Forrest was well aware of the effect his body produced on his audiences. When he first stepped on the stage as Spartacus, he would pause and let the audience look at his body before he began to speak. A critic in Albany, New York, reported that Forrest

> stepped upon the stage in his naked fighting trim, his muscular coating unified all over him and quivering with vital power, his skin polished by exercise and friction to a smooth and marble hardness, conscious of his enormous potency, fearless of anything on the earth, proudly aware of the impression he knew his mere appearance, backed by his fame, would make on the audience [that] impatiently awaited him; he used to stand and receive the long and tumultuous cheering that greeted him, as immovable as a planted statue of Hercules. The spectacle was worthy the admiration it won.[7]

In both England and America Forrest's lack of physical and psychological delicacy was what set him apart from English actors. In England the critic of the *London Courier* wrote: 'He is tall, handsome, muscular, and admirably proportioned. Indeed we have no such figure on the stage. His legs are so totally unlike those spindleshanks we are accustomed to see on our boards, as at first sight to appear padded and unnatural'.[8] The New York *Morning Herald* critic wrote: 'No actor in England can at all compare with Forrest except Macready. Forrest is all nature and Macready all art. The latter may give the more finishing touches but give me Yankee Doodle still'.[9]

By 1834 Forrest had made enough money to take a two-year grand tour of France, Italy, England, Germany, Russia, the Near East and Greece. The

6 Joe Cowell, *Thirty Years Passed Among the Players in England and America* (New York: Harper & Brothers, 1842), 74.

7 *The Evening Post* (24 November 1836), 2.

8 Reprinted from the *London Courier* in *The Western Times* (29 October 1836), 2.

9 Moody, *Edwin Forrest*, 167.

tour was designed to ameliorate his lack of cultural education and ended in England. There, as Forrest told a Philadelphia audience:

> I was repeatedly importuned with solicitations, and the most liberal offers were made to me. I finally consented not for my own sake – for my ambition is satisfied with the applause of my own countrymen – but partly in compliance with the wishes of a number of American friends, and partly to solve a doubt which is entertained by many of our citizens – whether Englishmen would receive an American actor with the same favour which is here extended to them. The doubt, so far as I have had an opportunity of judging is, I think, without foundation. During my residence in England, I found among the English people the most unbounded hospitality, and the warmest affection for my beloved country and her institutions. With this impression, I have resolved to present them an American tragedy, supported by the humble efforts of the individual who stands before you. If I fail, I fail. But whatever may be the result, the approbation of that public which first stamped the native dramatist and actor will ever be my proudest recollection.[10]

Forrest's Philadelphia speech was published in London four days before he opened at Drury Lane as Spartacus in *The Gladiator* by the American Robert Montgomery Bird on 17 October 1836. In effect he was laying down a challenge to English audiences and critics, and he was not disappointed. According to *The London Dispatch and People's Political and Social Reformer* of October 23:

> At the conclusion of the tragedy, Mr Forrest was loudly called for; obeying the summons, he told the audience that he felt sure that, in his exhausted state, they would excuse him if he failed in expressing all the thanks he felt for the very kind manner in which they had welcomed to the English stage an American performer [...]. The applause which succeeded changed into a slight show of disapprobation when Mr Forrest alluded to the handsome manner in which they had received the tragedy [...]. One gentleman in the boxes cried out: 'Let's see him in Shakespeare'.

English audiences were far more impressed with Forrest than with *The Gladiator*. The critic for *The Times* wrote:

10 *The Standard* (13 October 1836), n.p.

> Mr Forrest was received with a hearty warmth which, from the first moment of his appearance, left no doubt if any could have been entertained, that the audience [was] well disposed to accept his exertions for their entertainment. He is a tall, rather robust man, of some thirty years of age, not remarkably handsome but with expressive features […]. His voice is remarkably powerful, his figure rather vigorous than elegant […]. In concentrating the […] action of the play in […] Spartacus, [Bird] has bestowed very slight pains in the delineation of the other characters. The consequence of this is that all the scenes in which the hero is not in action are languid, and all the other personages in the play are very faintly sketched […]. The latter part of the play is less vigorous than the former […]. At the conclusion of the play Mr Forrest was called for, and began to address the audience, a practice not usual, nor safe, at least on this side of the Atlantic […]. When […] Mr Forrest, encouraged by the applause, began to thank them for the favours they had shown to the tragedy, he provoked some dissent, the audience not seeming to think as highly of the poet as of the player, so Mr Forrest made his bows and retired.[11]

The London *Morning Post*'s critic wrote that the thirty-year-old actor had astounded

> all eyes and ears by the overwhelming energy of his physical powers. Mr Forrest […] is tall, handsome, muscular and admirably proportioned. His declamation is perfectly free from the usual stage chaunt, catching, and points. Indeed nature alone seems to have been his only model. He is most certainly unlike any of our present actors […]. He was, indeed, from first to last, a magnanimous, a glorious barbarian […] of great prominence […] of muscle.

The reference to 'nature' indicates Forrest's most notable feature. Horatio Alger, Jr, the biographer whom Forrest paid to write his life story, wrote: 'In the same sense in which Forrest was melodramatic, God and Nature themselves are so.[12]

Forrest may have chosen Spartacus as his opening role in England not only because it showed off his body but also because Spartacus is the story of a slave revolt. Only three years before, the English parliament had abolished slavery throughout most of the British Empire. In actuality, as Jenna M. Gibbs has pointed out, 'the Emancipation Act of 1833 had been

11 *The Times* (18 October 1836), 3.

12 Alger, *Life of Edwin Forrest*, I, 197.

accomplished through a settlement whereby slave owners would be compensated and allowed to keep their slaves for an unpaid so-called apprenticeship of twelve years'.[13] In America the play was first produced while Nat Turner's slave rebellion was taking place in Southampton County, Virginia. While Spartacus is noble, he is also rebellious, and the play reflects its author's ambivalence about slavery. In a secret diary Bird wrote:

> If the Gladiator were produced in a slave state, the managers, players & perhaps myself into the bargain would be rewarded with the Penitentiary. Happy States. At this present moment there are 6[00] or 800 armed negroes marching through Southampton County, Va. murdering, ravishing, & burning those whom the Grace of God has made their owners – 70 killed, principally women & children. If they had but a Spartacus among them – to organize the half million of Virginia, the hundreds of thousands of [the] other states [and to] lead them on in the Crusade of Massacre, what a blessed example might they not give to the world of the excellence of slavery! What a field of interest to the playwriters [sic] of posterity! Someday we shall have it; and future generations will perhaps remember the horrors of Hayte [sic] as a farce compared with the tragedies of our own happy land! The *vis et amor sceleratus habendi* [force and criminal love of gain] will be repaid violence with violence, [&] avarice with blood. I had sooner live among bedbugs than negroes. But the play, the play – Ay the play's the thing. What a fool I was to think of writing plays! To be sure, they are much wanted.[14]

Americans saw in Spartacus a democratic hero fighting as an oppressed underdog for his freedom and family against a tyrannical government. Forrest, who had a reputation in America as the people's actor, blended his stage persona with that of the characters he played to voice American populism. American audiences might envision Rome as Britain and its slaves as their colonial ancestors, but the play's setting in classical Rome allowed English audiences to see it as a warning of what might happen if slaves were not free and as a vindication of their own decision in favor of abolition. At the same time, however, although the American Revolution

13 Jenna M. Gibbs, *Performing the Temple of Liberty: Slavery, Theater and Popular Culture in London and Philadelphia, 1760–1850* (Baltimore: John Hopkins University Press, 2014), 216.

14 Robert A. Bird, 'Secret Records', University of Pennsylvania.

had been successful, Spartacus has to die because Forrest was a tragedian, and because his death allowed American audiences to feel secure in light of Nat Turner's rebellion.

Although Forrest's reviews were personally positive, *The Gladiator* was not a success in London, and he abandoned playing the role in England after three performances, moving on to a series of Shakespearean characters (Othello, Lear, Macbeth) and roles in typical nineteenth-century pseudo-Shakespearean plays such as James Sheridan Knowles' *Virginius*, Richard Brinsley Sheridan's *Pizarro*, John Howard Payne's *Brutus* and John Banim's *Damon and Pythias*. He toured to Liverpool and Manchester before returning to London, where he became vice president of the Drury Lane Theatrical Fund and married an Englishwoman. He and his new wife left for America on 16 August 1837.

He returned to London and opened at the Princess's Theatre on 17 February 1845. On 26 March he appeared in John Augustus Stone's *Metamora or the Last of the Wampanoags*, a play that Forrest had not performed in England during his first tour (see Figure 3). Practical problems may have influenced his decision to introduce himself as Spartacus during the earlier visit rather than as Metamora. Bringing both *The Gladiator* and *Metamora* would have forced both Drury Lane and provincial English companies to get up two new plays. Forrest also had been uncertain of his English reception in 1836, only twenty-one years after the War of 1812 had ended. The villains of *Metamora* are the early Colonial English settlers in the process of exterminating the New World's Native Americans. Finally, he may have had some doubts about the play's merits. John Augustus Stone was a minor actor and hack writer, and Forrest had had Robert Montgomery Bird, who had a considerable literary reputation, to do revisions of the play before he took it abroad. Whatever reservations he may have had were fully justified. London's *Morning Post* described the play as

> a pure, unadulterated, genuine and unmistakable American tragic drama [...]. The Red Man of the vast wilderness, with his untamable love of liberty is shorn of all the ennobling qualities of his free nature and wild stoicism and becomes, in the stage process, a brawler and a butcher. We vainly essayed to follow the march of the piece – scene follows scene without the slightest attempt at forging a connecting link; there is neither development of character, dramatic construction, poetical imagery or interest

> of story – all is vague and inconsecutive. A number of personages, supposed to have existed in the days of the first Charles, and have emigrated to America – these are composed of Regicides and Roundheads – some dark mystery is shadowed forth, which is attached to the leading actors; but what it is, how they are implicated, and what is the result of the conflicting interests, was beyond our reflecting powers to fathom – it was confusion worse confounded. A young lady in white muslin is pursued through a 'pine barren' by an ancient gentleman in crimson velvet and silken hose – despite snags, swamps, gallinipers [huge mosquitoes], and rattlesnakes, the young lady in white muslin is saved by the Indian warrior – who we think announces his intention to watch over her future safety but all in honor, for our hero of the broad savannahs has a squaw and a papoose of his own, and is withal an unexceptionable husband and a doting parent; but the 'British' follow him to his hunting grounds; his squaw is about to fall into the power of the pale faces, and his papoose to be offered up as a peace offering to the hecatombs of scalps he has achieved, when driven to his last lair he tomahawks his better half, is unresistingly shot down like a rabid dog by the civilized Englishers, and expires uttering the most awful curses on his sacrificers. The entire drama is a most inartificial mass of coarse butchery, capable of affording recreation alone to the most brutified appetite, as does a Pennsylvania bond to a Bank of England note. [In both 1842 and 1845 the state of Pennsylvania had defaulted on its debts.] Mr Edwin Forrest gave an admirable portrait of the Indian *Metamora;* it was truthfully conceived and picturesquely embodied; there was the rude energy and repose – the abruptness and the ruggedness – the fellness and the stoicism – which we have been taught to consider as the grand elements in the character of the North American Indian – but all these various excellencies were wasted on this heterogeneous mass of turgid trash, which was suffered to proceed to its conclusion unhissed and unhooted.[15]

The [London] *Morning Chronicle*'s reviewer expressed doubts about even the validity of Forrest's characterization:

> Mr Edwin Forrest appeared last night in a new drama, wherein he sustained a part which is perhaps better adapted for the display of his energies and peculiar genius than the characters in Shakespeare's tragedies. The play, which we presume was written expressly for him, is in five acts, and entitled *Metamora, the Last of the Wampanogs.* The scene, as may be inferred from the title, is laid in North America, and the main action turns upon the contests between the emigrants from England, shortly after the execution of Charles I, and the red men of the soil. As the object appears solely

15 *The Morning Post* (27 March 1845), 6.

Figure 3: Drawing of the youthful Edwin Forrest as Metamora. University of Pennsylvania Library, Philadelphia, Pennsylvania.

> to give Mr Forrest the opportunity of appearing in the character of an Indian hero, and as both the admirers and detractors of that gentleman will no doubt go and see him in it, we may spare ourselves the trouble of attempting to describe a rather unintelligible plot, and of commenting upon a play which, considered as a literary production, seems to us to transcend criticism. We may, however, quietly wonder at the policy of elaborating, for the sake of legitimacy, into five dreary acts, materials which might have been much more effective if compressed into three [...]. Metamora is a savage warrior bold of heart and ready of hand, faithful and revengeful. He has gallantly resisted the encroachments of the English upon his territory, but the ranks of his tribe are thinned in the unequal contests and at last the miserable remnants are decoyed into a snare and massacred. *Metamora* and his wife alone remain. Her he solemnly devotes to death and stabs with his own hand, that she may not fall into the hands of his foes. He then presents himself to the muzzles of their fire and receives a dozen bullets, making, however, a longer and better dying speech than a man with so much lead in him could be reasonably supposed to utter. The admirers of Mr Forrest will be in raptures at his delineation of this character, while his detractors must, at least, admit that he may have presented a truthful impersonation of a genus of man which has not been represented, unless in caricature, upon any stage. Upon this point few of us have had the opportunity of deciding, and it appears unfair to test Mr Forrest's performance by the ordinary rules of stage criticism. The question seems to be this – has Mr Forrest presented a true picture of the red warrior of America; either a daguerreotype portrait, or one so far idealized as to suit the purpose of the artist, and gratify the eye of the spectator, yet still a resemblance? To judge this point fairly we ought, as in other cases, to see the original type, and it might not be discreet to venture an opinion upon the strength of a shilling's worth of comparison with the Ojibbeways.[16]

From 1843 through 1845, the American artist George Catlin, whose now revered Indian paintings were not selling well in England, spruced up his gallery by replacing the English actors whom he had disguised as Indians with a group of Ojibwa Native Americans designed to add 'spirit and reality' to the gallery. None were natural primitives plucked from the forest or the prairie. All were engaged in moneymaking tours 'playing Indian' for English audiences, just like Forrest.

The reviewer of [London's] *Lloyd's Weekly Newspaper*, quoting, in part, from the *Chronicle*'s review, wrote:

16 *The Morning Chronicle* (27 March 1845), 5.

> *Metamora, the Last of the Wampanoags* [...] has, we understand, been performed with considerable success at the principal theatres in the United States [...]. The principal character is to be found in the second volume of Washington Irving's sketch book, under the title of Philip of Pakanoket, and upon this Indian memoir does the drama in a great measure rest. It is one of those frightful and disgusting melodramatic productions, void of plot and character which used so signally to characterize the boards of the Coburg [one of London's unlicensed and consequently non-legitimate theatres] in its pristine days [...]. Washington Irving depicts the Wampanoags as a band of native untaught heroes who made the most generous struggle of which human nature is capable, fighting to the last gasp in the cause of their country without a hope of victory or a thought of renown. Worthy of an age of poetry and fit subject for local story and romantic fiction, they have left scarcely any authentic traces in the page of history but stalk the gigantic shadows in the dim twilight of tradition. This is the character of the tribe and Metamora who was their sovereign [...]. With heroic qualities and bold achievements that would have graced a civilized warrior and have rendered him the theme of the poet an historian, he lived a wanderer and a fugitive in his native land and went down like a lonely bark foundering amid darkness and tempest without a pitying eye to weep his fall, or having a friendly hand to record his struggle. Such are the grounds upon which the author has constructed his drama, which he has rendered a most inartificial mass of coarse butchery, capable of affording recreation only to the most brutified appetite.[17]

After three performances in London, Forrest abandoned performing Metamora regularly in England and embarked upon a provincial tour of Bristol, Bath, Dublin, Brighton, Manchester, Liverpool, Belfast, Glasgow, Carlisle and Cork, returning to *The Gladiator* and adding Shakespearean and other nineteenth-century standards. The mediocre reviews may have determined his decision, but it is also possible that the difficulty of touring to provincial English houses with two new plays (*Metamora* and *The Gladiator*) may have shifted his repertoire. Forrest's reviews in the English provinces were consistently positive, but he performed Metamora only once, relying on Spartacus and his Shakespearean and melodramatic parts. In Bath the local critic wrote of his Spartacus: 'The part which he took in the piece is sketched with considerable power, and his qualifications for representing it are such as to do it justice. His athletic figure, commanding

17 *Lloyd's Weekly Newspaper* (30 March 1845), 8.

mien, and powerful elocution, combined with his energy of action, give him advantages which are well turned to account'.[18]

Metamora reflects the dichotomy of the Caucasian vision of Native Americans as it evolved from the savagism depicted in eighteenth-century Colonial writing to the nostalgic romanticism that emerged in the early republic. James Fenimore Cooper's *The Last of the Mohicans*, published in 1826, only three years before Stone wrote *Metamora*, exemplifies the trend by contrasting the noble Uncas, defender of the pure-blooded blonde-haired Alice, with the despicable Magua, fatally attracted to the dark-haired mixed-blood Cora. If America was Arcadia, then the Native Americans had to be Arcadians; if, however, the English settlers were the proponents of a progressive civilization, then the Indians had to be lesser people designed to be colonized or obliterated. The solution to these opposing concepts was the noble savage, the physically magnificent and morally noble but potentially brutally savage American aboriginal.[19]

Just as tracts of land were set aside and remodeled in metropolitan areas so that the vestiges of the rapidly disappearing forest primeval could be retained (Central Park in New York City, Fairmount Park in Philadelphia), so too the Indian was appropriated and reconstructed to embody an idealized version of the qualities being lost in the gradual urbanization and industrialization of nineteenth-century America – the sanctity of land, the protection of women and children, reverence for ancestry, freedom of movement, the physical courage to endure hardship and the concept that a man's word was his bond. While in reality President Andrew Jackson's policy of Indian removal required that Native Americans be treated as inferior and dangerous beings so that their land could be appropriated, imaginatively they become superior, even heroic beings, of massive size and elevated diction, particularly as embodied by Edwin Forrest's Metamora. The Native American was thus appropriated as an object of white nostalgia

18 *Bath Chronicle and Weekly Gazette* (24 April 1845), 3.

19 Jeffrey D. Mason, *Melodrama and the Myth of America* (Bloomington: Indiana University Press, 1993), 32–3.

and Arcadian perfection.[20] Forrest brought to England the image of a mythic Indian that has a lengthy and continuing history in American culture – in American place names (the Lenape Valley, Malibu, Alabama), male fraternal organizations (the Order of Red Men founded in the 1820s), the rituals of scouting, political organizations (Tammany Hall named for a mythic Indian chief), Indian head nickels, Indian dress in Mardi Gras celebrations, professional and amateur sports teams (the Cleveland Indians, the Atlanta Braves, the Dartmouth College Indians, the Florida State University Seminoles), sixties counter-culture feathers and beads and above all the American motion picture in which the Indian could be savage or noble. Dialogue from a 1950s movie had the Indian chief saying: 'If I am not for myself, who will be for me?' – actually a quote from Rabbi Hillel. That this mythic view of the Indian is an illusion is best seen in a 1960s joke in which the Lone Ranger, watching a horde of Indian braves bear down on them in full battle fury, says to his Indian side-kick: 'Looks like we're in a heap of trouble, Tonto' and Tonto replies 'What you mean *we*, white man'?

Forrest performed both Spartacus and Metamora for his entire career. In these roles he brought to the English stage the exotic body of the perceived American – the American that Mrs Trollope saw – raw, natural, savage, untutored, strong, democratic, naturally moral, family-oriented, manly and, above all, free. In many respects it is still the way Americans perceive themselves and the way they are perceived in the world around them.

Bibliography

Alger, Horatio Jr. and Alger, William Rounseville, *Life of Edwin Forrest*, I (Philadelphia: J.B. Lippincott & Co., 1877).

Coleman, John, *Fifty Years of an Actor's Life* (New York: James Pott & Co., 1904).

20 Shari M. Hundorf, *Going Native: Indians in the American Cultural Imagination* (Ithaca: Cornell University Press, 2001), 6; Mason, *Melodrama and the Myth of America*, 25.

Cowell, Joe, *Thirty Years Passed among the Players in England and America* (New York: Harper & Brothers, 1842).

Hundorf, Shari M., *Going Native: Indians in the American Cultural Imagination* (Ithaca: Cornell University Press, 2001).

Mason, Jeffrey D., *Melodrama and the Myth of America* (Bloomington, Ind., Indiana University Press, 1993).

Moody, William, *Edwin Forrest: First Star of the American Stage* (New York: Alfred A. Knopf, 1960).

TIZIANA MOROSETTI

Constructing the Zulus: The 'African' Body and Its Narratives

ABSTRACT
As the ultimate theoretical goal of 'human zoos' or ethnological exhibitions was 'to demonstrate the superiority of the white race and/or of Western civilization' (Blanchard et al., *Human Zoos: Science and Spectacle in the Age of Colonial Empires*, 2008, 22), exhibits were presented to the public in their 'typical' environment, dressed in their 'distinctive' manner, and shown enjoying their 'routine'. The 'Zulu Kaffirs' exhibited by Charles Caldecott in 1853, as well as the 'Friendly Zulus' exhibited by Farini in 1880 are cases in point, but theatre is no exception, with titles such as Edward Fitzball's *Amakosa; or, Kaffir Warfare* (1853) C.S. James's *The Kaffir War* (1857), or the anonymous *The Grand Equestrian Spectacle of the War in Zululand* (1879) confirming, enhancing, and, sometimes, inspiring a politically oriented view of the Zulus. In this essay I will explore the narratives underlying both the exhibition of these 'exotic' bodies and their presence in the theatre, with particular attention paid to the visual features employed, as well as to their impact on (and relation to) the wider representation of 'Africans'. I will ultimately argue that portraits of the Zulus, both on the popular and theatrical stage, while responding to an increasingly historicized perception of specific African contexts, were nonetheless still used in Victorian entertainment as representative of the whole of Africa, thus reinforcing stereotypes of the continent dating back to before the nineteenth century.

***

In his 'cosmographical, visionary extravaganza, and dramatic review (in one act and four quarters)' *Mr Buckstone's Voyage around the Globe (in Leicester Square)*, first performed at Theatre Royal Haymarket on 17 April 1854, J.R. Planché presented his audience with a catalogue of the most renowned Southern African people in the city. 'One of the most agreeable entertainments the many and varied resources of the metropolis can offer',[1] that of

1 *Reynolds's Newspaper* (7 May 1854), 9.

the fictional Mr Buckstone (the real Mr Buckstone was at the time manager at the Haymarket) is a voyage to Wyld's Great Globe, which, between 1851 and 1862, was one of London's greatest attractions. 'On the principle [...] that a man may be a good astronomer and yet not live in a moon',[2] Mr Buckstone sets on a journey that is itself a reproduction of that undertaken by thousands of others, Londoners and visitors alike, to Leicester Square as well as, shortly before the Great Globe opened, to the Great Exhibition. That the stage at the Haymarket should provide audiences with a replica of that journey is typical of the inclusive nature of nineteenth-century entertainment, the various segments of which, like Chinese boxes, often served as *mise-en-abyme* perspectives on the overall combination. It is therefore unsurprising that *Mr Buckstone's Voyage around the Globe* should also contain a summary of the most popular 'exotic' performances available in London.

Mr Buckstone enjoys '"grand oriental spectacles," wise elephants of the East standing upon their heads, "feasts of dragons," and "wonderful performances of Chinese magicians"'[3]– all sights theatre audiences were familiar with.[4] As for Africa, he 'indulges in various ethnological reflections on the Bosjesmans, Zulu Kaffirs, Earthmen, and other unnatural curiosities',[5] as the *Morning Post* semi-seriously puts it, and indeed the 'Bushmen' (or San), the 'Kaffirs' (or Zulus), and the so-called 'Earthmen' did represent (alongside the 'Hottentots', as the Khoikhoi were commonly known)[6] the main 'unnatural curiosities' from the 'dark' continent. The actual nature of such 'reflections' is perhaps made clearer by the following passage, in

2 *Morning Post* (18 April 1854), 5.

3 Ibid.

4 The 'wise elephants' appeared at Astley's Amphitheatre from December 1853 to February 1854; see Kurt Koenigsberger, *The Novel and the Menagerie: Totality, Englishness, and Empire* (Columbus: The Ohio State University Press, 2007), 96; and Marty Gould, *Nineteenth-Century Theatre and the Imperial Encounter* (New York: Routledge, 2011), 19.

5 *Morning Post* (18 April 1854), 5.

6 See Bernth Lindfors, 'Hottentot, Bushman, Kaffir: Taxonomic Tendencies in Nineteenth-Century Racial Iconography', *Nordic Journal of African Studies* 5/2 (1996), 1–28.

which Planché is far more interested in arranging rhymes than providing his audiences with ethnological information:

CYBELE:	She [Africa] has many faults, no doubt, to be corrected— Her education has been so neglected. But niggers have proved that they do not lack art And music they have made almost a black art.
MR B:	I fear their arts are fitter for demolishing. What the stage wants is, not blacking—but polishing. Here in this zone, which you may call the Torrid, Have you no novelty, however horrid?
AFRICA:	De Bosjemans, dem berry horrid!
MR B:	Poh! Those gemmen were all bosh some time ago.
AFRICA:	De Zulu Kaffirs. (*the Zulu Kaffirs rush on L*)
MR B:	In town all last spring. They're done so brown, not one brown more they'd bring.
CYBELE:	Well, here are the peculiar sons of clay— The Earthmen.
MR B:	Earthmen! The earth babies, say; Poor little brats! their Mother Earth should be Ashamed to know they're out for folks to see.
AUTHOR:	Without a subject we must hence depart; Africa's still a desert as to art.
MR B:	How very odd! no spark of talent shining Under the Line—nothing worth underlining.
AFRICA:	Dis child hab noting buckra man tink good; Still workee—workee! How poor nigger could? As dat Boz-gemman, Massa Dickins, said; Me sure me wish dat Africa was dead.[7]

Having the Bushmen as 'berry horrid' reflects a widespread opinion that J.S. Tyler's *The Bosjemans: A Lecture on the Mental, Moral, and Physical Attributes of the Bushmen* (1847) summarizes when stating that they are

7 Act I, scene 2 in Planché, J.R., *Mr Buckstone's Voyage around the Globe (in Leicester Square)* (London: Thomas Hailes Lacy, s.d.), 19–20.

'[s]unk in the scale of humanity to the level almost of beasts of the forest'.[8] As beasts were also perceived the Earthmen, clearly distinguished from the Bushmen in the passage above, as well as in popular exhibitions such as that of Flora and Martinus,[9] compared to which, as we shall see, the Zulus were held on the contrary as a 'superior' race, their 'brown' complexion resulting as not at all aesthetically displeasing when combined with features that commentators across the media were prone to ascribe to a lesser stage of 'savagery'. But while it addresses, indeed parodies the 'ethnological' frenzy of the time, the passage above also reveals how the apparently diversified perception of African peoples still harboured the stereotype of a continent indistinctly inhabited by generally uncivilized 'niggers' addicted to music and with 'no spark of talent shining' – as stated by 'Africa' in the 'corrupted' English she interestingly speaks in *Mr Buckstone's Voyage around the Globe*.

Language reveals much of the overlapping narratives about Africa that informed the Victorian stage. 'Corrupted' English was commonly associated to slavery (just as the 'poor nigger' is in Planché's extravaganza associated to 'workee'), and by mid-century had become characteristic of Blacks more generally; 'Africans' on stage, however, had not always spoken that way, with Abyssinians or Ethiopians in particular usually employing standard English. Furthermore, while black characters speaking 'corrupted' English increasingly tend towards the caricature – under the influence of the blackface minstrel groups successfully touring Britain from as early as 1843,[10] and after 1852, under that of the several theatrical adaptations of *Uncle Tom's Cabin* – standard-speaking characters are generally tragic

8 J.S. Tyler, *The Bosjemans: A Lecture on the Mental, Moral, and Physical Attributes of the Bushmen, with Anecdotes by Their Guardian* (Leeds: C.A. Wilson and Co., 1847), 2.

9 Although Flora and Martinus – two alleged specimen of this 'elvish afrite race', as the *Morning Chronicle* puts it, that were exhibited at Regent-street in 1853 – were San, as too were Farini's 'Earthmen Pigmies', exhibited at the Royal Aquarium in 1884. *Morning Chronicle* (10 May 1853), 6.

10 1843 saw 'the first full- fledged minstrel troupe', Dan Emmett's Virginia Minstrels, appearing at the Adelphi. J.S Bratton, 'English Ethiopians: British Audiences and Black-Face Acts, 1835–1865', *The Yearbook of English Studies* 11 (1981), Literature and Its Audience, II Special Number, 127–42, 131.

figures, whose appearance does not necessarily call for mockery, and whose names and environment are more often associated with the 'Orient', as with the wronged protagonist of Edward Fitzball's *Nitocris; or, The Ethiop's Revenge* (1855). This is hardly surprising, given that already '[i]n the imaginative geography of the eighteenth century, Ethiopia (often a synonym for Africa) seems to migrate from Africa to Arabia and back again. It is sometimes contiguous to Egypt and sometimes depicted on the western side of the continent'.[11] The ambiguity for which 'the omnipresent turban [...] migrates [...] across the apparent divide between Oriental and black, across East and West Indian, symbolizing a generalized exotic'[12] is not lost on the Victorian stage, with such an interesting example as E.G. Burton's *The Blind Child of Africa; or, the Last Prince of Abyssinia and the True British Seaman* (1851), in which a 'black cook' predictably speaking 'corrupted' English appears aside the protagonist Achmet, a 'prince', who, equally predictably, speaks standard English.

But as with the populations of Southern Africa, who are at the same time portrayed as different but also equal in their general lack of civilization, Abyssinians too undergo a similar fate, with scientific texts such as H. Blanc's 'The Native Races of Abyssinia' (1869) juxtaposing them to the rest of the continent (Southern Africa especially),[13] while declaring them, overall, a 'degraded race',[14] and *as such*, still synonym for the whole

11 Felicity A. Nussbaum, 'Between "Oriental" and "Blacks So Called", 1688–1788', in Daniel Carey and Lynn Festa, eds, *The Postcolonial Enlightenment: Eighteenth-Century Colonialism and Postcolonial Theory* (Oxford: Oxford University Press, 2009), 137–66, 149.

12 Nussbaum, 'Between "Oriental" and "Blacks So Called"', 146.

13 'In Africa, more than in any other part of the known world, we generally find native races in their greater purity. The Hottentots, the Zulus, the Caffres, etc, taken separately, are so well defined as to appear fashioned on one mould,—see one, you see the tribe; in manners, customs, religion, they are one, and any difference in species seems as if absorbed in the classic type. The Abyssinian, on the contrary, presents much analogy to many European nations, the offspring of divers invaders'. H. Blanc, 'The Native Races of Abyssinia', *Transactions of the Ethnological Society of London* 7 (1869), 291–8, 291.

14 Blanc, 'The Native Races of Abyssinia', 298.

of Africa (although in the course of the century the term 'Ethiopian' came to refer almost exclusively to blackface minstrel shows).[15] This double-faceted view finds a parallel also in the theatre, with, for example, Francis Burnand's extravaganza *The White Fawn*, which opened at the Holborn on Easter Monday 1868 (the year of the British Expedition to Abyssinia), associating Abyssinians with the caricature of Africa that had been typical of 'corrupt'-English-speaking portraits of the continent. The villain of the piece, Princess Nigressa, although speaking standard English, represents a quintessence of the African ridicule and the stereotyped Black more generally, her origin, Abyssinia, allowing for some rather obvious jokes:

> Prince [in his first dialogue with Nigressa]: '*Fair* words suit only a *light* conversation'.
> [...]
> 'Nigres: You're mighty great in your opinion
> But dread the anger of this Abyssinian;
> That girl and you will meet a fate most tragic,
> I know more than the A B C of magic.
> [...]
> Dande: This *A-B-C-nian* means she can *spell*'.[16]

The Africa that emerges from Burnand's, as well as Burton's and Planché's work, is therefore as multifaceted as it is, in the end, consistently reduced to the usual narrative of 'backwardness', to which the mocking touch of the exaggeration so typical of genres like the extravaganza, the farce and the pantomime is also added.

These increasingly clashing images of Africa were mainly due to theatre responding to textual stereotypes of the continent already circulating on stage, while addressing the challenges posed by conflicts in Southern Africa especially. The changing attitude towards theatre more generally, however,

15 See Bratton, 'English Ethiopians', 138; Campbell's *More Ethiopians!! Or, 'Jenny Lind' in New York*, first performed at the Grecian on 17 May 1847; Hazel Waters, *Racism on the Victorian Stage: Representation of Slavery and the Black Character* (Cambridge: Cambridge University Press, 2007), 118–20.

16 Francis Burnand, *The White Fawn; or, the Loves of Prince Buttercup and the Princess Daisy* (London: Tomas Hailes Lacy, s.d.), 10.

must also be relevant, as in the second half of the century the public was 'exposed to an increasing volume of information, much of it visual, concerning the exploits of Empire',[17] so that it when it came to the theatre 'it was to confirm what they had seen and read elsewhere'.[18] The war fronts in Africa are no exception to this, with the eighth 'Kaffir' or Xhosa War (1850–3), the British Expedition to Abyssinia (1868), the third Anglo-Ashanti War (1873–4), the ninth Xhosa War (1877–9), the Anglo-Zulu War (1879), and the Sudan campaign (1898), inspiring productions such as Stocqueler's *The Conquest of Magdala* and Travers's *The Abyssinian War and the Death of King Theodore* (both 1868), Elphinstone's *King Coffee; or, the Ashantee War* and Sandford's *The Ashantee War* (both 1874), and Stanhope's *The Zulu War; or, The Fight for the Queen's Colours* (1881), the texts of which have unfortunately not always survived. The wars of the 1860s and 1870s in particular led to a contradictory idea about Africa, one that again saw the continent as located within history while at the same time living outside its reach. This view is held by numerous texts that, no doubt to highlight the valour of the British and their rights above all in Southern Africa, portrayed African conflicts as unreasonable and therefore unavoidable. In his *The History of the Battles and Adventures of the British, the Boers, and the Zulus, in Southern Africa* (1879), for example, Duncan Moodie observes that 'With savages wars do not arise from political causes, but chiefly from the wish of the young men to distinguish themselves and become warriors',[19] while the aggressive attitude of the Zulus is largely represented as the outcome of a natural disposition. As Clinton Parry states in *African Pets; or, Chats about Our Animal Friends in Natal* (1880), Cetshwayo had decided

17 Heidi J. Holder, 'Melodrama, Realism and Empire on the British Stage', in J.S. Bratton, Richard Allen Cave, Breandan Gregory, Heidi J. Holder and Michael Pickering, eds, *Acts of Supremacy: The British Empire and the Stage, 1790–1930* (Manchester and New York: Manchester University Press, 1991), 129–49, 133.

18 Ibid.

19 Duncan Campbell Francis Moodie, *The History of the Battles and Adventures of the British, the Boers, and the Zulus, in Southern Africa, from 1495 to 1879, Including Every Particular of the Zulu War of 1879, with a Chronology* (Sydney, Melbourne and Adelaide: George Robertson Publisher, 1879), 72.

to resume his hostility for the English as he 'has got tired, I suppose, of his quiet life',[20] while earlier in the century, commenting on Caldecott's exhibition of the 'Zulu Kaffirs' in 1853, the *Morning Post* informed readers that the Zulus 'have an awkward habit of cracking skulls on the slightest provocation, or, just as often, on no provocation at all'.[21]

In the theatre, this attitude meant that while, to match audiences' expectations as for the historical accuracy of performances, increasing 'authenticity' was employed on stage – with public lectures accompanying popular entertainment, and theatre coming to be interpreted, as I will argue, as *evidence* within debates on Empire – an array of recurrent representational strategies was employed so as to emphasize the enemy's illogical and all in all a-historical character. In the following pages, I shall focus on the specific case of the Zulus, and the 'Kaffirs' more generally, as symptomatic of the ambivalent attitude towards Africa that I have delineated above.

The threat posed by the Zulus, as well as the 'relative lack of contact between Europeans and the Zulus until the mid-nineteenth century',[22] as Sadiah Qureshi observes, were responsible for much of the success of the 'Zulu Kaffirs', both in live displays and on the theatrical stage, between 1853 and 1880. The very term 'Kaffir' – regarded today as highly offensive, but largely employed in both Georgian and Victorian Britain – can be of problematic definition, both for the wide range of the meanings implied in its etymology, and its widespread use from the sixteenth century onward, the word being used to indicate now the populations of the British Kaffraria, now the Zulus alone'. Nicholas Hudson reminds us that it was Johann Friedrich Blumenbach that introduced, at the end of the eighteenth century, 'the practice of bunching the Hottentots with all the neighbouring peoples

20 Clinton Parry, *African Pets; or, Chats about Our Animal Friends in Natal: With a Sketch of Kaffir Life*, ill. by R.H. Moore (London: Griffith and Farran, 1880), 152.

21 *Morning Post* (17 May 1853), 5.

22 Sadiah Qureshi, *Peoples on Parade: Exhibitions, Empire, and Anthropology in Nineteenth-Century Britain* (Chicago: The University of Chicago Press, 2011), 170. Compared to the San and the Khoikhoi, 'the Zulus lived further inland and were only routinely observed by settlers from the early to mid-nineteenth century onward' (ibid.).

of southern Africa (including, prominently, the "Bushmen"' and "Caffres"), whom he classified together as "woolly-haired African nations"'.[23] Scientific milestones such as Buffon's *Natural History* (translated in English in 1828), or Prichard's *The Natural History of Men* (1855) further tend to suggest that the Hottentots and the Kaffirs are one race, although neither of the two are seen as 'Negros' proper, which Buffon and Prichard mainly locate in Central and West Africa. The notion that the Kaffirs are not 'Negros' is taken further by the Rev. H. Calderwood in his *Caffres and Caffre Missions* (1858) and by Moodie, the former stating that 'as the term Kaffir is of Arabian origin, so are the features of many of the Zulus strictly Arabian [...]. The Zulu proper has no characteristic of the negro in feature, *i.e.*, receding forehead, blubber lips, and flat nose',[24] while the latter writes that

> When we consider the appearance of the Caffres, their language, and some of their customs, it is rather difficult to assign with certainty their true position among the different races of men. They have the woolly hair, and many of them have the thick lip and the flattened nose of the negro. Not a few of them are very dark. A large proportion of them, however, have none of the characteristics of the negro, excepting the woolly hair.[25]

The Rev. William Holden's *The Past and Future of the Kaffir Races* (1866) also discusses Kaffir and Hottentots as different races, 'their [the Zulus'] physical and mental character [...] having no affinity with the Negro'.[26]

Kaffirs can therefore include 'The numerous and warlike Zulu tribes beyond the Natal Colony',[27] but also the 'Amaxosa Kaffirs of British

23 Nicholas Hudson, 'Hottentots and the Evolution of European Racism', *Journal of European Studies* 34/4 (2004), 308–32, 323.

24 Moodie, *The History of the Battles and Adventures of the British*, 157.

25 Rev. H. Calderwood, *Caffres and Caffre Missions; with Preliminary Chapters on the Cape Colony as a Field for Migration, and Basis of Missionary Operation* (London: James Nisbet and Co., 1858), 32.

26 Rev. William C., Holden, *The Past and Future of the Kaffir Races; in Three Parts: I. Their History. II. Their Manners and Customs. III. The Means Needful for Their Preservation and Improvement* (London, 1866). 3.

27 Calderwood, *Caffres and Caffre Missions*, 32.

Kaffraria',[28] because although 'much misconception exists as to the terms Kaffirs, Zulus, &c. [...] once for all, we will perhaps be allowed to lay down that "Kaffir" is the *generic* appellation, and all the other names of the different tribes *specific*',[29] as Moodie puts it. The two terms, 'Kaffir' and 'Zulu', tended nonetheless to be used separately when it came to the wars, with the *Historical Records of the 2nd Battalion, 24th Regiment, for the Campaign in South Africa, 1877–78–79: Embracing the Kaffir & Zulu Wars* (1882), for instance, distinguishing between the 'Kaffir' 1878 campaign against Mgolombane Sandile (1820–1878) and the 'Zulu' wars against Cetshwayo kaMpande (c. 1826–1884).[30] On the popular and theatrical stage, 'Kaffir' and 'Zulu' are on the other hand either used in combination, or as synonyms, an ambiguity that must be kept in mind when dealing with performances such as the 'Grand Military Spectacular Drama' *The Kaffir War* (1879), as we will see shortly.

Common to all texts, fictional and non-fictional, is a perception of the Zulus as superior to their neighbouring groups, a notion that is central to stage portraits of the Zulus, and is confirmed by writings as different as George French Angas's *The Kafirs Illustrated* (1849), and Parry's already mentioned *African Pets* (1880), the former describing the Zulus as 'a fine race of Kafirs, superior in stature and physical strength',[31] the latter as 'the most intelligent, the best looking, and of the lightest colour'.[32] The reception of the physical appearance of the exhibits in the ethnic shows is analogous, Caldecott's Zulus being described by the *Lloyd's Weekly Newspaper*

28 Moodie, *The History of the Battles and Adventures of the British*, 57.

29 Moodie, *The History of the Battles and Adventures of the British*, 157.

30 Similarly, the memoir *A Zulu Boy's Recollections of the Zulu War* (1884) suggests that 'Kafirs' is 'a contemptuous term applied by the Zulus to the Natal natives'. *A Zulu Boy's Recollections of the Zulu War, and of Cetshwayo's Return*, transl. by George H. Swinny (London: George Bell and Sons, 1884), 77.

31 George French Angas, *The Kafirs Illustrated in a Series of Drawings Taken among the Amazulu, Malay, Fingo, and Other Races Inhabiting Southern Africa: Together with Sketches of Landscape Scenery in the Zulu Country, Natal, and the Cape Colony* (London: J. Hogarth, 1849), 25.

32 Parry, *African Pets*, 145.

as 'remarkably well-made',[33] whereas Farini's Zulus, exhibited in 1879, are said to be 'unquestionably a fine lot of men',[34] 'athletic and by no means repulsive-looking',[35] and 'as lissom as panthers, and almost as graceful'.[36] This is relevant within narratives of the 'savage' that were centred primarily on the body and the bodily: that is, the appearance of the 'natives', their feeding, coupling, and clothing habits, their physical abilities, etc.

When focusing on these narratives, at least three types of body must be taken into account: the political and the scientific on the one hand – how the various tribes and nations from Southern Africa were perceived by the British public within the frame of the recurring conflicts in southern Africa, as well as within the scientific discourse on race – and, on the other, the theatrical body, that is, the actual body of the people (be it on stage or in live exhibitions) presented to the public as representative of the other two. Although obviously differing from theatre in providing the public with 'genuine' bodies, I have included ethnological exhibitions under the expression 'theatrical body' in consideration of the fact that 'Exhibitions were commonly marketed as if the performances were unmediated representations of life abroad, yet all were evidently quite carefully choreographed and managed'.[37] Representational strategies included introducing the exhibits, as well as their substitutes on stage, in what was presumed to be their 'typical' environment, dressed in their 'distinctive' manner, and carrying out their 'routine'. Such a metonymic approach applied to the body of the individual or group, which often stood for the 'backwardness' of Africa, as well as to single objects or acts that *per se* signified that backwardness.

What is interesting in the case of the 'Zulu Kaffirs' is that most theatrical productions, however, actually came *before* ethnological exhibitions, thus suggesting that – if mutual influence and the building of a tradition in portraying the Zulus is to be envisaged – it may have been theatre setting the pace for live exhibitions, rather than the other way round. The Kaffir

33 *Lloyd's Weekly Newspaper* (22 May 1853), 8.

34 *Reynolds's Newspaper* (13 July 1879), 5.

35 *Nottinghamshire Guardian* (11 July 1879), 5.

36 *Evening News – Portsmouth* (10 July 1879), 2.

37 Qureshi, *Peoples on Parade*, 122.

Wars inspired in particular two dramatic performances, C.S. James's *The Kaffir War* (1851) at the Queen's Theatre, and Edward Fitzball's *Amakosa; or, Scenes of Kaffir Warfare* (1853) at Astley's Amphitheatre. In both plays the action revolves around a love story, featuring, in the case of *Amakosa*, a rebel chief who, for the sake of a British woman, fights against his own people. In neither of the two the 'Kaffirs' speak 'bad' English, probably to highlight the heroism of the British, seen as fighting no helpless savages, but a well-organized, thinking enemy; the language spoken by the 'Noble Kaffir Chief' Amakosa, who in the end chooses the British, is in particular highly dignified ('thou hast spoken well') and made more striking by the comparison with that of another character, Jawboo ('a Kaffir Boer'), who significantly speaks 'corrupted' English.

These clearly politically driven distinctions are not, however, matched by any exact portrait of sceneries and customs: scene 3, act II of James's *The Kaffir War*, for instance, opens on '[a]n Indian view. In the centre of stage is a Kaffir Idol. A Gigantic head supposed to be formed out of wood – large eyes and mouth partly open. As savage and [...] [the writing is illegible] as possible'. As the curtains rise on *Amakosa*, we similarly find 'Hottentots and Blacks' of no better description scattered on stage, joined, later on, by a 'Bosjeman', Mokhanna, also talking of 'sacrificing our victims to the Idols' (scene 1, act II). When the landscape is meant to be properly 'African', as in scene 3 of act I of *The Abyssinian War and the Death of King Theodore*, set in an 'Abyssinian landscape', sceneries may have been equally vague or incongruent, although it is debatable whether any lack of specification in the text should correspond to an equally vague scenery on stage. In a theatre characterized by a cannibalistic attitude towards past plays and performances it is in fact safe to assume that while such directions may not mean anything to us today, they may nonetheless have suggested a lot to their contemporaries. What these sceneries may have been like should then be deduced not only by reviews of the plays, but also those of the live exhibitions that followed.

This is the case with Charles Caldecott's 'Zulu Kaffirs' at St George's Gallery in May 1853, the costumes and arrangements of which are representative of the general way in which the Zulus came to be portrayed in the second half of the century. This exhibition – featuring 11 men, a woman and a child – was meant, as the *Morning Post* has it, 'to represent the domestic manners, mode of hunting the tiger, war dances, superstitions, witch-finding, &c., of this wild and savage race',[38] and the performance did in fact include a Zulu marriage, a council of war, and a combat – love and war being the two leading elements of the narrative around the Zulus, both on stage and in live exhibitions. Costumes in particular stood for the 'wild' character of the Zulus; in Caldecott's show they appear to have been 'mostly of a furry nature',[39] with patches of animal skins, and the 'usual' feathers and armlets, to say it with the *Morning Post*.[40] Thirty years later, Farini's 'friendly' Zulus would also wear 'fur drapery around the waist, feathers and flowers in the hair, together with armlets and strange ornaments in the ear'.[41] In both exhibitions, the fiery nature of the 'savage' is furthermore represented by the employment of a wide range of weapons: clubs, knives, arrows, and the famous assegai, to which – in Farini's show – the equally characteristic shields are added.

During the Anglo-Zulu Wars, the Zulus came to prominence on stage as 'larger-than-life warriors of nearly superhuman capabilities';[42] before being exhibited in Farini's show, however, these warriors were again introduced to the public at the theatre, with a 'Grand Military Spectacular Drama' entitled *The Kaffir War*, first performed on 26 April 1879 at Astley's Amphitheatre. Centred on the famous battle of Rorke's Drift on 22 and 23 January 1879,[43] this play is *not* about the Kaffirs that appeared in the two

38 *Morning Post* (3 May 1853), 6.

39 *Lloyd's Weekly Newspaper* (22 May 1853), 8.

40 *Morning Post* (17 May 1853), 5.

41 *Reynolds's Newspaper* (13 July 1879), 5.

42 Shane Peacock, 'Africa Meets the Great Farini', in Bernth Lindfors, ed., *Africans on Stage: Studies in Ethnological Show Business* (Bloomington and Indianapolis: Indiana University Press; Cape Town: David Philip, 1999), 81–106, 86.

43 'Although the battle was little more than a botched mopping-up operation from the Zulu perspective, the courage of the defenders allowed the British a propaganda victory and, more significantly, proffered tactical lessons which were to have ominous implications for the future Zulu conduct of the war'. Knight, Ian, '"What Do You Red-Jackets Want in Our Country?": The Zulu Response to the British Invasion of 1879', in Benedict Carton, John Laband and Jabulani Sithole, eds, *Zulu Identities:*

plays of 1851 and 1853; yet this drama, originally entitled *Rorke's Drift*, was renamed *The Kaffir War* '[f]or reasons, which to many will be obvious',[44] thus showing full awareness of the ambiguity, as well as the commercial potential, of the term 'Kaffir'.

The public's excitement for the *Kaffir War* is guaranteed 'by the smell of gunpowder, by hand-to-hand struggles, by patriotic songs and choruses, and, of course, by the triumphant victory of the British against their savage foes'.[45] A similar programme, in the overlapping of influences that characterized portraits of the Zulus in the latter part of the century, can be found in *The Grand Equestrian Spectacle of the War in Zululand*, performed in Manchester from 1 November 1879, which featured a Grand Concourse of Zulu warriors, chieftains and people; the arrival of King Cetshwayo, with a war dance, a Grand Review of the Zulu Warriors and a Congress of Chieftains; the introduction of an Army of Real Soldiers facing the 'Overwhelming number of the enemy',[46] followed by the Death of Two Brave Heroes; and, last but certainly not least, the Defence of Rorke's Drift and Repulse of the Enemy. In this spectacle, as Jacky Bratton observes, 'the Zulus are reduced to an item of local colour by the resolution of the scene into a spectacle in which they dance and sing, in the same way that nineteenth-century productions of *Henry V* included entertainments in the French camp to underline their frivolity'.[47] Bratton is referring here to a scene in which Cetshwayo is explaining the reasons for the war but is promptly interrupted by dances and songs, further evidence that the body and the bodily are not only at the core of narratives about the 'savage', but also contribute to silencing the 'savage' when s/he tries to speak (in an age, it may be furthermore argued, in which the distinction between 'spoken'

Being Zulu, Past and Present (Scottsville: University of KwaZulu-Natal Press, 2008), 177–89, 183.

44 *The Era* (4 May 1879), 10.

45 *The Era* (4 May 1879), 12.

46 *Aberdeen Journal* (26 May 1879), 1.

47 Bratton, J.S., Richard Allen Cave, Breandan Gregory, Heidi J. Holder, Michael Pickering, eds, *Acts of Supremacy: The British Empire and the Stage, 1790–1930* (Manchester: Manchester University Press, 1991), 25.

and 'illegitimate' drama, although dissolved by the Theatres Act of 1843, still evoked different ideas of respectability and 'value' attached to the use of speech on stage).

When Farini started displaying the Zulus, first at St James's Hall and then at the Royal Aquarium, warfare was also the focus of action, as it would have been later on. After an introduction from Farini himself, as it was customary to have exhibitions introduced by public lectures on the cultural, anthropological, and scientific aspects of the peoples exhibited, the Zulus, although named 'friendly', came on stage 'shouting and jumping with formidable energy'.[48] Something similar also happened at the South of England Palace, Portsmouth, in September 1880, where the group performed 'wild guttural songs and energetic ohs! intermingled with savage dances, contortion of the bodies, and vehement rattlings and shakings of their shields, assegais, and other rude implements of war'.[49]

These representational strategies would have found confirmation, at the very end of the century, at the 1899 Greater Britain Exhibition, where the fictional construction of the 'Kaffir' would be given further ground by the display of an entire 'Kaffir Kraal' with 174 people inside it. The exhibition also featured a *Savage South Africa* to be staged by the impresario Frank Fillis at the Empress Theatre at Earl's Court. The show, which then transferred to St Louis in 1904, and was here introduced by 'the Lecturer, Peter James Visser',[50] went on between May and October 1899, and included 'Matabele, Basotho, Zulu and Swazi "warriors" in full regalia (including knobkerries and assegais) singing songs and doing war dances'.[51] The tradition established by past performances and exhibitions, though, meant that this show too was marked by what was in fact the recognized 'authenticity' of these people, rather than being informed by actual

48 *Reynolds's Newspaper* (13 July 1879), 5.

49 *Evening News – Portsmouth* (28 September 1880), 2.

50 *The South African Boer War Exhibition: Official Program, Historical Libretto* (World's Fair St Louis, 1904), 5.

51 Bett Pacey, 'Battles of War as Amusement Enterprise: Fillis' Spectacles in London and St Louis', unpublished paper presented at the IFTR 'Theatre and Stratification' conference (2014), 3. I am grateful to the author for letting me quote from her paper.

faithfulness to 'real' costumes. Although the pamphlet for the 1904 show confidently boasts that 'All the natives will appear in their native costumes, exactly as worn by them in Darkest Africa',[52] these costumes are far from 'authentic', as observed by Bett Pacey:

> From the available photographs, the traditional clothes which were worn seem to be Zulu. While the Matabele are kin to the Zulus, the Swazis and Basothos had completely different traditional dress and one wonders what they made of having to wear those 'costumes'. As the Basotho and Swazi war dances are not as ferocious and are executed in a different style to that of the Zulus, they would have had to adapt rather drastically.[53]

Savage South Africa is a good example of how theatre 'proper' and live exhibitions often went hand in hand in nineteenth-century entertainment. Within this context, whereas on the one hand live exhibitions were promoted by their managers as evidence, with theatre proper being generally understood to be mainly entertainment, *both* ethnological exhibitions and the theatre, however, were given full credit by the public with regards to the performances' resemblance to reality, as if there were in fact no difference between the 'real' body of the exhibits and its reduplication on the theatrical stage. For both, 'what is at stake is not opinions or ideas but the sense of what is real, embodied in what is patently fictional', as Bratton has it.[54]

'Authenticity' was an obvious concern of non-fictional texts alike, with Duncan Moodie explaining for instance that he was 'a resident in South Africa for twenty years […]. I speak the Zulu language fluently […] and having intimate general knowledge of the matter in hand, I now respectfully and confidently place before the public at large the following pages';[55] while Rev. Holden similarly highlights that he had 'for the last *twenty-six years* been placed in the most favourable circumstances for acquiring correct and extensive information on the topics brought under review'.[56] But

52 *The South African Boer War Exhibition*, 17.

53 Pacey, 'Battles of War', note 11.

54 Bratton et al., *Acts of Supremacy*, 27.

55 Moodie, *The History of the Battles and Adventures of the British*, viii–ix.

56 Holden, *The Past and Future of the Kaffir Races*, iv.

first-hand knowledge is central also within popular entertainment, with audiences in Portsmouth, for example, being invited by Nat Beherens, who was Farini's associate at the time, to ask questions to the Zulus so as to test 'their nationality', while the *Nottinghamshire Guardian* speculated that 'that they are genuine Zulus is not only evident by their appearance, but the fact is attested by some seventy ladies and gentlemen who travelled to Europe with them'.[57] Witnesses were often mentioned in support of the exhibits and their story, but what is interesting here is that the *appearance* of the exhibits is mentioned as *evidence* of their truthfulness. This created a paradox: that what audiences expected on the basis of what was presented to them as 'real' also served as scientific demonstration: the Zulus appeared according to public expectations, and as they met such expectations, they must therefore necessarily be Zulus.

It also mattered, however, what experts had to say – be it the managers, who willingly introduced themselves as authorities on their subjects, or the various scientific and non-scientific texts, travelogues included, that may have circulated beforehand, and here again, it is interesting to note that dramatists were included in this list. According to the *Era*, for example, Edward Fitzball's experience as a melo-dramatic writer offered 'sufficient guarantee for a startling and *truthful* picture of the stirring scenes and events in Kaffir life';[58] while commenting on the 1879 military drama *The Kaffir War*, the *Era* again states that if one is to believe that Cetshwayo resembled the Zulu king on stage, he was therefore 'not so black and so ugly as he has been painted by some of his artistic opponents'.[59] Both comments, although with different approaches, reveal a habit of equalling theatre productions to commentaries on given events or peoples comparable to those provided by journalism and science.

Central to the enjoyment of these performances was in any case the careful monitoring of entertainment in its various forms, a central feature of Victorian society that could only happen, however, within venues that

57 *Nottinghamshire Guardian* (11 July 1879), 5.

58 *The Era* (3 April 1853), 1. Emphasis added.

59 Ibid.

provided 'exotic' performances with that liminal space, in Victor Turner's term, necessary to construct a coherent portrait of 'savages'. As soon as the protagonists of these performances stepped off stage and the magic was over, the people exhibited in live ethnic shows, in particular, were liable to be perceived as posing a serious threat to the community. This is best illustrated by two incidents that occurred during Caldecott's and Farini's shows, when their exhibits at some point claimed some liberty. Manyos, the chief of Caldecott's 'Zulu Kaffirs', appeared before a magistrate in September 1853,[60] as Caldecott had apparently forced the Zulus to come back from a stroll in Hyde Park. Farini's Zulus, on the other hand, were charged in April 1880 'with causing an obstruction in the streets'[61] when leaving a coffee-house where they had been asked to wait for their manager; a small crowd was naturally attracted to the Zulus, and one of them 'drew a knife and gesticulated with it in a threatening manner'.[62] In both cases, 'consequences to the public' were advocated for preventing the Zulus from wandering around, and in both cases magistrates invited *all* parts to respect the existing contracts, which did not mention the need, for the exhibits, to be kept inside; in the case of Manyos, for example, '[t]he judge, William Broderip, a well-known naturalist, ruled that Caldecott had no legal right to prevent Manyos from choosing to go outdoors, even if it was intended for his protection'.[63]

It is arguable, however, that the reaction to the perspective of the Zulus roaming around London unchecked was due not only to the practical problems that may have arisen, but also to the risk represented by the Zulus when facing the British public somewhat unmediated. When the encounter with the real, physical body of the Zulu occurred outside the theatrical, fictional framework in which the Zulus were presented to the audience, the political body of the Zulu was at stake. The encounter with the real Zulus was thus prevented from taking place, while that with the

60 *Morning Post* (29 September 1853), 7.

61 *Pall Mall Gazette* (29 April 1880), 5.

62 Ibid.

63 Qureshi, *Peoples on Parade*, 140.

fictional Zulu, which often represented the only actual, physical encounter of the general public with the 'exotic' Other, was amply encouraged.

As Bratton has it, 'while one formal requirement of such displays [the ethnic shows] is that they claim authenticity, the unmediated presentation of reality, they always determine what is seen through other formal means and structures which make the display conform to the demands of the discourse'.[64] These 'formal lenses' were provided by the experts: in the persons of managers (who introduced the exhibits to the public), scientists and explorers (who provided accounts of their habits and customs), the police and the magistrates (who served to assess the veracity of the exhibited 'specimens'), but also, last but not least, playwrights – who provided the public with a long-lasting, but also very controversial, portrait of the 'natives' of the British Empire.

Aside and before famous examples of live exhibitions such as Caldecott's and Farini's, theatre contributed, in its portrait of the Zulus, to establish traditions that made use of recurrent representational strategies. These strategies, independently on their 'truthfulness', ended up constructing, both on the popular and the theatrical stage, metonymic narratives of the *fictional* body of the African that, although seemingly discussing specific incidents in the life of the Empire, and encompassing 'ethnological' detail, consciously reinforced a vision of the *political* body of Africa as altogether unstable, unreliable, and all in all needing close supervision.

Bibliography

Aberdeen Journal (26 May 1879), 1.

Angas, George French, *The Kafirs Illustrated in a Series of Drawings Taken among the Amazulu, Malay, Fingo, and Other Races Inhabiting Southern Africa: Together with Sketches of Landscape Scenery in the Zulu Country, Natal, and the Cape Colony* (London: J. Hogarth, 1849).

64 Bratton et al., *Acts of Supremacy*, 4.

Blanc, H., 'The Native Races of Abyssinia', *Transactions of the Ethnological Society of London* 7 (1869), 291–8.

Booth, Michael R., *English Melodrama* (London: Herbert Jenkins, 1965).

Bratton, J.S., 'English Ethiopians: British Audiences and Black-Face Acts, 1835–1865', *The Yearbook of English Studies* 11 (1981), 127–42.

Bratton, J.S., Richard Allen Cave, Breandan Gregory, Heidi J. Holder, Michael Pickering, eds, *Acts of Supremacy: The British Empire and the Stage, 1790–1930* (Manchester and New York: Manchester University Press, 1991).

Burnand, Francis, *The White Fawn; or, the Loves of Prince Buttercup and the Princess Daisy* (London: Tomas Hailes Lacy, s.d.)

Burton, E.G. *The Blind Child of Africa; or, the Last Prince of Abyssinia and the True British Seaman* (British Library: Add. MS. 43034, 1851).

——, *The Nubian Captive; or, the Royal Slave* (1857).

Bryant, Alfred T., *A Zulu-English Dictionary with Notes on Pronunciation, a Revised Orthography and Derivations and Cognate Words from Many Languages; including also a Vocabulary of Hlonipa Words, Tribal Names, etc., a Synopsis of Zulu Grammar and a Concise History of the Zulu People from the Most Ancient Times* (Maritzburg and Durban: P. Davis & Sons, 1905).

Calderwood, Rev. H., *Caffres and Caffre Missions; with Preliminary Chapters on the Cape Colony as a Field for Migration, and Basis of Missionary Operation* (London: James Nisbet and Co., 1858).

Daily News (15 September 1853), 4.

Davis, Rev. William J., *A Dictionary of the Kaffir Language: Including the Xosa and Zulu Dialects* (London: The Wesleyan Mission House), 1872.

Durbach, Nadja, *Spectacle of Deformity: Freak Shows and Modern British Culture* (Berkeley: University of California Press, 2010).

Elphinstone, J., *King Coffee; or, The Ashantee War: Spectacle* (1874).

The Era (3 April 1853), 1.

——(4 May 1879), 10, 12.

——(11 January 1880), 4.

Evening News – Portsmouth (10 July 1879), 2.

——(28 September 1880), 2.

Fitzball, Edward, *Amakosa; or, Kaffir Warfare: Spectacle* (British Library: Add. MS. 52938 K, 1853).

——, *Nitocris; or, The Ethiop's Revenge: Grand Original Historical Play* (British Library: Add. MS. 52956 B, 1855).

Fulton, Richard, 'The Sudan Sensation of 1898', *Victorian Periodicals Review* 42 (1) (2009), 37–63.

Gould, Marty, *Nineteenth-Century Theatre and the Imperial Encounter* (New York: Routledge, 2011).

Historical Records of the 2nd Battalion, 24th Regiment, for the Campaign in South Africa, 1877–78–79: Embracing the Kaffir & Zulu Wars (Secunderabad, Deccan: printed by 2nd Battalion, 'The South Wales Borderers', 1882).

Holden, Rev. William C., *The Past and Future of the Kaffir Races; in Three Parts: I. Their History. II. Their Manners and Customs. III. The Means Needful for Their Preservation and Improvement* (London, 1866).

Holder, Heidi J., 'Melodrama, Realism and Empire on the British Stage', in J.S. Bratton, Richard Allen Cave, Breandan Gregory, Heidi J. Holder and Michael Pickering, eds, *Acts of Supremacy: The British Empire and the Stage, 1790–1930* (Manchester and New York: Manchester University Press, 1991), 129–49.

Hudson, Nicholas, 'Hottentots and the Evolution of European Racism', *Journal of European Studies*, 34 (4) (2009), 308–32.

James, Charles Stanfield, *The Kaffir War: Drama* (British Library: Add. MS. 43036, 1857).

Jones, Eldred Durosimi, *Othello's Countrymen: The African in English Renaissance Drama* (Oxford: Oxford University Press, 1965).

The Kaffir War: Grand Military Spectacular Drama (Rorke's Drift; or, the Zulu War (1879).

Knight, Ian, '"What Do You Red-Jackets Want in Our Country?": The Zulu Response to the British Invasion of 1879', ch. 15 in Benedict Carton, John Laband and Jabulani Sithole, eds, *Zulu Identities: Being Zulu, Past and Present* (Scottsville: University of KwaZulu-Natal Press, 2008), 177–89.

Koenigsberger, Kurt, *The Novel and the Menagerie: Totality, Englishness, and Empire* (Columbus: The Ohio State University Press, 2007).

Lindfors, Bernth, 'Hottentot, Bushman, Kaffir: Taxonomic Tendencies in Nineteenth-Century Racial Iconography', *Nordic Journal of African Studies* 5 (2) (1996), 1–28.

Lloyd's Weekly Newspaper (22 May 1853), 8.

MacKenzie, John M., 'The Imperial Exhibitions of Great Britain', in Pascal Blanchard, Nicolas Bancel, Gilles Boëtsch, Eric Deroo, Sandrine Lemaire, and Charles Forsdick, eds, *Human Zoos: Science and Spectacle in the Age of Colonial Empires* (Liverpool: Liverpool University Press, 2008), 259–68.

Moodie, Duncan Campbell Francis, *The History of the Battles and Adventures of the British, the Boers, and the Zulus, in Southern Africa, from 1495 to 1879, Including Every Particular of the Zulu War of 1879, with a Chronology* (Sydney, Melbourne and Adelaide: George Robertson Publisher, 1879).

Moody, Jane, *Illegitimate Theatre in London, 1770–1840* (Cambridge: Cambridge University Press, 2000).

Morning Chronicle (10 May 1853), 6.
——(15 September 1853), 1.
Morning Post (3 May 1853), 6.
——(17 May 1853), 5.
——(15 June 1853), 5.
——(29 September 1853), 7.
——(18 April 1854), 5.
Nottinghamshire Guardian (11 July 1879), 5.
——(19 December 1879), 3.
Nussbaum, Felicity A., 'Between "Oriental" and "Blacks So Called", 1688–1788', in Daniel Carey and Lynn Festa, eds, *The Postcolonial Enlightenment: Eighteenth-century Colonialism and Postcolonial Theory* (Oxford: Oxford University Press, 2009), 137–66.
Pacey, Bett, 'Battles of War as Amusement Enterprise: Fillis' Spectacles in London and St Louis', unpublished paper presented at the IFTR 'Theatre and Stratification' conference (2014).
Pall Mall Gazette (29 April 1880), 5.
Parry, F. Clinton, *African Pets; or, Chats about Our Animal Friends in Natal: With a Sketch of Kaffir Life*, ill. by R.H. Moore (London: Griffith and Farran, 1880).
Peacock, Shane, 'Africa Meets the Great Farini', in Bernth Lindfors, ed., *Africans on Stage: Studies in Ethnological Show Business* (Bloomington and Indianapolis: Indiana University Press; Cape Town: David Philip, 2009), 81–106.
Planché, J.R., *Mr Buckstone's Voyage around the Globe (in Leicester Square)* (London: Thomas Hailes Lacy, s.d.).
Qureshi, Sadiah, *Peoples on Parade: Exhibitions, Empire, and Anthropology in Nineteenth-Century Britain* (Chicago: The University of Chicago Press, 2011).
Reynolds's Newspaper (7 September 1851), 9.
——(7 May 1854), 9.
——(13 July 1879), 5.
Sandford, J., *The Ashantee War: Burlesque* (1874).
The South African Boer War Exhibition: Official Program, Historical Libretto (World's Fair St Louis, 1904).
Stanhope, B., *The Zulu War; or, The Fight for the Queen's Colours: Drama* (1881).
Stocqueler, J.H., *The Conquest of Magdala; or, The Fall of Theodore: Drama* (1868).
Travers, William, *The Abyssinian War and the Death of King Theodore* (British Library: Add. MS. 53068 M, 1868).
Tyler, J.S., *The Bosjemans: A Lecture on the Mental, Moral, and Physical Attributes of the Bushmen, with Anecdotes by Their Guardian* (Leeds: C.A. Wilson and Co., 1847).

The War in Zululand, Massacre at Isandula and Defence of Rorke's Drift (aka *The Grand Equestrian Spectacle of the War in Zululand*, Manchester, 1879).

Waters, Hazel, *Racism on the Victorian Stage: Representation of Slavery and the Black Character* (Cambridge: Cambridge University Press, 2007).

The Western Daily Press – Bristol (7 February 1881), 3.

A Zulu Boy's Recollections of the Zulu War, and of Cetshwayo's Return, transl. by George H. Swinny (London: George Bell and Sons, 1884).

MARIANNE SCHULTZ

'An Interest Must Be Strong Now-a days to Raise Much Enthusiasm in an Audience, but It May Be, at the Same Time, of an Unpleasant Nature': Māori, New Zealand and Empire on Stage 1862–1864

ABSTRACT

In July 1862 as Governor Sir George Grey prepared to arm British Militia and local Volunteer forces against Māori (indigenous New Zealander) in New Zealand's North Island, a 'troupe of Maori Warrior Chiefs, Wives and Children' appeared in melodramas in Sydney and Melbourne. At the conclusion of their Australian run, the Māori performers travelled to the United Kingdom and performed from London to Edinburgh until June 1864. This essay focuses on performance events by Māori and European entertainers between 1862–1864 and highlights the corporeal representations of New Zealand on stage that reflected the purposes of the 1860s wars, namely 'to establish the rule of British law and promote racial "amalgamation"' (Alan Ward, *A Show of Justice: Racial Amalgamation in Nineteenth-Century New Zealand*, 1974, p. 164). Though a vision emerged in these melodramas that reflected successful settlement, co-operative natives and beautiful landscape, this essay addresses questions of imperialism and colonialism overlaid with contemporary ideas of race and 'civilized' culture versus 'savage' authenticity. The presentation of melodramas featuring Māori performing songs, games and war dances, i.e. acting 'Māori', and non-Māori acting 'British', reflect not only contemporary modes of popular theatricality but also illustrate the way that 'Empire' and 'Colony' came together on stage. The dramas that the New Zealanders appeared in – *Whakeau, the Pakeha Chief*, *The Maori Queen* and *The Emigrant's Trials or Life in New Zealand* as well as the pantomime *Robinson Crusoe* – reveal other dimensions of constructed representations of New Zealand and New Zealanders. As this essay shows, the participation of Māori in Victorian melodramas abroad coincided with the New Zealand Wars, contributing visceral and tangible representations of New Zealand that augmented newspaper accounts of the battles between Imperial forces and Māori.

***

The 19 June 1864 edition of *The Era* alerted readers to the latest offering on show at London's Marylebone Theatre, *The Emigrant's Trial or Life in New*

Zealand, from the pen of J.B. Johnstone. As *The Era* reported, following the shock of an 'essentially animal' sound emitted by some cast members, 'something more like horror appeared to be experienced for a short time by everybody'.[1] The cast of Māori actors, portraying both 'hostile natives' and Māori 'friendly to the whites', proved to be the highlight of the drama. *The Era* noted how the Māori were 'vociferously applauded', especially at the conclusion of the 'The Festival Scene', where the 'muscular development' of the men elicited 'strong sensations' from the audience.[2] Without the inclusion of its Māori cast it seems likely that Johnstone's play might never have garnered notice in the London press, as it vied for attention with other productions such as *The Factory Girl*, featuring a 'good looking and fascinating young actress', and Rossini's *Otello*, attended by the Prince and Princess of Wales.

Popular entertainments of the British Empire of the nineteenth century encompassed a wide range of spectacle and drama. Melodrama, offering vivid characterizations and exaggerated representations of good and evil, has been described as an 'almost perfect instrument for propaganda'.[3] Johnstone's *Emigrant's Trial* followed on from his other melodramas such as *Life's Luck or The Navigator's Bride* (1854) and *Gale Breezely or The Tale of a Tar* (1850) where travellers encountered strange and unexpected circumstances and people in foreign lands. In 1864 Johnstone imagined the experience of the English emigrant to New Zealand as both dangerous and exciting, not least of all because of his encounters with the Māori.

From the early half of the century, prior to melodramas such as Johnstone's, performance of the 'Other' took many forms, from exhibitions and dime museum displays to ethnological shows. The inclusion of indigenous peoples in forms of popular entertainment evolved over the course of the century. The ethnologically based entertainments developed from almost static exhibition to the 'performance' of daily rituals and

1 *The Era* (19 June 1864), 10.

2 *The Era* (19 June 1864), 10. J.B. Johnstone (birth name John Southbeer, aka John Beer, born 1806 in Southwark, London) wrote over 20 plays between 1849 and the 1880s.

3 Frank Rahill, *The World of Melodrama* (University Park: Pennsylvania University Press, 1967), xvi.

ceremonies. The next logical step, then, for producers in the latter half of the century was to incorporate real 'savages' into melodrama rather than merely present them as objects for display. The melodramas and pantomimes explored here – *Whakeau, the Pakeha Chief, Rangatira Wahena or The Maori Queen* and *The Emigrant's Trials or Life in New Zealand* – not only reflected contemporary modes of popular theatricality but also narrated and dramatized the meeting of 'Empire' and 'Colony'. Marty Gould, in his discussion of empire and drama in the Victorian age, has argued that 'for many nineteenth-century Britons [...] performances were their only contact with the people and lands under British dominion [...] theatre is precisely the site at which empire was exhibited, celebrated, and challenged in the nineteenth century'.[4]

The melodramas featured here, performed between July 1862 and June 1864, imagined New Zealand and its inhabitants for audiences in distant lands. At a time when English and Australian actors were able to portray non-indigenous New Zealanders (Pākehā) how did the cultural expression of Māori (indigenous New Zealander) adapt to European performance conventions of the nineteenth century? More importantly, how was it possible that as Māori and Pākehā engaged in battles over land ownership and natural resources in some parts of New Zealand, mock battles and daring rescues drew audiences to theatres in main cities and small towns across the Australian colonies and in the United Kingdom? Against backdrops of 'authentic scenery and panoramic views' and displays of male flesh not usually seen on British and Australian stages, these performances allowed audiences to experience New Zealand vividly and viscerally. As Gould has stated, imperialist dramas 'served as sites of contact between the imperial center and its peripheral possessions'.[5] The melodramas of the 1860s featured Māori acting Māori while highlighting the relationship of colonial outposts, the plight of the settler and the pursuit of civilization via Christian missionaries. This essay highlights the means in which these diverse groups

4 Marty Gould, *Nineteenth-Century Theatre and the Imperial Encounter* (New York: Routledge, 2011), 3.

5 Ibid.

of people, forms of culture and ideologies came together through a communal expression on stage. While Māori and Imperial troops engaged in battles throughout New Zealand, Māori and non-Māori collaborated to construct a vision of New Zealand on stage that portrayed harmonious race relations, strong, healthy bodies, beautiful and magical scenery in a Christian-focused colony.

Whakeau, the Pakeha Chief and *The Māori Queen*

In July 1862 as tensions rose between settlers and Māori in New Zealand's North Island, a 'troupe of Maori Warrior Chiefs, Wives and Children' appeared in Robert P. Whitworth's drama *Whakeau, the Pakeha Chief* at Sydney's Royal Lyceum Theatre. Advertisements for the production enticed audiences with assurances of 'exciting war dances, sacred ceremonies, extraordinary choruses and beautiful new scenery'.[6] The nineteen 'New Zealanders' (the term for Māori at the time) disembarked at Sydney harbour from Auckland on board the passenger ship *Gazelle* on 27 June 1862.[7] Described as 'a party of highly interesting and superior class of men and women, all more or less holding positions of honour and distinction in their native country', the visitors drew interest before setting foot in the theatre.[8] The diversity of cast members, drawn from North Island tribes, as well as the Australian thespian community, promised an eclectic evening

6 *Sydney Morning Herald* (12 July 1862), 1.

7 The term 'New Zealander' applied to Māori is commonly attributed to English historian Lord Macauley, who wrote, in his 1840 article on the Catholic Church for the *Edinburgh Review*, of a Māori man who sat on the future remains of London Bridge, sketching the ruins of St Paul's. As Ron Palenski explains Macauley's 'some traveller from New Zealand' subsequently became in retelling a 'New Zealander', Ron Palenski, *The Making of New Zealanders* (Auckland: Auckland University Press, 2012), 2–3.

8 *The Argus* (17 September 1862), p. 8.

of entertainment combined with the allure of the unknown. At the conclusion of its successful run in Sydney, the show moved onto Melbourne in September, with a different cast of European actors but with the same cast of Māori.[9] In Melbourne, the premiere of another drama, *The Maori Queen*, followed performances of *Whakeau*.[10]

From the start, the Māori performers who arrived in Australia were distinguished as different from indigenous Australians, the Aboriginal, considered 'barbarous' and 'uncivilized' at this time.[11] New Zealand historian Keith Sorrenson describes the comparison: 'the Aboriginal was despised as a rural pest' while the 'Maori was respected as a warrior'.[12] Advertising for the 'somewhat novel exhibition, namely a dramatic entertainment' promised that there 'is no savage race so interesting as the Maori. He proves himself capable of education and civilization'.[13] Uniqueness, ferociousness and unfamiliar physical traits were employed as descriptive elements in promotional material as is seen in this 1862 advertisement for *Whakeau* from the Melbourne newspaper the *Age*: 'there is no savage race as interesting as the Maori [...] the novelty of the entertainment will doubtless prove attractive for some time'.[14] The rhetoric surrounding the theatrical representation of the 'New Zealanders' – the 'physically, powerfully framed

9 The *Argus* listed 'Mr T. Andrews as Mr Mortimer, Mrs Harry Jackson as his daughter Alice Mortimer, and Whakeau, the Pakeha chief (alias Mark Thornton), Mr Fitzgerald', *The Argus*, 17 September, 1862, 8.

10 Sydney newspapers advertised a twelve- night season (the *Sydney Morning Herald* 15 July, 3 announced that the engagement would be 'limited to twelve nights' as the play was scheduled for Melbourne on 9 August) but according to Brian Mackrell, this was extended to 37 days, *Daily Post*, 1 May, 1978, np, clippings, Tourism file, Don Stafford Collection, Rotorua Public Library.

11 Mark. F. Lindley, *The Acquisition and Government of Backward Territory in International Law: Being a Treatise on the Law and Practice Relating to Colonial Expansion*, London, 1926, p. 41, cited in <http://kudnarto.tripod.com/ch30.htm#e> accessed 28 January 2014.

12 Keith Sorrenson, 'Māori and Pākeha', in Geoffrey Rice, ed., *The Oxford History of New Zealand* (Auckland: Oxford University Press, 1992), 142.

13 The *Argus* (17 September 1862), 8.

14 The *Age* (18 September 1862), 5.

men' and 'native-born gentlemen' who possessed 'the beauty of diction' with 'the elegance of the rhyme, in their war songs' – highlight the difference in perception of Māori with Australian Aboriginals.[15]

The cast of *Whakeau* who played 'New Zealanders, Chiefs etc.' portrayed both 'hostile' and 'friendly' tribes. In newspaper promotions of the drama, such as in the *Argus*, all actors were listed individually, along with their tribal affiliations, so that the public could be assured of authenticity of race and *mana* (prestige) of genealogy. The 'names of the Maoris' appeared with short explanations such as 'a chief of rank and influence; ancestors very great warriors'. Defined by their rank within Māori culture, the language describing the cast of *Whakeau* is crucial in understanding how the Māori were viewed and understood in performance. This convention of listing ancestral connections and tribal rankings refers back to earlier ethnographic displays. Sadiah Qureshi highlights similar cast listings in notices of ethnographic displays in London in 1844, such as George Catlin's Ojibbeway Indians, and explains, 'the names of the Indians' in newspapers offered 'other opportunities for consumption without attendance', with their claims to rank verifying authenticity. From the consumers' point of view this was 'one of the most pressing initial concerns'.[16] This blurring of reality and showmanship crystalizes the theatrical conventions of this era when fresh ideas of what characterized 'us' and 'them' emerged at the intersection of evolutionary science, the industrial revolution and popular entertainment.

When the curtain parted at the Lyceum Theatre on 19 July 1862, images of New Zealand flora and fauna emerged, illuminated by the limelight that outlined the spectral shape of Mount Egmont. The three-act *Whakeau* illustrated the story of British settlers to New Zealand, and their encounters with the native inhabitants. Act I introduced an English settler, Mortimer, his daughter and their friend the missionary who interacted peacefully

15 Ibid.

16 Sadiah Qureshi, *People on Parade: Exhibitions, Empire, and Anthropology in Nineteenth-Century Britain* (Chicago: The University of Chicago Press, 2011), 63; 166.

with the Māori men, women and children as they moved within the surroundings, playing games and conducting 'ceremonies'. Idealized colonial civilization unfolded on stage. Suddenly, the peaceful setting was shattered by the appearance of the 'Pakeha Maori' chief, an Englishman who, living amongst the natives, led a 'hostile tribe' of Māori. His evil scheme to kidnap the settler's daughter soon emerged. 'Pakeha Maori' is a nineteenth century term describing settlers who lived as Māori and who were accepted into some tribes, either by marriage, through fighting of a mutual enemy or for protection in return of service to the tribe.[17] The 'Pakeha Maori', as depicted in Whitworth's drama, was a rogue escaped convict who embraced the 'warrior' aspect of Māori culture.

Act II of *Whakeau* opened against a backdrop of a spectacular waterfall. This is where the Pākehā chief has hidden his captive. A secret entrance, known only to Whakeau and his accomplice, Red Bill, protects access to the waterfall. However, Peter Jenkins, a 'nondescript cockney' who has followed Red Bill, discovers the secret. Meanwhile, as Miss Mortimer pleads for her release, Whakeau 'assumes the garb of a sorcerer and consecrates the entrance and waters near the cave'.[18] Just then the friendly tribe discover the waterfall and, recognizing Whakeau impersonating Kopare, render him powerless. A 'war-dance inspired with real fury' transpires prior to the battle between the tribes.[19] Whakeau is slain, and in the dénouement, Miss Mortimer is freed and returned to the care of her father and fiancé. The inclusion of Māori acting Māori on-stage added to the excitement of the story, while the satisfactory and peaceful ending reinforced the successful settlement of the Antipodes.

Nine days after the premiere of *Whakeau* the second of the specially written dramas by Mr Whitworth opened in Sydney. *The Maori Queen* again served as a vehicle to feature games, ceremonies and war dances of Māori, but the play also ventured into social commentary with its narrative

17 Vincent O'Malley, *The Meeting Place: Māori and Pākehā Encounters*, 1642–1840 (Auckland: Auckland University Press, 2012), 9–10.

18 The *Argus* (17 September 1862), 8.

19 The *Age* (18 September 1862), 5.

of interracial marriage, the status of native women and race relations in a settler society. The character of the Māori Queen, Hine Matioro, played by the white Australian actress Fanny Morgan, shared her name with the historical Ngati Porou chieftainess, Hinematioro, who died in 1823.[20] *The Maori Queen* depicted Hine Matioro and her Pākehā husband entangled in a plot that again contained a clash of friendly and hostile Māori, dramatized via *haka* (dance) battle scenes. With her the interracial marriage crumbling, Hine Maitoro attempts a violent revenge on her husband for his second marriage to a Pākehā woman. Nonetheless, a peaceful resolution is achieved when Hinematioro is unable to inflict pain on the man that she still loves. Though *The Maori Queen* presented an antipodean take on a familiar dramatic trope, its native heroine added an extra element of racial expression to a common melodramatic plot. The heroine perishes but not before amends are made with her former husband, enabling her to die in peace.

Ostensibly, the performers and performances discussed here displayed corporeal representations of New Zealand, while also promoting what historian Alan Ward has identified as one of the main purposes of the conflicts of the 1860s – 'to establish the rule of British law'.[21] Thus, these works could be characterized as propaganda that supported colonization and settlement. However, acknowledging the agency of the performers, who entertained with their mix of 'amusement and instruction', the reception and the recorded observations thereof challenges previous interpretations of relations between Māori and Pākekā, Māori and the Crown and representations of New Zealand in Australia and the United Kingdom in the nineteenth century.[22]

The Māori performers all hailed from upper North Island tribes including Te Arawa, Ngati Whakaue, and Ngapuhi, tribes commonly identified as

20 Angela Ballara, *Hinematioro*, Dictionary of New Zealand Biography, Te Ara- the Encyclopedia of New Zealand, 30 October 2012 <http://www.TeAra.govt.nz/en/biographies/1h23/hinematioro> accessed 22 February, 2013.

21 Alan Ward, *A Show of Justice: Racial 'Ammalgamation' in Nineteenth Century New Zealand* (Canberra: Australian National University Press, 1974), 164.

22 The *Age* (18 September 1862), 5; *The Empire* (11 July 1862), 5.

'loyalist' during the wars. But as a historian of the wars, Vincent O'Malley, explained, this division is not clear-cut since 'many Maori defied categorisation' at this time. O'Malley describes

> problems of definition surround the concept of 'loyalist' or 'kupapa' (Māori who fought on the Pākehā side, also known as 'friendly Maori'). Many simply tried to keep from being caught up in the conflict. Others chose to cooperate with the Crown's forces or Crown's officials out of the complexity of inter-hapu rivalry. Many changed sides during the course of the conflicts.[23]

Thus, while many of the performers might have been 'Queen's Maoris', loyal to Queen Victoria, some could have come from tribes loyal to the Māori King (the so-called 'King's Maoris'). Therefore, tribal and *hapu* (sub-tribe) affiliations of the performers cannot unequivocally establish their individual allegiance in the conflicts.[24] Nonetheless, while deadly skirmishes over allegiance to the British Crown occurred in New Zealand, elaborate war dances and mock battles took place on stage between Māori and British subjects, portrayed by Australian and English actors.

Pre-European contact and cultural encounters

Prior to the 1840 signing of the Treaty of Waitangi between the British Crown and some Māori tribes, which made all Māori British subjects, settlers and explorers had seen a *haka* only in impromptu or ceremonial circumstances. Early European accounts of New Zealand record the dances of the native inhabitants. From initial contact in the seventeenth century, Māori dance and song played important roles in communication and formation of identities. Anne Salmond surmises that the 'rough, loud calling'

23 Vincent O'Malley, *Te Rohe Potae War and Raupatu*, Wai 898, #A22, Waitangi Tribunal Report, Wellington, December 2010, 30.

24 Belich, *The New Zealand Wars* (Auckland: Auckland University Press, 1986), 125–6.

described in Henrik Haelbos's account of Dutch explorer Abel Tasman's landing in 1642 was a *haka*.[25] In 1827 Louis Auguste de Sainson, an artist on the French charter ship *Astrolabe*, described in his diary the way that Māori 'ran up taking their place in a single line ... stamping their feet one after the other in perfect time and at the same time striking the top of their thighs'.[26] Accounts from Cook's landing of the *Endeavour* in New Zealand shores in October 1769 described 'a dancing war song': 'They seemed formed in ranks, each man jump'd with a swinging motion at the same instant of time to the right and left alternately accommodating a war song in very just time to each motion'.[27] These European descriptions are an important contribution to historical representations of Māori as they demonstrate how *haka* has been integral to first encounters. *Haka*, then, represent significant experiences where Māori and non-Māori met via a physical language of movement and sound (see Figure 1).[28]

Over time, Pākehā came to the realization that *haka* could be welcoming as well as aggressive. The sharing of *haka* between Māori and non-Māori men is mentioned in early nineteenth-century accounts of Pākehā Māori. Perhaps the most well-known Pākehā Māori, Frederick Edward Maning, wrote in 1863 of 'his' tribe as he became 'Maorified' in the 1840s: 'the newcomers perform another demon dance; then my tribe give another'.[29] Thus, interactions between Māori and non-Māori, viewed through this sharing of corporeal expression via *haka*, relied on the comprehension of and participation in movement, gestures, sounds and songs.

25 Anne Salmond, *Two Worlds: First Meetings Between Maori and Europeans 1642–1772* (Auckland: Viking Press, 1991), 81.

26 Gardiner, p. 44. See also Jennifer Shennan, *Maori Action Song* (Wellington: New Zealand Council for Educational Research, 1984), 3–4.

27 Salmond, *Two Worlds*, 126.

28 There are many types of *haka*, not all performed by men and not all are 'war dances'. See Wira Gardiner, *Haka: A Living Tradition* (Auckland: Hodder Moa Beckett, 2005) especially 26–34; also Suzanne Youngerman, 'Maori Dancing since the Eighteenth Century', *Ethnomusicology*, 18, 1, 1974, 87–9.

29 Frederick Edward Maning, *Old Time New Zealand: Being Incidents of Native Customs and Character in the Old Times by a Pakeha Maori*, 1863 <http://www.nzetc.org/tm/scholarly/tei-ManPake> accessed 8 June, 2007.

Figure 1: An early interpretation of haka as witnessed by Europeans, with men and women performing together. Augustus Earle, 1793–1838, *A Dance of New Zealanders*, drawn by A. Earle. Engraved by J. Stewart. Published by Longman & Co., London, May 1832, from *Narrative of a Nine Months Residence in New Zealand*, opposite p. 70. PUBL-0022-3, Alexander Turnbull Library (ATL), Wellington. Permission of the Alexander Turnbull Library, Wellington, New Zealand, must be obtained before any reuse of the image.

With the influx of settlers to New Zealand increasing from the mid-nineteenth century, the transmission and transcultural exchange of British performance form, content and style led to hybrid forms of entertainment on popular stages, both domestically and internationally. Māori cultural expression was integrated into plot development, with *haka* and *waiata* (song) signifying both Māori and New Zealand for spectators. At the same time, Māori adapted European forms of singing and dancing, while British and other composers and writers incorporated Māori proper names, place names, and mythologies into their works.[30] From the mid- nineteenth cen-

30 Peter Gibbons presents a cogent argument on the process of 'cultural colonization' of Māori by settlers. Peter Gibbons, 'Cultural Colonization and National Identity',

tury Pākeha appropriated and integrated Māori cultural expression into works of fiction, the naming of places and people, and design. Māori also used and adapted European forms, especially in performance, for their own ends. For instance, the introduction of Christianity in the early nineteenth century influenced the adaptation of hymns and European chord and metre structure to Māori singing, likewise, the use of accordion, harmonica and brass instruments as accompaniment to Māori *haka* and *waiata* at gatherings and communal activities point to this widespread cross-cultural exchange.[31] A deeper understanding of New Zealand's cultural history can emerge by considering these performance events and by centralizing performance in historical inquiry. Thus, this exploration of melodramas expands what we know of the shared histories of Māori and Pākehā from the nineteenth century.

Māori in the United Kingdom/Empire on stage

Meanwhile, in Australia, financial disagreements broke out amongst the group appearing in *The Maori Queen*. In December the dispute ended up in the Melbourne courts, which found in favour of the Māori performers, who claimed their producer, McGauran, owed them wages. McGauran, forced to abandon the enterprise, was replaced with a new producer, M. G. Hegarty and a 'group of Melbourne speculators'. With only three performers from the original nineteen – Tomati Hapimana, Aperahama Pungatura and Pene Tutu – remaining, the entourage set sail for London in mid-1863. In July, the same month as Governor Grey ordered the invasion of the Waikato region in New Zealand, Hegarty's troupe premiered at the

---

New Zealand Journal of History, 36, 1, 2002, 5–17. I explore this concept further in Marianne Schultz, *Performing Indigenous Culture on Stage and Screen: A Harmony of Frenzy* (Basingstoke: Palgrave Macmillan, 2016).

31 Mervyn McLean, *Maori Music* (Auckland: Auckland University Press,1996), 270–308.

Alhambra Palace Theatre, Leicester Square billed as the 'Maori Warrior Chiefs'.[32] In February 1863, only a few months before Hegarty and the six Māori performers departed Melbourne for the United Kingdom, another group of Māori had embarked for London. Led by William Jenkins, an English cabinetmaker-turned-lay-preacher for the Wesleyan Missionary Society and interpreter for the New Zealand government. Jenkins had resided in New Zealand since the early 1840s and nurtured a relationship with Māori by learning *te reo Māori* (the Māori language). His fourteen 'New Zealand Native Chiefs' were assembled so that they could lecture on Māori culture in the United Kingdom and to expose them to 'the work of England which is not seen by multitudes of men'.[33]

Reflecting contemporary missionary objectives as well as personal ambition, Jenkins hoped that his chosen group might, on their return to New Zealand, extoll the virtues of English Christian civilization to other Māori, while he would win favour with Royalty and people in power both in New Zealand and Britain. Jenkins aspired to gain the support of both the New Zealand government and the British Crown once in London, but as a letter to Governor Grey from the Duke of Newcastle, Secretary of State of the Colonies, made clear, this support was not forthcoming. The Duke spoke of his alarm at the 'discovery that Mr Jenkins is going to take them about the country and introduce them to "illustrate lectures". Which I perceive to mean to make a *show* of them a la "Barnum"'.[34] This reference to Barnum evoked the proliferation of live theatrical performances in the United Kingdom and United States of indigenous peoples and curiosities inspired by the famous impresario P.T. Barnum. By the Duke's estimation, Jenkins's endeavour was not worthy of royal endorsement.

Though Jenkins professed that his 'Native Chiefs' would present lectures on New Zealand throughout the United Kingdom, as opposed to exhibitions for entertainment, it became clear that his plan was fraught.

32 *The Era* (12 July 1863), 6.

33 Brian Mackrell, *Hariru Wikitoria! An illustrated history of the Maori tour of England, 1863* (Auckland: Oxford University Press, 1985), 19–22.

34 Mackrell, *Hariru Wikitoria!*, 45.

The fundamental problems lay with the chiefs' lack of understanding of the tour's purpose coupled with inadequate resources. It also became increasingly clear to the Māori themselves that Jenkins required them to 'act' Māori, most notably in their style of dress. Jenkins directed the presentation and representation of the Māori to encourage a historical image of this race. An account from a member of the group emphasizes the need for historical 'authenticity' over contemporary style. Although the 'Maori party possessed European clothing', the 'majority of invitations they received requested their attendance in native costume'.[35] A mat was a woven flax cloak draped across the body, but in the period of colonization this practice became less widespread amongst Māori. Reihana Te Taukawau, a member of Jenkins's lecture group, wrote in 1864 of the theatricality that Jenkins demanded from his: 'In New Zealand I never had a mat, before I knew Jenkins I disliked all sorts of mats for mostly they are many years old, being not much made now, and the things are nasty, they are often filled with vermin. Jenkins said, "You must wear the mats, people like it"'.[36] Jenkins's group acutely felt the loss of their *mana*, as related in this excerpt from Paula Morris' fictional account of this venture, *Rangatira*. The eldest chief, the Rangatira, reflects on Jenkins' treatment of his charges: 'in England we were little better than slaves [...] displayed in public places like trophies of war'.[37]

Not surprisingly, the paths of both Hegarty's and Jenkins's groups crossed as they toured the United Kingdom in 1863–1864, leading to comparisons which troubled Jenkins; he had hoped that in the mind of the public there would be a distinct difference between the two groups of Māori. While Jenkins manufactured lectures presumably in an attempt to educate both Māori and their English audiences, there could be no mistaking Hegarty's 'Six Maori Chiefs' for anything but performers. A major insult to Jenkins's pride occurred when three of his group – Wiremu Pou, Hirini Pakia and his wife Tere Pakia (Hariata Te Iringa) – defected to Hegarty's

35 Mackrell, *Hariru Wikitoria!*, 50.

36 Statement by Reihana Te Taukawau, 8 March 1864, Mackrell, Brian MS-Papers-10953-2, Research papers concerning visit to England of Maori Chiefs, Alexander Turnbull Library (ATL), Wellington.

37 Paula Morris, *Rangatira* (Auckland: ReadHowYouWant, 2011), 154.

'Warrior Chiefs' in August 1863, citing money as the incentive. Jenkins tried his best to prevent this desertion becoming public knowledge. Kamariera Wharepapa, a spokesman for the Māori of Jenkins's group, urged Jenkins to 'confess publicly that some of our party have joined the Alhambra people'. Jenkins's response that 'we need not publicise it, it will do us harm' points to the less than respectable reputation that adhered to Music Hall performing artists at this time.[38] Alongside the issue of payment (Hegarty's performers received £2 per week plus 'board and lodging', compared to Jenkins's payment of tobacco and £1 5s), Hegarty's group proved a much more up front way to 'see England, the work of England'.[39] Regardless of the difference in pay, Hegarty's honesty in the motive for his enterprise excelled Jenkins's. Whereas Hegarty's 'Warrior Chiefs' willingly assumed their roles as performers in theatrical settings, Jenkins did not explain to his 'Native Chiefs' that they would be *performing as* Māori in their lectures in England. In April 1864 Jenkins's disheartened and ill chiefs left the United Kingdom to return to New Zealand, while Hegarty's troupe of 'Six Maori Chiefs' continued to perform throughout England and Scotland, from London to Edinburgh.

Warriors and cannibals

Overlapping with the 'Chiefs' engagement at the Alhambra and Jenkins's 'Native Chiefs' illustrated lectures in London, the 29 August 1863 edition of the *Illustrated London News* featured an engraving showing a *Pa* (fortress) engulfed in flames against the backdrop of Mount Taranaki (Egmont) with Imperial soldiers surrounding and capturing armed Māori warriors. The

38 Letter from Kamariera Wharepapa translated by Mrs Colenso and Mr W. George Maunsell, Brian Mackrell, Research papers concerning the visit to England of Māori Chiefs, MS-Papers-10953-2, ATL, Wellington.

39 Mackrell, *Hariru Wikitoria!*, 64–5.

woodcut shows Māori outnumbered by British forces. For white British subjects, a Māori victory in these conflicts was inconceivable. As historian James Belich explains, 'the Pakeha believed it was their destiny to rule New Zealand fully' and illustrations such this emphasized Pākehā and British superiority.[40] That same month Hegarty's troupe were performing 'two Dramas along with an English company' as advertised in the 23 August edition of *The Era*, including *Wahena, The Maori Queen.*[41] The poster advertising their season at the Princess's Theatre in September reminded the public [of the] 'great attraction of these Maori Warrior Chiefs is the interest attached through the present calamitous Rebellious War in New Zealand'.[42] The conflation of the melodrama with the real conflict 12,000 miles away proved to be a major drawcard for the show. These dramas presented an idealized vision of settler New Zealand that augmented and exaggerated newspapers' representations of the conflicts in the colony.[43] (See Figure 2.)

From mid-1863 to mid-1864, as Imperial troops spread across the upper North Island of New Zealand engaging in battles with local tribes, Hegarty's Māori performers traversed the Empire with engagements ranging from one night to several weeks, presenting a vision of a harmonious settler society on stage. On 21 September, 1863 'Supported by the Resident Corps Dramatique' with 'Appropriate music', *Wahena or The Maori Queen* opened at Edinburgh's Princess's Theatre.[44] Their performances were,

40 Belich, 'The Governors and the Maori' in Keith Sinclair ed., *The Oxford Illustrated History of New Zealand* (Auckland: Oxford University Press, 1990), 88.

41 *The Era* (23 August 1863), 1. The notice, signed 'D. Morton, 18a Wolcot Place, Kennington Road, S.' regularly appeared throughout the next eleven months in *The Era*, Garrick Club Library, London.

42 Royal Princess's Theatre (Edinburgh), photocopies of six posters advertising performances by Māori warrior chiefs, Eph-C-MAORI-1863-01/06, ATL, Wellington.

43 Theatres where the Māori performers appeared between July 1863 and July 1864: Alhambra Palace, Leicester Square, London; Theatre Royal, North Shields; New Theatre, High Jarrow; Theatre Royal, Seaham Harbour; Theatre Royal, Stockton; Theatre Royal, Bradford; Theatre Royal, Leeds; New Adelphi Theatre, Liverpool; Royal Princess's Theatre, Edinburgh; Theatre Royal, Accrington, Preston.

44 Eph-C-MAORI-1863-01/06, ATL, Wellington.

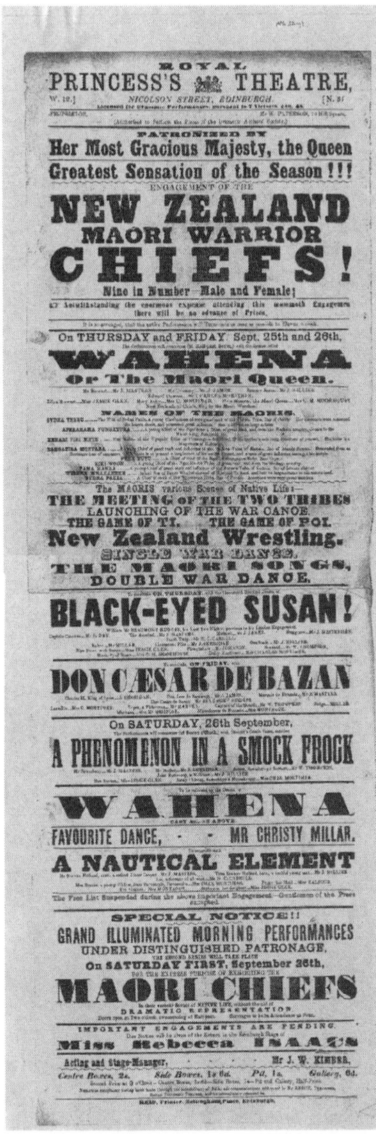

Figure 2: Royal Princess's Theatre (Edinburgh): photocopies of six posters advertising performances by Māori warrior chiefs, Eph- C-Maori -1863-01/06, ATL, Wellington. Permission of the Alexander Turnbull Library, Wellington, New Zealand, must be obtained before any reuse of the image.

first and foremost, entertainment and displayed the pre-requisites for nineteenth-century popular performance as outlined by Jane R. Goodall: 'spectacle, humour, variety, eroticism and surprise'.[45] The poster for the Edinburgh season described the appearance of the nine Māori as 'intensely thrilling'. (Three performers had joined the group: Henari Mete, Rangatira Moetara and Riki Woon). *The Era*'s extensive review commented on the authenticity of the 'Maori Warrior Chiefs' as well as the theatricality and acting skills of all the main characters, Māori and European alike (as with the Australian production, a European woman played the part of the Māori Queen). The Māori had become seasoned performers, especially in regard to the rule to always leave the audience wanting more. The audience on 26 September expressed 'a warm desire to have several of the "illustrations of savage life" repeated, but singular to state, the artistes, like certain great English vocalists, always appeared grateful for the applause they had created, but shrewdly declined the honour of an encore'.[46]

From Edinburgh the actors travelled to Liverpool and performed *Wahena* at the New Adelphi Theatre in November. A small item in the *The Era* during this appearance reported '[T]hey have also appeared in the drama of *Robinson Crusoe*'. This diversion from their previous productions is noteworthy. When the Māori actors assumed the roles of characters symbolizing submission, colonization and conversion to Christianity they stepped outside the representation of their own race and became instead, to borrow performing arts theorist Joseph Roach's term, the 'signifying body' of uncivilized society by portraying the 'cannibal savages' of the story.[47] English literature scholar Ann Marie Fallon believes that the phenomenon of the 'Robinsonade', a genre of texts produced following the

45 Jane R.Goodall, *Performance and Evolution in the Age of Darwin* (London: Routledge, 2002), 8.

46 *The Era* (27 September 1863), 11.

47 Joseph Roach explains that 'the signifying body is central to theatrical representation in any form'. Joseph Roach, 'Power's Body: The Inscription of Morality as Style' in Thomas Postlewait and Bruce A McConachie, eds, *Interpreting The Theatrical Past* (Iowa City: University of Iowa Press, 1989), 101. In Defoe's novel the island is an imagined one situated somewhere in the Carribean.

1719 publication of Daniel Defoe's novel, 'established the Crusoe myth as a story of celebratory colonialism'. Therefore, by the time the Māori performers appeared in the Crusoe pantomime, the story had evolved from a tale of one man's heroism involving shipwreck, domination and colonization to what Gould refers to as a 'transformative encounter with indigenous peoples'.[48] This 'mischievous' relationship between the 'popular stage and the world of ideas' of the nineteenth century, highlights the collisions of cultures and ideas permissible in theatrical ventures of the era.[49]

By June 1864 Hegarty's group of nine performers were back in London, appearing at the Marylebone Theatre in *The Emigrant's Trials or Life in New Zealand*, the play by the English playwright, J.B Johnstone.[50] Described as 'expressly written for the introduction of this party' the plot of Johnstone's drama nonetheless mirrors almost exactly that of *The Pakeha Chief* performed two years earlier in Australia by some of the Māori. Johnstone's plays were conventional melodrama, reflecting his interest in colonial settings and nautical themes, such as *Ned Kelly or The Perils of the Bush* (1880).[51] The cast of characters in *The Emigrant's Trials* included New Zealand settlers, Godfrey Oldacre, and his daughter, Eleanor, who arrived in New Zealand as forced emigrants due to loss of their estate through unscrupulous dealings. A former suitor of Eleanor, Landrogue is an escaped convict. Making his way to New Zealand, Landrogue, like Whakeau in Whitworth's drama, has become a 'chief of a party of natives'.[52] The cast also included a Māori 'friendly to the whites' and two young Englishmen.[53] Landrogue is

48 Ann Marie Fallon, *Global Crusoe: Comparative Literature, Post Colonial Theory and Transnational Aesthetics* (Farnham: Ashgate, 2011), 3; Gould, *Nineteenth-Century Theatre*, 52.

49 Fallon, *Global Crusoe*, 6. Māori did practice cannibalism in inter-tribal warfare and in excursions with early explorers.

50 After extensive research to locate this play and Whitworth's works in theatre archives in the UK and Australia no copies were found. Synopses were obtained from newspaper articles. *The Emigrant's Trials* does not appear in the Lord Chamberlain list of plays.

51 <http://karenphotographs.com/afamilyalbum/johnelizasouthbeer.htm> accessed 7 January 2013.

52 *The Era* (19 June 1864), 10.

53 Ibid.

in possession of a document that will clear the name of Oldacre, allowing him and his daughter to return home. Pursued for the document by the two young Englishmen and the 'friendly' Māori, the convict is shot and killed, thus, restoring justice for the Oldacres.

As with *Whakeau*, the interest in *The Emigrant's Trial* arose from the participation of the Māori performers. *The Era* explained that though the 'drama is of very ordinary description' the presence of the 'New Zealand savages' presented 'striking situations' with 'some rather astonishing feats of strength, [including] a wrestling match'.[54] Competition for audiences in London during the run of *The Emigrant's Trials* was fierce. Contemporaneous offerings such as Monsieur Henrequez's Windsor Castle Troupe of Performing Dogs and Monkeys and W.H. Wieland's, the 'Prince of Niggers-Ethiopean Delineators', lured those seeking novelty and excitement of an evening. Thus, it is understandable why a commentator, after attending Johnstone's play stated: '[A]n interest must be strong now-a days to raise much enthusiasm in an audience, but it may be, at the same time, of an unpleasant nature'.[55] The Festival Scene, in which the 'New Zealanders had the stage to themselves' was 'vociferously applauded', and included a *haka*. While the Māori actors were integrated into the plot, delivering lines and providing action scenes, they also added elements of danger and suspense to an otherwise ordinary melodrama.

Conclusion

The examination of these melodramas reveals untold facets of constructed representations of New Zealand and New Zealanders, both Māori and Pākehā, in the nineteenth century. The stage offered white British subjects

54 Ibid.

55 *The Era* (19 June 1864), p. 10.

a proximity to Māori that augmented the news of the conflicts involving imperial forces and Māori and filled in gaps of knowledge about the colony and its inhabitants, native and settler. While Jenkins's group spoke of the benefits of colonization in a lecture format, there is no doubt that the dramas discussed here promoted British superiority, Christian morality and the civilizing influence of both. These melodramas reflected familiar melodramatic tropes while also provoking questions regarding imperial conflicts and race relations. Written and produced by Australians and Englishmen, *Whakeau, the Pakeha Chief*, *The Emigrant's Trials or Life in New Zealand* and *Rangatira Wahena or The Maori Queen*, disseminated views of successful colonization and settlement of New Zealand. However, the presence of Māori in Imperial theatres interacting with non-Māori, added a layer of complexity to formations of race and culture. Pulling back the curtain on these dramas sheds new light on Māori and Pākehā shared histories and demonstrate the ability of theatre to create perceptions of people, places, and power. In the theatre, 'savage' and settler celebrated the Empire. While the presence of the Other on stage represented the reach of colonization, New Zealand came alive in sight and sound in ways that newspaper reports could only hint at.

Bibliography

Ballara, Angela, 'Hinematioro', *Dictionary of New Zealand Biography, Te Ara–The Encyclopedia of New Zealand* <http://www.TeAra.govt.nz/en/biographies/1h23/hinematioro> accessed 30 October 2012.

Belich, James, *The New Zealand Wars and the Victorian Interpretation of Racial Conflict* (Auckland: Auckland University Press, 1986).

——, 'The Governors and the Maori' in Keith Sinclair ed., *The Oxford Illustrated History of New Zealand* (Auckland: Oxford University Press, 1990), 75–98.

Goodall, Jane R., *Performance and Evolution in the Age of Darwin* (London: Routledge, 2002).

Gould, Marty, 'Role Britannia: Theatricality and Empire in the Victorian Period', PhD thesis (University of Iowa, 2005).

——, *Nineteenth-Century Theatre and the Imperial Encounter* (New York: Routledge, 2011).

Lindley, Mark. F., *The Acquisition and Government of Backward Territory in International Law: Being a Treatise on the Law and Practice Relating to Colonial Expansion* (London, 1926), 41, cited in <http://kudnarto.tripod.com/ch30.htm#e>.

Mackrell, Brian, *Hariru Wikitoria! An Illustrated History of the Maori Tour of England, 1863* (Auckland: Oxford University Press, 1985).

McLean, Mervyn, *Maori Music* (Auckland: Auckland University Press, 1996).

O'Malley, Vincent, *Te Rohe Potae War and Raupatu*, Wai 898, #A22, Waitangi Tribunal Report, Wellington, December 2010.

——, *The Meeting Place: Māori and Pākehā Encounters, 1642–1840* (Auckland: Auckland University Press, 2012).

Qureshi, Sadiah, *People on Parade: Exhibitions, Empire, and Anthropology in Nineteenth-Century Britain* (Chicago: University of Chicago Press, 2011).

Rahill, Frank, *The World of Melodrama* (University Park: Pennsylvania State University, 1967).

Salmond, Anne, *Two Worlds: First Meetings between Maori and Europeans 1642–1772* (Auckland: Viking Press, 1991).

Sorrenson, Keith, 'Māori and Pākeha', in Geoffrey Rice, ed., *The Oxford History of New Zealand* (Auckland: Oxford University Press, 1992).

Ward, Alan, *A Show of Justice: Racial 'Ammalgamation' in Nineteenth-Century New Zealand* (Canberra: Australian National University Press, 1974).

PETER YEANDLE

Performing the Other on the Popular London Stage: Exotic People and Places in Victorian Pantomime

ABSTRACT

Pantomime was one of the most enduring and popular forms of public entertainment in the nineteenth century. As a performance genre, it was both sensitive, and reactive, to political developments – indeed, much of its appeal owed to its topical commentary on current affairs and its staged negotiations of prevailing ideological attitudes. Topical allusions to empire increased exponentially after 1880 – the timing of such a rise is coterminous with the Scramble for Africa and deliberate attempts to sow imperial enthusiasm across society writ-large.

In this essay, I trace the ways in which dominant – and less dominant – ideologies of imperialism were played out in the pantomime. We know from several existing studies, for instance, that the pantomimes *Aladdin* and *Robinson Crusoe* evolved over the nineteenth century to reflect shifting attitudes to China, the Chinese, Africa and Africans. If it is a secure supposition that pantomime became increasingly exotic in its articulation of imperial topics, more might be said on how the pantomime implemented a visual display of colonial landscapes and the people that inhabited these spaces. This essay, then, investigates the interrelationship of exotic people and exotic places in the context of late-Victorian visual culture. In particular, I focus on pantomimic responses to the Indian Rebellion of 1857 and trace the evolution of the *Jack and the Beanstalk* story as it was presented in London's pantomimes. I am interested in how topical references to the empire were incorporated into performances, and pay particular attention to the role of the Giant, as villain, as allegory of imperial ideology.

These questions guide analysis of reviews published in the national press and trade periodicals. These sources reveal much about how performances were received by the audience; they also often provide detailed coverage of the technical production of pantomimes. They provide, therefore, a rich source for the study of the theatrical display of the exotic.

***

Introduction: Pantomime and popular imperialism

In 1879, Britain was gripped by debates about its empire. William Gladstone, 'the Grand Old Man' of British politics, provoked national discussion in a series of speeches about the ethics of foreign policy, particularly in Afghanistan. Meanwhile, British forces in Africa had suffered setbacks against the Zulus but, by the end of the year, had emerged victorious and the Zulu leader Cetewayo was captured. This is how events were raised in the *Era*'s review of the *Jack and the Giant Killer; or, Good King Arthur and the Knights of the Round Table* at the Crystal Palace's children's pantomime of Christmas 1879:

> Children do not want to hear anything of Mr Gladstone's speeches, neither do they understand much about Cetewayo and the conditions of Zululand. But they, one and all, are well up in the story of Jack, that delightful youth who made short work of the terrible Giant, and who was raised to the peerage of the period by his grateful monarch for the valuable services he rendered. We want a few such heroes at the present day, for there are plenty of giants to be slaughtered if we could only find Jacks equal to the task. (28 December 1879)

This essay explores pantomime responses to key events in British imperial history with particular focus on the interrelationship of exotic bodies and exotic spaces in Victorian performance culture. Pantomime was the most popular and commercially profitable theatrical form of the nineteenth century, often financing theatres for the year.[1] It was a core ritual of Victorian Christmas.[2] As George Lancaster, a contemporary theatre critic, noted in 1883: 'Boxing Day without pantomime would be as empty as Christmas

1 The most recent academic study, and most detailed to date, is See also the essays in Jim Davis, ed., *Victorian Pantomime: A Collection of Critical Essays* (Basingstoke: Palgrave, 2010), as well as Jeffrey Richards, *The Golden Age of Pantomime: Slapstick, Subversion and Spectacle in Victorian England* (London: I.B. Tauris, 2015).

2 Mark Connelly, *Christmas: A History* (London: I.B. Tauris, 2012), 44–60. See also Jim Davis, 'Boxing Day', in Tracy C. Davis and Peter Holland, eds, *The Performing Century: Nineteenth-Century Theatre's History* (Basingstoke: Palgrave, 2010), 13–31.

Day without dinner'.[3] Another critic, for the *Daily Telegraph*, had also embraced the analogy of festive food: 'an exceedingly large proportion of the community would as soon think of giving up their plum pudding on Christmas Day as abandoning their pantomime the night after'.[4] The pantomime was popular with people of all ages and from all social classes, from Queen Victoria herself to the poorest of her subjects.

Pantomime was popular because it was a spectacular, extravagant and anarchic theatrical form. Its popularity was also owed to its remarkable sensitivity to topical news: productions poked fun at local, national and imperial events, often sending up politicians and offering critique of current and foreign affairs. Pantomime was popular entertainment, but it was much more than *just* entertainment. As David Mayer argues for the early nineteenth century: 'like the tabloid of today, the pantomime leaned towards the *immediate*, the *sensational*, the *most readily apparent* or *easily understood*'. It was 'an unofficial and informal chronicle of the age'.[5] In her study of the politics of regional pantomime, Jill Sullivan demonstrates that pantomime encompassed 'references to aspects of mid- to late-Victorian culture' which mirrored the audiences' 'various experiences and understandings' of the world.[6] Pantomime would continue to thrive because it was uniquely placed, amongst theatrical forms, to operate as a form for broadcasting and interpreting the news – pantomime was satirical, but it also reflected, and sought to direct, public opinion. Simply put, its success depended not only on its fantastic spectacle but on the accessibility and popularity of its topical commentary. It is precisely this contemporaneity of pantomime that makes it such a rich source for analysis of Victorian attitudes to race and empire.

3 'Notes on Pantomimes', *The Theatre* (January, 1883), 13.

4 Cited in Davis, 'Boxing Day', 14.

5 David Mayer, *Harlequin in His Element: English Pantomime, 1806–36* (Cambridge, MA: Harvard University Press, 1969), 6–7. My emphases.

6 Jill A. Sullivan, *The Politics of the Pantomime: Regional Identity in Theatre, 1860–1900* (Hatfield: University of Hertfordshire Press, 2011), 15.

When invited to contribute an essay on Victorian pantomime to this volume, I was initially hesitant. Given the surge of recent academic research into the history of the popular Victorian theatre – including pantomime – I was unsure what I could contribute that was interpretively new. Provoked by Bernard Porter's misleading argument that the empire was almost entirely absent from Victorian performance culture,[7] a spate of recent studies has emerged confirming popular entertainments not only reflected imperial themes but consciously sought to inform and enthuse audiences about the empire.[8] Marty Gould, for instance, has located hundreds of nineteenth-century plays in which plot and characterization dramatized imperial events and conveyed ideologies. Moreover, his case study of the *Robinson Crusoe* story, adapted into one of the most popular Victorian pantomime franchises, reveals changing attitudes to the empire – particularly Africa – over the course of the nineteenth century: the Crusoe character transitions from explorer to colonizer, and from colonial administrator to conquistador, functioning throughout as a 'current and contemporary embodiment of British imperialism'.[9] Edward Ziter's meticulous study of the *Orient on the Victorian Stage* illustrates how melodrama and pantomime responded to imperial wars in East Africa in the mid-1880s.[10] Anne Witchard's reading of the evolution of the *Aladdin* and *Ali Baba* pantomime adaptations of the *Arabian Nights* stories demonstrates that the popular theatre directed as well as reflected public attitudes to China and the Chinese. Witchard's study is particularly rich for its emphasis on the development of oriental

7 Bernard Porter, *The Absent-Minded Imperialists: What the British Really Thought about the Empire* (Oxford: Oxford University Press, 2004), 140.

8 For work that pre-dated Porter, see for instance, Michael Booth on melodrama, 'Soldiers of the Queen' in Michael Hays and Anastasia Nikolopolou, eds, *Melodrama: The Cultural Emergence of a Genre* (New York: St Martins Press, 1996), 3–20; Jeffrey Richards, *Imperialism and Music, Britain 1876–1953* (Manchester: Manchester University Press, 2001). For work that post-dates Porter, see below.

9 Marty Gould, *Nineteenth-Century Theatre and the Imperial Encounter* (London: Routledge, 2011), 72.

10 Edward Ziter, *The Orient on the Victorian Stage* (Cambridge: Cambridge University Press, 2003), 164–95.

pantomime characters in the context of Opium Wars and Yellow Peril.[11] Jim Davis and Jennifer Schacker have both used the relocation of Giantland to South Africa in the 1899 Drury Lane production of *Jack and the Beanstalk*, in the context of the second Boer War, to investigate pantomime's negotiation of ideologies of race and gender.[12] Jeffrey Richards' powerfully argued essay shows how pantomime responded to the imperial wars of the late-Victorian pantomime; productions not only provided a digest of foreign affairs and topical comment on them but also, according the evidence found in theatrical reviews, stoked the patriotism of the audience by presenting to them a series of imperial heroes and colonial villains.[13] My initial hesitancy, then, is well founded: in the present state of research, the argument that pantomime operated as a cultural site for the dissemination of imperial ideology is seemingly irrefutable. That would suggest a privileged place for the performance of race, and exotic bodies, in Victorian theatres.

My aim is to problematize our understanding of the interrelationship of imperialism and performance culture by arguing the significance of those exotic bodies – so dramatically depicted in the rough and tumble of pantomime – is advanced by examining their relationship to theatrical depictions of place. Pantomime was popular because, as a humorous performance genre that staged and invoked intense emotional reactions, it exceeded Victorian parameters of theatrical authenticity. Pantomime created performative space for crudely drawn and vulgar topical commentaries on race and imperialism and the form thrived on its freedom to

11 Anne Witchard, *Thomas Burke's Dark Chinoiserie: Limehouse Nights and the Queer Spell of Chinatown* (Farnham: Ashgate, 2009), especially 58–9, 68–77, 84–7.

12 Jim Davis, 'Imperial Transgressions: The Ideology of Drury Lane Pantomime in the Late Nineteenth Century', *New Theatre Quarterly* 12 (1996), 147– 55; Jennifer Schacker, 'Slaying Blunderboer: Cross-dressed Heroes, National Identities and Wartime Pantomime', *Marvels and Tales* 27/1 (2013), 52–64.

13 Jeffrey Richards, 'Drury Lane Imperialism', in Peter Yeandle, Katherine Newey and Jeffrey Richards, eds, *Politics, Performance and Popular Culture: Theatre and Society in Nineteenth-Century Britain*, chapter 9 (Manchester: Manchester University Press, forthcoming).

fashion fun through invocations of fairy tale traditions. Pantomime was, as Katherine Newey argues, 'licensed mayhem'; the 'enduring attraction of pantomime in the nineteenth century was precisely [its] mix of frivolity and topicality'.[14] Its pursuit of pleasure included social and artistic licence to trade in grotesque characters and exaggerated stereotypes; melodramatic modes of good versus bad were translated into fantastical forms of pantomime heroes and villains.[15]

However, the location of 'exotic' bodies in exoticized landscapes animated stage representations of race in ways that sharpened delineations of 'us' and 'them'. Linda Colley defines the 'other' and 'otherness' as conceptual modes in which the cultural construction of 'us' as a national community was defined in opposition to constant iterations of what 'we are [were] not'. If we take this definition, then the contrast of 'home' and 'foreign' bodies reveals Victorian pantomime's contributions to collective identity formation.[16] This was particularly the case by the end of the nineteenth century as pantomime increasingly sought to sow imperial patriotism, holding up the image of the colonial body to public view in order to justify colonial wars and promote British solidarities around racial identity. To add to this, I follow Edward Ziter's argument that the theatre 'helped constitute the modern British colonial imaginary'.[17] Audiences were conditioned to locate bodies within particular geographical contexts; race and place were contingent factors in staging the exotic body in pantomime and this relationship became increasingly evident as the century progressed. I investigate these issues through two case studies: of pantomime's responses to

14 Katherine Newey, '"Bubbles of the Day": The Pantomimic and the Melodramatic', in Yeandle, Newey and Richards, eds, *Politics, Performance and Popular Culture*, chapter 3 (forthcoming).

15 Perhaps the most immediately obvious example of the pantomimic play on realism is the gender subversion in the roles of the pantomime dame and the principal boy. In both instances, it was clear to audiences that key roles were played by people of the opposite sex. See Jim Davis, '"Slap On! Slap Ever!" Victorian Pantomime, Gender Variance, and Cross Dressing', *New Theatre Quarterly* 30/3 (2014), 218–30.

16 Linda Colley, *Britons: Forging the Nation* (London: Pimlico, 1994); 'British and Otherness: An Argument', *Journal of British Studies* 31/4 (1992), 309–29.

17 Ziter, *Orient on the Victorian Stage*, 6.

a key event in British imperial history (what Victorians called the Indian 'Mutiny', of 1857); and the imaginative use made of a famous pantomime location (Giant-Land, in *Jack and the Beanstalk* productions from the 1870s to the 1890s). But, first, a note on methodology, further elaboration of the significances of place and visual culture, and an explanation for why I have chosen these case studies.

Quantitative trends: The importance of place

This essay draws from research I conducted as a postdoctoral researcher on Professors Katherine Newey and Jeffrey Richards's AHRC-funded project 'The Cultural History of Victorian Pantomime'.[18] Part of my task was to build a database of pantomime performance in London, recording productions staged across London between 1820 and 1910. The initial purpose of the database was twofold: first, to document performance titles, playwrights, theatres and, where information was available, set painters, musical directors and choreographers; second, the database was to double up as an easy-reference catalogue of over a terabyte's worth of digitized newspaper and periodical reviews. However, the database also enables simple quantitative analysis of change over time.[19] In the mid-Victorian period pantomimes derived their titles from mixed traditions – the burlesque, the extravaganza, French, German and Scandinavian folk stories adapted to an English audience, and in some cases, traditional English and

18 <http://www.ahrc.ac.uk/News-and-Events/News/Pages/Pantomimes-enduring-appeal-put-through-academic-scrutiny.aspx> accessed 9 May 2015.

19 In order to draw up the database, I used advertisements and reviews in the national and theatrical press, including the *Era*, the *Stage* (for the years after 1880 in which it was launched), *The Times* and the *Daily News*. I also cross referenced against the Lord Chamberlain's collection of plays. Although lists are as comprehensive as possible, I cannot claim to have documented *every* pantomime that was staged in London. Not all were recorded in the press or submitted to the censor.

Celtic folk stories.[20] The chart below details titles, subtitles and the theatres in which pantomimes were produced for the Christmas season 1851–2.

Title	Subtitle	Theatre
Harlequin Hogarth	*Or the Two London Apprentices*	Drury Lane
Princess Radiant	*Or the Story of Mayflowers by the Brothers Brough*	Haymarket
The Prince of Happy Land	*Or the Fawn in the Forest*	Lyceum
Harlequin Billy Taylor	*Or The Flying Dutchman and the King of Raritongo*	Princess's
The Mandarin's Daughter	*Or the Story of the Willow Pattern Plate*	Punch's Playhouse
Red Rufus	*Or Harlequin Fact, Fiction and Fancy*	Olympic
Harlequin and the Yellow Dwarf	*Or the Enchanted Grove*	Sadler's Wells
Mr and Mrs Briggs	*Or Harlequin Punch's Festival*	Astleys
Harlequin Bluecap and the King of the Golden Waters	*Or the Three Kingdoms, Animal, Vegetable and Mineral*	Surrey
The Lion and the Unicorn	*Or Harlequin Britannia, True Blue and Merry England*	Victoria

20 For a brisk explanation and analysis of the development of the pantomime genre, see Jennifer Schacker, 'Unruly Tales: Ideology, Anxiety and the Regulation of Genre', *Journal of American Folklore* 120 (2007), 381–400.

Title	Subtitle	Theatre
Sir John Barleycorn	*Or Harlequin Champagne and the Fairies of Hop and Vince*	Marylebone
Oliver Cromwell	*Or Harlequin and Charlie over the Water*	City of London
Beauty and the Beast		Queens (Tottenham Court Rd)
Hoddy Toddy, All Head and no Body	*Or Harlequin and the Fairy of the Magic Pippin*	Standard
Cowardy, Cowardy Custard, Ate His Father's Mustard	*Or Harlequin the Demon Vice and the Fairy Queen of Virtue*	Pavilion
Little Red Riding Hood		Adelphi
Queen Mab		Grecian Saloon

By the end of the century, recognizably modern and anglicized productions of *Aladdin*, *Cinderella*, *Jack and the Beanstalk* and *Dick Whittington* dominated calendars. The chart below documents pantomimes in London in the season 1899–1900.

Title	Theatre
Jack and the Beanstalk	Drury Lane
Cinderella and the Little Glass Slipper	Standard
The Forty Thieves	Grand (Islington)
Puss in Boots	Garrick
Goody Two Shoes	Surrey
Dick Whittington and His Cat	Elephant and Castle
Robinson Crusoe	Shakespeare (Clapham)
Dick Whittington.	Kennington

Title	Theatre
Cinderella.	Grand (Fulham)
Cinderella	Crown (Peckham)
Magic Moonstone	Britannia
Sinbad	Lyric (Hammersmith)
Babes in the Wood	Coronet
Dick Whittington and His Cat	Pavilion
Dick Whittington	Borough (Stratford)
Jack of Hearts	West London
Dick Whittington and His Cat	Lyric (Ealing)
Puss in Boots	New Cross
Sinbad	Stoke Newington
Aladdin	Morton's (Greenwich)
Dick Whittington	Terriss Theatre (Rotherhithe)
Dick Whittington	Dalston
Puss in Boots	Richmond
Babes in the Wood	Kingston
Aladdin and the Sleeping Beauty	Royal Artillery (Woolwich)

Two trends are immediately obvious: titles were shortened as harlequinades all but disappeared from productions and more suburban theatres produced pantomime. The third trend, and the trend of most relevance to this essay, is the vivid increase in productions set nominally in overseas contexts. In the 1890s, 54 out of the documented 120 pantomimes staged in London were set – according to the admittedly crude measurement of title – abroad: of which *Robinson Crusoe*, *Ali Baba*, *Sinbad*, and *Aladdin* predominated (these formed less than a tenth of productions in the 1850s). The two most popular pantomimes of the 1890s were *Cinderella* (31) and *Dick Whittington* (27), both of which increasingly incorporated comment on imperial events and, in the case of *Dick Whittington*, almost always involved foreign travel. In 1882, *Cinderella* at the Pavilion theatre introduced audiences to British and enemy protagonists of the Egyptian campaign (30 December 1882). The Adelphi's production of *Dick Whittington* in 1898 was staged in the aftermath of Britain's brutal victory at Omdurman in the Sudan. In a reflection of near-contemporary events, the hero was pitted in battle against Arabic slave traders in East Africa (*Era*, 31 December 1898). Titles alone, then, are not indicative of content and should not be presumed to be; however the mammoth increase in oriental pantomimes as the century progressed is clearly noteworthy. The huge rise in the number of performances staged overseas can be taken as a crude indicator of the persuasiveness of Gould's and Richards' arguments (outlined in the introduction) that pantomime became increasingly imperialistic towards the end of the century. This correlation confirms further analysis of place is an essential complement to the study of pantomime's exotic bodies.

In recent years, theatre historians have persuasively argued that scholars need to place more significance on the reciprocal relationship between Victorian theatrical and visual culture.[21] Vision, according to Lynda Nead, was the 'universal language' by which the Victorians would learn about their world.[22] Increasingly given to classification of the environment and its bodies, the Victorian period was an age – in Jonathan Smith's words – that was 'relentlessly, explosively visual'.[23] The reciprocity of visual and theatrical culture is crucial to the study of popular imperialism. Visual culture increasingly illustrated foreign spaces and bodies: from extensive public fascination with Victorian explorers of the 1860s,[24] through to the dominance of exotic landscapes as scenic devices for picturing out crude racial stereotypes

21 See, for instance, Katherine Newey, 'Speaking Pictures: The Victorian Stage and Visual Culture', in Anselm Heinrich, Katherine Newey and Jeffrey Richards, eds, *Ruskin, the Theatre and Victorian Visual Culture* (Basingstoke: Palgrave, 2009), 1–18.

22 Lynda Nead, *Victorian Babylon: People, Streets and Images in Nineteenth-Century London* (New Haven: Yale University Press, 2000), 59.

23 Jonathan Smith, *Charles Darwin and Victorian Visual Culture* (Cambridge: Cambridge University Press, 2006), 30.

24 See Felix Driver, *Geography Militant: Cultures of Exploration and Empire* (Oxford: Blackwell, 2001).

in late-century advertising.[25] By the end of the century, it is no surprise that reporting about the empire and foreign affairs was dominated by visual and theatrical culture – this included line drawing, coloured illustrations and war photography in the graphic press on the one hand, and historical and contemporary re-enactments, and topical dramatizations in and out of the theatre, on the other.[26] The interplay of the theatrical and the visual contributed to what Ziter calls the cultivation of a 'pictorial vocabulary' of 'authentic' imperial knowledge.[27] Ziter explains:

> It was not simply that the theatre rallied support for Britain's imperial wars or that in doing so it familiarised audiences with distant regions; the theatre adopted an emerging conception of geography that was informed by the growth and popularisation of the discipline at a time when new racial theories were coming to the fore.[28]

For an understanding of Victorian knowingness about the empire, stereotypes of place were as crucial as racial stereotypes of people.

The following two sections are driven by the project's quantitative data. They investigate the interrelationship of people and places through detailed investigation of how pantomimes made topical allusion to an event (the Indian Rebellion) and a fantasy location (Giant-Land). There

25 Anandi Ramamurthy, *Imperial Persuaders: Images of Africa and Asia in British Advertising* (Manchester: Manchester University Press, 2003). On visual culture and imperialism more generally, see Ashley Jackson and David Tomkins, *Illustrating Empire: a Visual History of British imperialism* (Oxford: Bodleian, 2011).

26 Simon Popple, '"Fresh from the Front": Performance, War News and Popular Culture during the Boer War', *Early Popular Visual Culture* 8/4 (2010), 401–18; Kenneth Morgan, 'The Boer War and the Media', *Twentieth Century British History* 13/1 (2002), 1–16; Jane Pritchard and Peter Yeandle, '"Executed with Remarkable Care and Artistic Feeling": Popular Imperialism and the Music Hall Ballet', in Yeandle, Newey and Richards, eds, *Politics, Performance and Popular Culture*, chapter 8 (forthcoming).

27 Ziter, *Orient on the Victorian Stage*, 3. This may explain why D.W. Griffith, the only film director granted official access to the Western Front to film during the First World War, 'was disappointed with the reality of the battlefield'. See Michael Hammond, '"A Soul Stirring Appeal to Every Briton": The Reception of *The Birth of a Nation* in Britain (1915–6)', *Film History* 11/3 (1999), 353–70 (at 359).

28 Ziter, *Orient on the Victorian Stage*, 165.

are two reasons to examine what the Victorians called the Indian 'Mutiny'. First, barring one exception, no pantomime title in 1857 gives any indication whatsoever to the dramatic events that had occurred in India that year: titles alone are no signifier of content.[29] Second, the Mutiny was one of the most horrifying events in British colonial history. That a great number of London's pantomimes were able to make the horror humorous through the representation of the dismembered Indian body illustrates the argument that pantomime both told the news but also adapted the news through exaggerated caricatures and by drawing contrasts between 'us' and 'them'. Indian bodies were transported into the anarchic world of the mid-Victorian harlequinade. By the end of the century the harlequinade had all but disappeared from performance calendars; instead topical allusion to people and events was incorporated within the plotting and staging of the pantomime. That required theatrical signification of place. My second case study, then, focuses on the *Jack and Beanstalk* story examining the opportunity for the presentation of foreignness and exoticism afforded by Giant-Land.[30]

As noted, Jim Davis and Jennifer Schacker have both drawn our attention to the theatrical use of Giant-Land space in the 1899 production of *Jack* at Drury Lane. In 1899, Britain was at war in South Africa against the Boer republics. Paul Kruger, the Boer President, was represented as the pantomime villain: the Giant Blunderbore of fairy-tale lore replaced, seamlessly, by the Blunderboer. When defeated, the Giant was draped in a Union Jack flag as hundreds of child actors, dressed in the various colours of British and colonial troops, emerged from his pocket leading a

29 One of the methodological weaknesses of Porter's research is that, on a study of play *titles* alone, he claimed theatrical culture was not influenced by imperialism. Clearly it is problematic to rule out the potential of a text to reveal ideological discourses without due attention to its content. See Gould, *Nineteenth-Century and the Imperial Encounter*, 3–9.

30 Allegorical use of *Jack* stories was an ever present in political discourse. See, for instance, Caroline Sumpter's analysis of how socialists took up the story and used to frame critique of the Giants of capitalism. *The Victorian Press and the Fairy Tale* (Basingstoke: Palgrave, 2012), 118–30.

rousing singalong of 'Rule Britannia' and 'God Save the Queen' (British troops had been besieged in key garrison towns and Kruger claimed to have had the British army in his pocket). If 1899 enabled the imaginative staging of South Africa on the pantomime stage, and the imposition of imperial ideology onto the body of the colonial enemy in a militaristic crescendo, was this a novelty or an extension of a tradition? Analysis of how *Jack* pantomimes became increasingly bombastic in representations of imperialism, I demonstrate, underlines the significance of combined depictions of people and places.

Act I: India, 1857

The majority of pantomimes staged in London in 1857 included topical reference to what Victorians called the Indian Mutiny. The 'Mutiny' became, for mid-Victorian Britons, an enthralling unfolding drama of treachery, total villainy and absolute heroism; it was, according to James Ryan, 'the single most important influence in the making of British images of India in the nineteenth century'.[31] As various sieges were relieved, battles won, and reprisals meted out to mutinous sepoys, news was greeted in Britain with a mixture of relief and celebration. Tales of horror, shock and despair had been captured in various genres of popular print culture including hundreds of published sermons, pamphlets, novels, and stories and images in the graphic press.[32] Hero cults developed around key military

31 James Ryan, *Picturing Empire: Photography and the Visualisation of the British Empire* (Chicago: Chicago University Press, 1997), 197.

32 Gautam Chakravarty, *The Indian Mutiny and the British Imagination* (Cambridge: Cambridge University Press, 2005); Neil Hultgren, *Melodramatic Imperial Writing: from the Sepoy Rebellion to Cecil Rhodes* (Athens, OH: University of Ohio Press, 2014).

leaders – especially Sir Henry Havelock.[33] Yet, as Marty Gould demonstrates, 'the energies of this colonial crisis exceeded the narrow limits of pen and page' as news of the uprising was 'carefully choreographed and politically reinterpreted' in dozens of plays staged in theatres across the country.[34]

Gould traces theatrical representations of the Mutiny in melodrama, including those which responded with incredible speed to events. Melodrama played on serious themes of inter-racial children (*Vermuh Kareeda*, performed at the Victoria in November 1857) and sought to explain the history and development of events (*The Storming and Capture of Delhi* at Astley's in December 1857). Melodramas took on a pseudo-documentary function, situating audiences in India and bridging, in Gould's words, 'the worlds of journalism and entertainment' by inviting audiences 'to think of themselves not merely as playgoers but as eyewitnesses'.[35] London's pantomimes also responded to the profound sense of revulsion at atrocities committed by rebellious sepoys and, like melodramas, served as theatrical sites for the playing out of acts of ferocious retribution. Unlike melodrama, however, they merged celebration with sadistic humour. The violence of revenge scenes in pantomime was made possible by the incorporation of mutinous Indians into harlequinades.[36] At the City of London Theatre, the otherwise historical pantomime *William the Second and the Fayre Maid of Honour* contained a scene in its harlequinade in which sepoys were captured and Nana Sahib, villain-in-chief, was fired from a canon 'to the great satisfaction of the delighted audience' (*Times*, 28 December 1857). The Surrey pantomime *Queen Mab; or, Harlequin Romeo and Juliet* included a gruesome scene in which a sepoy was killed by the Clown, amusingly dressed in Grenadier's costume, 'rammed into

33 Graham Dawson, *Soldier Heroes: British Adventure, Empire and the Imagining of Masculinities* (London: Routledge, 1994), especially 79–116.

34 Gould, *Nineteenth-Century Theatre*, 155–6.

35 Gould, *Nineteenth-Century Theatre*, 174.

36 The following paragraph draws from but extends Jeffrey Richards' analysis. See his, *The Golden Age of Pantomime*, 25–6; and 'Drury Lane Imperialism' (forthcoming).

a mortar, and fired at the butcher's shop, where his disjointed body suddenly replaces the mutton and beef on the hooks' (*Era*, 27 December 1857). 'The patriotism of the audience rose to a fever pitch' in response to this scene, reported the *Standard*, as the Clown 'besplattered the walls with his [Nana Sahib's] members' (28 December 1857). In a remarkably swift response to the headlines of the day that the siege of Lucknow had been lifted, British soldiers shelled sepoys in the Grecian Theatre's *Peter Wilkins and the Flying Indians* and Nana Sahib was labelled 'out of Luck–now'. The 'flying Indians' of the title, according to the *Era* (27 December) were not 'retreating Sepoys' yet the title must have appealed to the 'exigencies' of the moment.

Of the topical references to India in *Joe Miller; or, Harlequin Mirth, Jollity and Satire* at the Marylebone theatre, the *Standard* reported:

> It may be worth mentioning, as showing the temper and tone of the public mind, that every reference in the course of the piece to the events now passing in India, and the heroes who are fighting our battles there, was eagerly caught up by the audience, in a manner which proves that the people at any rate are not disposed to distribute to our heroes any niggard measure of praise or award (28 December 1857).

Productions clearly aimed to generate patriotic reactions and on the evidence of reviews, they more than succeeded. The *Era* reviewer even noted that 'much dissatisfaction' was 'expressed' by the audience at the Princess's Theatre for the lack 'of political allusions' in its pantomime *The White Cat* (27 December 1857). However, the nature of the comedic dismemberment of the Indian body exceeded the usual bounds of patriotic emotions unleashed by military victory. This was a celebration of retribution and violence that both reported acts of vengeance actually carried out by British troops in India but also sanitized them by reducing the act to humour. The unprovoked murder of British women and children had demanded an equally violent response: this was not just the gratuitous and spectacular execution of foreign bodies but the symbolic execution of Britain's moral duty. The relocation of Indian bodies into butcher's shops was a particularly crude comment on one of the causes of the Mutiny: Muslim and Hindu soldiers had refused to bite open ammunition cartridges because they contained fat from cows and pigs. Although conflict in India would last long into the following year, these acts of revenge constituted a suitably dramatic finale for British audiences at home: the melodramatic narrative of the story had reached its conclusion as good had overcome evil and moral order was restored.

It is clear that in these pantomimes it is the body – or the enacted body – of the villainous Nana Sahib that serves as the site for physical comedy. Nana Sahib represents mutinous Indians writ-large and British generals embodied the entirety of the British army. At Sadler's Wells, *Harlequin Beauty and the Beast* featured the embodied figure of 'Justice' in a sign–painter's establishment awakening (from ignorance) to award a peerage and a pension to the Mutiny heroes General Havelock and Sir Colin Campbell. In *Queen Mab*, Harlequin and Pantaloon played cribbage with 'immense conversation cards': '"General Havelock" played over "Nana Sahib" secured enthusiastic applause; so did "Wilson taking Delhi"' (*Era*, 27 December 1857). The physical comedy in these scenes was derived from the traditional rough and tumble anarchy of harlequinade scenes. Indian bodies became characters in a fantasy realm starring Clown, Pantaloon and Harlequin. In these, the melodramatic structure of 'goodies' versus 'baddies' takes on new meaning. The humour of these pieces was prefaced upon audience knowledge of, and shared emotional revulsion, at the horrors committed by the sepoys; laughter and patriotic cheering was both the expression of collective joy at the defeat of the sepoys and shared celebration in acts of retaliation. Indian bodies became expendable theatrical props both to 'other' the enemy as brutal and immoral but also to hold a mirror up to the British as heroic and honourable.

That comic retribution was enacted in harlequinades, however, is significant. As noted, quantitative analysis demonstrates that whereas harlequinades dominated in the 1850s they had almost all but disappeared by the end of the century. How did later-century pantomime incorporate its topical referencing not into harlequinades but pantomime plot and staging? The answer relates to the theatrical use of landscapes and bodies, especially in the form of the pantomime villain, and this is made manifest by a study of the evolution of the *Jack and the Beanstalk* pantomime from the 1870s to the Drury Lane spectacular of 1899.

Act II: Giant-Land, 1870–1899

The *Daily Mail*'s review of the 1899 Drury Lane production of *Jack and the Beanstalk* confirms that the production was an emphatic patriotic statement of intent. The review both captures the jingoism of the performance but also pantomime's flexibility to respond to the news. After the defeat of Blunderboer, child actors emerged from the Giant's pocket:

> Soldiers in red, soldiers in khaki, soldiers in kilts, colonials on the tiniest little ponies, sailors with their Maxims [guns] – on, on they come, in a long stream, marching, drilling, manoeuvring. Such an animated scene as these scores of perfectly drilled children, so full of life and energy, has surely never been seen [...]. They begin to shout and cheer and scramble back again till they cover the Giant, and the Union Jack is waved, – the effect is indescribably exciting. It is an open secret that the original giant was to have represented Mr Kruger, and, of course, the meaning of the scene suffers through the alteration rendered necessary by our temporary check in South Africa. All the same, this scene is the triumph of triumphs of pantomime. (27 December 1899)

Here, the Giant *is* Kruger even though the intended pantomime mask slips for the sake of expediency: it would not do to predict so definitive a victory over the Boers at a time in which Britain was suffering major reverses in the field. However, there was a clear depiction of a military victory: the pantomime 'catches the martial mood' reported the *Stage*, continuing that 'the pitch of patriotism enthusiasm' meant that 'the audience find it a very inspiriting scene' (28 December 1899). The contrast of innocent and healthy children to the corpse of the despoiled immoral enemy served clear propagandistic purpose. Concerns about the health of soldiers had combined with trepidation about the decline of the 'race' to dominate contemporary domestic debates about imperialism.[37] This was especially so because, as was the case in Mutiny pantomimes, the othering

37 See Anna Davin, 'Imperialism and Motherhood', *History Workshop Journal* 5 (1978), 9–65.

of the enemy took place while combat was ongoing, providing comfort by merging humour and violence.

Jack had not always found the Giant's kingdom and castle atop the beanstalk. In some productions, Giant-Land was cast either as a fairy kingdom, 'cloud land', or as an historical utopia. *Jack and the Beanstalk* at the Adelphi (1872) invoked 'The Verdant Valley of the Variegated Beans' and in *Jack the Giant Killer* at the Surrey (1875) Jack emerged in Camelot. Even in these productions, however, the fusion of Christianity and imperialism was implied by Jack's recruitment of knights in his crusade against a barbaric and uncivilized enemy (*Era*, 28 December 1872; 26 December 1875). However, as the century progressed and in tandem with the increased influence exercised by imperial propagandists over popular performance culture, Jack more often than not found himself located in the giant's domain. As key scenes of castles that required annexation, treasures claiming, and face-to-face battles became commonplace, the *Jack* genre incorporated a greater frequency of topical references to the empire and foreign affairs. This development is neatly encapsulated by juxtaposition of the 1899 production of *Jack and the Beanstalk* at Drury Lane and the quotation, from the *Era*'s review of *Jack* at the Crystal Palace in 1879, given at the beginning of this essay. In 1899, the articulation of imperial ideology could not have been more explicit; it was central to the pantomime's action and given as the central explanation for the production's success. In 1879, however, it was the authorial voice of the reviewer that wished for more Jacks to combat allegorical giants. When empire was referenced in 1879 it was not by direct allusion to violent conquest but by celebration of the gorgeousness of Indian scenery; the transformation scene, 'The Shrine of Schiva', incorporated elephants, camels and 'groups of figures emblematic of the various races under our dominion in East'. In a clear nod to Victoria having recently been made Empress of India, the Queen dominated the 'centre of the scene' and sat regally on top of a giant silver globe (*Era*, 28 December 1879). In 1875, similarly at the Crystal Palace, *Jack in Wonderland* included both topical commentaries and exotic scenery. Set in a venue that also exhibited Egyptian and Byzantine decorations, the pantomime reprised the Prince of Wales' tour of India of that year. Nautch girls, dressed in 'handsome Indian robes of gold-spangled crimson or white' joined elephants, monkeys and camels in a parade in front of the 'sacred river' and a 'vast domed palace'; to their number was added 'natives, Indian soldiers, serpent charmers' and Britannia in a chariot. This was, according the reviewer in the *Morning Post* a 'laudable effort to make us at home realize to the full some of the scenes which the future Emperor of India has witnessed'. The scene painters and costume designers deserved 'all possible credit' (23 December 1875). For *The Sunday Times*, the pantomime had 'fully revealed' the gorgeous 'splendour of eastern magnificence' (26 December 1875). With the Indian Rebellion still fresh in the mind, the pantomime was a show of stability and beneficent colonization. Indians soldiers had become subservient. Indian subjects held up a banner proclaiming 'tell Mama we are happy', a 'significant message for the Prince of Wales to carry home to the Queen' commented the *Era*, 'and one we trust would be echoed by the natives in reality' (26 December 1875). By the end of the 1890s, however, *Jack* pantomimes had evolved to display levels of brutality evident in the 1899 Drury Lane production. How?

In 1878, various *Jack* pantomimes alluded to events in Bulgaria as Russia became Britain's main diplomatic adversary. Productions at both Covent Garden and the Gaiety included audience singalongs to G.W. Hunt's widely popular song, 'By Jingo', which had been popularized by the Great MacDermott (G.H. Farrell).[38] Topical allusions, according to *The Times* 'elicited roars of merriment' (27 December 1878). *Jack and the Giant Killer* at the Imperial Theatre (1882) included a procession of flags depicting the colonies; so, too, did *Jack and the Beanstalk* productions at the Grand in 1883 and the Surrey in 1886. In 1886 the Bulgarian question re-emerged as a significant dilemma for the British and the pantomime at Sadler's Wells addressed the issue: Jack's mother was called Dame Europa, the villain 'Blunderbore Russia', and all participants were transported to Buckingham Palace where Britannia delivered a lecture to them (and the audience) on the foreign policy issues of the day. The *Stage* commented that the pantomime concluded 'with an edifying picture' of 'virtue triumphant and vice

38 See Richards, *Imperialism and Music*, 325–6. See reviews in *The Times* (27 December 1878) and the *Era* (29 December 1878).

defeated, ultimately resulting in peace and reconciliation all round' (31 December 1886). Clearly, the pantomime reflected Britain's contemporary understanding of itself as a moral arbiter. In 1887, the recent celebrations of the Queen's Golden jubilee spilled over into the pantomime at Covent Garden as children, dressed in the national costumes of 'England and her colonies', paraded in a spectacular display as cast and audience together sang 'Rule Britannia' and 'God Save the Queen' (*Daily News*, 27 December 1887). The transformation scene in *Jack* at the Grand, Islington, in 1893 was similarly given over to a display of Britain and colonies; on this occasion, however, it was not national dress worn but emblematic military uniforms (*Stage*, 28 December 1893). By 1897, the militarization of *Jack and the Beanstalk* was complete. The production at the Pavilion included a 'grand bombardment of the Giant's castle' and audience participation in 'patriotic songs' (*Stage*, 30 December). The *Era* took delight in reporting that the audience knew the words to the popular song poem 'Soldiers of the Queen' (1 January 1898) and *The Times* commented that topical allusions to President Kruger, the Klondike Gold Rush and the Indian frontier were enthusiastically and 'quickly taken up by the audience' (28 December 1897). Pantomime clearly had its finger firmly on the pulse of imperial developments and reflected current affairs to audiences accordingly.

Authentic images of exotic colonial landscapes were thus increasingly incorporated into productions, setting scenic context for allusion to topical imperial affairs. Pantomime did not only trade in crude imagery, however, it also revealed tensions in imperial ideology and this is evident in various treatments of the exotic body of the Giant. The process by which Kruger's body was othered through its representation as Giant provides fascinating insights into pantomime's ability to construct binary opposites of heroes and villains; between 'us' and 'them'. Visual propaganda had successfully used demarcations of race to contrast the British and their black African foes, most recently and most explicitly in recent wars in Egypt and the Sudan.[39] Such techniques of picturing the colonized body as subhuman and

39 Richard Fulton, 'The Sudan Sensation', *Victorian Periodicals Review* 42/1 (2009), 37–63.

barbaric helped to justify British military campaigns.[40] Visual othering, in the context of social Darwinism, also endorsed a racial hierarchy in which military conquest could be explained as the legitimate extension of British superiority. Depicting racial difference through visual and performance culture was not so straightforward for the second Boer War, however, given the Boers were – like the British – white, Christian, European colonists. The pantomime Giant had emerged from across nineteenth-century adaptations of the *Jack* story as a thief, a murderer, a tyrant and a cannibal (he was even called Giant Gobble-All at the Surrey Theatre's production of 1886). The pantomime Giant in general, and Kruger specifically, was stripped of all the characteristics of a civilized European: as a cannibal, he was actively dehumanized. The key line of 'Fe-Fi-Fo-Fum, I smell the blood of an Englishman', had become a well-established pantomime trope by the end of the century; so too the pantomime scene set in the Giant's kitchen in which the bones of humans are crushed to create flour. The elision of Kruger and Giant served not only to animalize Kruger but to also attribute characteristics to him that had previously been used to describe black colonial adversaries: savage, cannibalistic, beyond the reach of civilization. The villain contributed to the creation of its mirror image, the hero: Jack's transformation from lazy child to masculine warrior served a didactic function specially geared to children in the audience; salutary attributes of courage, civic duty and national pride were clearly established in an obvious metaphor of imperial manhood.

Imperial propaganda, however, traded not only in tales of ruthless military conquest but also the conversion and civilization of the colonized. This perhaps explains why pantomimic depictions of Indians and India could be both heartlessly inhumane in response to the 'Mutiny' but sentimentally affectionate in later years. In his study of race relations, *Taming Cannibals* (2011), Patrick Brantlinger's observes this 'central contradiction

40 Ziter, *The Orient on the Victorian Stage*, 180–1. On racism, see Hazel Waters's study of the years 1830–60, *Racism on the Victorian Stage: Representation of Slavery and the Black Character* (Cambridge: Cambridge University Press, 2007).

in the racist and imperialistic ideology'.[41] Treatment of Kruger-as-Giant as a savage colonial tyrant to be defeated certainly reflected the brutality of turn-of-the-twentieth-century militarism. In the majority of productions Jack killed the Giant. However a few pantomimes in the 1880s made reference not to the death of the Giant, but his conversion and resultant emergence as part of civilized society. In the Standard's *Fi Fo Fum; or Harlequin Jack and the Giant Killer* (1887) 'the wicked giant was not imbued with an excess of wickedness'; indeed he ultimately 'proved to be a very amiable monster' and partook in Jack's wedding celebrations suitably attired in 'evening dress' (*Era*, 31 December 1887). The *Stage* described the Giant as a 'converted ogre' (30 December 1887). In the same year, *Jack* was presented at the Covent Garden theatre and there, too, the Giant's life was spared; the Giant, in formal evening wear and now a member of the Salvation Army, returning to the stage to join the final (teetotal) celebration scene (*Stage*, 30 December 1887). In 1889, the Giant in Drury Lane's *Jack and the Beanstalk* was a bookworm, and in particular a fan of Shakespeare. That love of learning and English classics may explain why the Giant did not want to devour the princess, whom he had taken prisoner, but marry her.[42] When defeated by Jack, not in a battle of weapons but wits, the Giant 'renounces his claim to the princess' and is invited to join the entirety of the cast at a lavish feast. What is noticeable, clearly, is that the incorporation of distinctively British symbols – Shakespeare, evening wear, Salvation Army – allowed both for the civilization of the giant but also the assimilation of the 'other' into national culture. As the reintegration of the Giant into civil society demonstrates, the core component of the othering of the pantomime villain as an enemy was his location within exotic landscapes: place positioned the 'other' beyond civilization itself. Such was the flexibility of pantomime that it was able to embody various

41 Patrick Brantlinger, *Taming Cannibals: Race and the Victorians* (London: Cornell University Press, 2011), 2.

42 None of the reviews suggested the production was a mash up of *Jack* and *Beauty and the Beast* but the plot suggests certain similarities.

ideological manifestations of empire and apply these to those foreign bodies onto which colonial ideologies were written.

Conclusion

It has been my contention that topical references in pantomime reveal various ways in which imperialism permeated popular performance culture. Exotic bodies, in relation to visual signifiers of imperial places, served to enforce colonial ideologies and help generate support for British foreign policy. The pantomime was both illustrated imperialism in practice – the civilizing mission of the empire project – and a performance technique that gave British audiences scope for a whole range of emotional responses from horror and revulsion, to sensations of comfort, assurance and superiority. Pantomime could both shock and thrill. But, ultimately, it was intended to make people laugh. Such an objective required a performance format that was flexible but could concomitantly blend the realistic and the hyper-real. Pantomime encapsulated what Lynn Voskuil labels the 'enigmatic doubleness' of Victorian sensation theatre, making possible a 'dual emphasis on authenticity and heightened spectacle'.[43] Such doubleness was enhanced by a performance culture that emphasized the visual truthfulness of scenery within which exaggerated racial stereotypes could perform their roles. When applied to pantomimic depictions of race, and the location of race, this allowed for both the comedic and the serious, and the abstract and the corporeal.

In his study of the nineteenth-century evolution of *Jack and the Beanstalk* in children's literature, Brian Szumsky argues that different versions 'can be read as the history of literary responses to socio-political

43 Lynn Voskuil, *Acting Naturally: Victorian Theatricality and Authenticity* (Charlottesville, VA: University of Virginia Press, 2004), 76.

circumstances, in particular [...] colonial practice and ideology'.[44] The evidence of pantomime *Jacks* presented in this essay certainly support this view. Yet pantomime, watched by large audiences and demanding boos, hisses, applause, cheers, and singalongs, was able to reach further than the written word. Pantomime was able not only to adapt the story to incorporate plot and character variation but also to integrate surplus and seemingly unrelated scenes. Going to the pantomime was an immersive experience, to which the visual was vital. This is perhaps why pantomime was so suitably positioned to both report and revel in popular imperialism.

Bibliography

Booth, Michael, 'Soldiers of the Queen' in Michael Hays and Anastasia Nikolopolou, eds, *Melodrama: The Cultural Emergence Of A Genre* (New York: St Martins Press, 1996), 3–20.

Brantlinger, Patrick, *Taming Cannibals: Race and the Victorians* (London: Cornell University Press, 2011).

Chakravarty, Gautam, *The Indian Mutiny and the British Imagination* (Cambridge: Cambridge University Press, 2005).

Colley, Linda, *Britons: Forging the Nation* (London: Pimlico, 1994).

——, 'British and Otherness: An Argument', *Journal of British Studies* 31/4 (1992), 309–29.

Connelly, Mark, *Christmas: a History* (London: I.B. Tauris, 2012).

Davin, Anna, 'Imperialism and Motherhood', *History Workshop Journal* 5 (1978), 9–65.

Davis, Jim, 'Imperial Transgressions: The Ideology of Drury Lane Pantomime in the Late Nineteenth Century', *New Theatre Quarterly* 12 (February 1996), 147–55.

——, 'Boxing Day', in Tracy C. Davis and Peter Holland, eds, *The Performing Century: Nineteenth-Century Theatre's History* (Basingstoke: Palgrave, 2010), 13–31.

——, '"Slap On! Slap Ever!" Victorian Pantomime, Gender Variance, and Cross Dressing', *New Theatre Quarterly* 30/3 (2014), 218–30.

44 Brian Szumsky, 'The House that Jack Built: Empire and Ideology in British Versions of "Jack and the Beanstalk"', *Marvels and Tales* 13/1 (1999), 11–30 (at 12).

Dawson, Graham, *Soldier Heroes: British Adventure, Empire and the Imagining of Masculinities* (London: Routledge, 1994).

Driver, Felix, *Geography Militant: Cultures of Exploration and Empire* (Oxford: Blackwell, 2001).

Fulton, Richard, 'The Sudan Sensation', *Victorian Periodicals Review* 42/1 (2009), 37–63.

Gould, Marty, *Nineteenth-Century Theatre and the Imperial Encounter* (London: Routledge, 2011).

Hammond, Michael, '"A Soul Stirring Appeal to Every Briton": The Reception of *The Birth of a Nation* in Britain (1915–6)', *Film History* 11/3 (1999), 353–70.

Hultgren, Neil, *Melodramatic Imperial Writing: From the Sepoy Rebellion to Cecil Rhodes* (Athens, OH: University of Ohio Press, 2014).

Jackson, Ashley, and David Tomkins, *Illustrating Empire: A Visual History of British imperialism* (Oxford: Bodleian, 2011).

Mayer, David, *Harlequin in His Element: English Pantomime, 1806–36* (Cambridge, MA: Harvard University Press, 1969).

Morgan, Kenneth, 'The Boer War and the Media', *Twentieth Century British History* 13/1 (2002), 1–16.

Nead, Lynda, *Victorian Babylon: People, Streets and Images in Nineteenth-Century London* (New Haven: Yale University Press, 2000)

Newey, Katherine, 'Speaking Pictures: The Victorian Stage and Visual Culture', in Anselm Heinrich, Katherine Newey and Jeffrey Richards, eds, *Ruskin, the Theatre and Victorian Visual Culture* (Basingstoke: Palgrave, 2009), 1–18.

——, '"Bubbles of the Day": The Pantomimic and the Melodramatic', in Peter Yeandle, Katherine Newey and Jeffrey Richards, eds, *Politics, Performance and Popular Culture: Theatre and Society in Nineteenth-Century Britain* (Manchester: Manchester University Press, forthcoming), chapter 3.

Popple, Simon, '"Fresh from the Front": Performance, War News and Popular Culture during the Boer War', *Early Popular Visual Culture* 8/4 (2010), 401–18.

Porter, Bernard, *The Absent-Minded Imperialists: What the British Really Thought about the Empire* (Oxford: Oxford University Press, 2004).

Pritchard, Jane, and Peter Yeandle, '"Executed with Remarkable Care and Artistic Feeling": Popular Imperialism and the Music Hall Ballet', in Peter Yeandle, Katherine Newey and Jeffrey Richards, eds, *Politics, Performance and Popular Culture: Theatre and Society in Nineteenth-Century Britain* (Manchester: Manchester University Press, forthcoming), chapter 8.

Ramamurthy, Anandi, *Imperial Persuaders: Images of Africa and Asia in British Advertising* (Manchester: Manchester University Press, 2003).

Richards, Jeffrey. *Imperialism and Music, Britain 1876–1953* (Manchester: Manchester University Press, 2001).

——, *The Golden Age of Pantomime: Slapstick, Subversion and Spectacle in Victorian England* (London: I.B. Tauris, 2015).

——, 'Drury Lane Imperialism', in Peter Yeandle, Katherine Newey and Jeffrey Richards, eds, *Politics, Performance and Popular Culture: Theatre and Society in Nineteenth-Century Britain* (Manchester: Manchester University Press, forthcoming), chapter 9.

Ryan, James, *Picturing Empire: Photography and the Visualisation of the British Empire* (Chicago: Chicago University Press, 1997).

Schacker, Jennifer. 'Unruly Tales: Ideology, Anxiety and the Regulation of Genre', *Journal of American Folklore* 120 (2007), 381–400.

Schacker, Jennifer. 'Slaying Blunderboer: Cross-Dressed Heroes, National Identities and Wartime Pantomime', *Marvels and Tales* 27/1 (2013), 52–64.

Smith, Jonathan, *Charles Darwin and Victorian Visual Culture* (Cambridge: Cambridge University Press, 2006).

Sullivan, Jill A., *The Politics of the Pantomime: Regional Identity in Theatre, 1860–1900* (Hatfield: University of Hertfordshire Press, 2011).

Sumpter, Jennifer, *The Victorian Press and the Fairy Tale* (Basingstoke: Palgrave, 2012).

Szumsky, Brian, 'The House that Jack Built: Empire and Ideology in British Versions of "Jack and the Beanstalk"', *Marvels and Tales* 13/1 (1999), 11–30.

Voskuil, Lynn, *Acting Naturally: Victorian Theatricality and Authenticity* (Charlottesville, VA: University of Virginia Press, 2004).

Waters, Hazel, *Racism on the Victorian Stage: Representation of Slavery and the Black Character* (Cambridge: Cambridge University Press, 2007).

Witchard, Anne, *Thomas Burke's Dark Chinoiserie: Limehouse Nights and the Queer Spell of Chinatown* (Farnham: Ashgate, 2009).

Ziter, Edward, *The Orient on the Victorian Stage* (Cambridge: Cambridge University Press, 2003).

SARA MALTON

Impressment, Exoticism and Enslavement: Revisiting the Theatre of War through Thomas Hardy's *The Trumpet-Major* (1880)

ABSTRACT

Although it fell into disuse in 1815, naval impressment played a crucial role in Britain's achievements during the Napoleonic era. By some estimates, half of the average crew was comprised of pressed sailors (M. Lincoln, *Representing the Royal Navy: British Sea Power, 1750–1815*, 2003, p. 5). Often indicted as a practice akin to slavery, impressment was seen by many to 'constitut[e] the grossest imposition, any free people ever submitted to' (J.R. Hutchinson, *The Press Gang: Afloat and Ashore*, 1914, p. 17). This essay shall consider how the treatment of impressment in the Victorian period complicates earlier renderings of the iconic 'jolly tar' that emerged in an era of postwar triumphalism. Long overlooked in discussions of impressment is the degree to which later authors frequently revisit and revise earlier dramatic forms in order to foreground the pressed sailor's exoticism, particularly his kinship with the African slave.

The representation of impressment in Thomas Hardy's *The Trumpet-Major* (1880) serves as an especially resonant illustration, drawing as it does on the Italian pantomime, or *commedia dell'arte*, in its treatment of the press gang affray. Importantly, Hardy thus invokes the cultural legacy of the Harlequin, a figure often located at 'the intersection of slave culture' (E. Lott, *Love and Theft: Blackface Minstrelsy and the American Working Class*, 1993, p. 22), alongside the black minstrel, the clown, and the 'blackman' of English folk drama.

In considering the representation of the pressed sailor across the century, I shall urge a renewed consideration of race and exoticism in the works of some of the period's most prominent authors, and, furthermore, emphasize the wealth of connections yet to be drawn between nineteenth-century fiction and drama.

***

I want to thank the staff of the Huntington Library for their support and assistance, especially for the opportunity to spend a summer with the Larpent collection. This essay would not be possible without them.

> 'Anne would have liked to take her into their own house, so as to acquire some of that practical knowledge of the history of England which the lady possessed [...] and which could not be got from books'.
>
> — THOMAS HARDY, *The Trumpet-Major*[1]

I.

In her rejection of the usual texts of history, Anne Garland herself might be a good reader of the novel that she inhabits. For even as it situates the rival affections of two brothers in the context of a specific historical moment – the anticipated invasion of England by Napoleon in the early nineteenth century – Hardy's *The Trumpet-Major* (1880) characterizes the process of historical accounting as one perpetually informed by absence. Exemplifying what Nicholas Dames refers to as 'Hardy's elaborately memory-scarred narratives',[2] the novel's portrayal of this particular moment in history is akin in many ways to a ghost story, a kind of extended *danse macabre*, in which 'layers of ancient smells linger', characters emerge as skeletons with 'no life in the bones', and literally and figuratively move between walls. History thus appears as an ephemeral, transient ghost – something, as our heroine suspects, that cannot merely 'be got from books'.[3]

The novel's representation of history in terms of absence and negation constitutes what Tim Armstrong identifies elsewhere in Hardy's works as

I wish to acknowledge the generous support of the Social Sciences and Humanities Research Council, whose grant has facilitated much of the research for this project. I am also grateful to the enthusiastic and timely assistance of Katherine Crooks and to Keith Wilson for his ongoing thoughtful responses to my queries on Thomas Hardy's life and work.

1 Thomas Hardy, *The Trumpet-Major* (1880), ed., Linda M. Shires (London: Penguin, 1997), 23–4.

2 Nicholas Dames, *Amnesiac Selves: Nostalgia, Forgetting, and British Fiction, 1810–1870* (Oxford: Oxford University Press, 2001), 11.

3 Hardy, *The Trumpet-Major*, 11, 144, 60.

the portrayal of the 'entry into history, the trauma of *becoming-historical*'.[4] For figures throughout the novel, especially those most closely connected with the war, such as John Loveday, the trumpet-major, are perpetually shadowed of the narrator's anticipation of their deaths, which will occur 'at a distance of many years after, when they lay wounded and weak in foreign lands'.[5] Historical representation in *The Trumpet-Major* thus emerges an act of disinterment that permits the dead to speak before us of their 'treasury of experience', as Anne would have it, and give voice to a more nuanced, if elusive version of cultural memory.[6]

As I shall show in the essay that follows, the sensitivity of Anne's suspicion of recorded history is underscored by the novel's theatrical treatment of a military practice that has a rather haunting, elusive history of its own: naval impressment. Impressment – enforced or coerced naval service – was a matter of much controversy during the Napoleonic era, when its widespread use was necessary to meet the manning requirements of the British fleet. Press gang affrays were matters of great violence and much social disruption, representing a frightening and devastating 'intrusion into the lives of ordinary citizens'.[7] Press gangs often swiftly removed men from their communities and livelihoods, leaving the pressed man's whereabouts or possibility of return matters of great uncertainty for the families left behind. Although no longer a military imperative beyond 1815, naval impressment played a crucial role in Britain's achievements during the Napoleonic wars. Discussing the 'enormous sacrifices common seamen made for imperial gain'[8] during this period, sacrifices that have often been

4 Tim Armstrong, *Haunted Hardy: Poetry, History, Memory* (Houndsmills: Palgrave, 2000), 2.

5 Hardy, *The Trumpet-Major*, 26.

6 Hardy, *The Trumpet-Major*, 24.

7 Nicholas Rogers, *The Press Gang: Naval Impressment and Its Opponents in Georgian Britain* (London: Continuum, 2007), 8.

8 Denver Brunsman, *The Evil Necessity: British Naval Impressment in the Eighteenth-Century Atlantic World* (Charlottesville and London: University of Virginia Press, 2013), 7.

overlooked,[9] Denver Brunsman estimates that 'approximately 250,000 British seamen were impressed during the long eighteenth century – many more than once'.[10]

Hardy's rendering the press gang's pursuit of the sailor Bob Loveday in *The Trumpet-Major* captures in miniature the ongoing haunting of the text and its characters by the menace of uncertain invasion and attack. Far more than a mere farcical interlude in a novel often noted for its generic instability,[11] the press gang's arrival constitutes, I would argue, a crucial moment in the novel, once more emphatically associating history with arbitrariness, violence, and absence.[12] Hardy imagines the spectacle of the press-gang affray as the visible intervention of the strong arm of the law and, we might say, the hand of history, as it produces a confrontation that is sudden, arbitrary, and violent. Abducted and taken aboard ship, the pressed sailor is ultimately absorbed into a version of history that denies his individual identity, telling instead the national, triumphalist tale of Britannia's prowess.

Seemingly subverting such grandiose claims through comic deflation and bathos, the press gang sequence in *The Trumpet-Major* has frequently been noted for its similarity to the structure of the English pantomime, especially given its hilarity and physicality. As I shall show, in its very

9 Rogers identifies impressment as a longstanding 'embarrassment' to many naval historians, who have been more apt to accept it as a 'necessary evil' in the conduct of war. Rogers, *The Press Gang: Naval Impressment and Its Opponents in Georgian Britain*, 3, 13.

10 Brunsman, *The Evil Necessity: British Naval Impressment in the Eighteenth-Century Atlantic World*, 6. By some estimates, half of the average crew was comprised of pressed sailors. See also Margarette Lincoln, *Representing the Royal Navy: British Sea Power, 1750–1815* (Aldershot: Ashgate, 2003), 5.

11 See, for instance, Edward Neill on *The Trumpet-Major* as 'historical entertainment': Edward Neill, 'Mixed Modes in *The Trumpet-Major*', *Essays in Criticism* 56/4 (October 2006), 351.

12 Linda M. Shires likewise claims that 'the greatest emotional crisis in *The Trumpet-Major* is the press-gang's chasing of Bob'. Linda M. Shires, introduction to *The Trumpet-Major* (1880) by Thomas Hardy, ed., Linda M. Shires (London: Penguin, 1997), xxxi.

mode – its proximity to farce and a form highly dependent on spectacle, trope, and type – Hardy's treatment of the press gang emphasizes the absurdity of authorized history and the farcical nature of the claims to authority made by such arbitrary action as impressment.

According to its critics, impressment 'undoubtedly constitute[d] the grossest imposition, any free people ever submitted to'.[13] The manning problems that confronted the Royal Navy during the long eighteenth century helped rationalize this 'imposition', but so too did widespread perceptions of the sailor, who was often conceived as a primitive being dwelling on the margins of civilization. An 1827 article from *The Naval and Military Magazine* tells us, for example, that the sailor 'is but a kind of naturalized fish. He is of no place, but a mere citizen of the sea, as vagabonds are of the world'.[14] N.A.M. Rodger points out that 'Seamen have always dwelt on the fringes of settled society'.[15] The realities of their working lives little understood by the broader citizenry. In the words of Gillian Russell, 'sailors were often perceived as dangerously aberrant [...] a distinctive subcultural group in Georgian society'.[16] The often tortuous physical[17] treatment faced by the sailor aboard ship attests to the persistent cultural denial of his individual identity.

Subject to 'attack, seizure, and incarceration',[18] the *pressed* sailor, I would suggest, constitutes a specialized category of this forgotten 'subaltern

13 J.R. Hutchinson, *The Press Gang: Afloat and Ashore* (New York: E.P. Dutton, 1914), 14.

14 'Characteristics of the Sailor', *The Naval and Military Magazine* (March 1827), 94.

15 N.A.M. Rodger, *The Wooden World: Anatomy of the Georgian* Navy (Annapolis, MD: Naval Institute Press, 1986), 15.

16 Gillian Russell, *Theatres of War: Performance, Politics, and Society 1793–1815* (Oxford: Oxford University Press, 1995), 9.

17 See, for instance, Denver Brunsman on the 'mind-boggling array of violent bodily punishments' to which sailors were subject aboard ship. Denver Brunsman, 'Men of War: British Sailors and the Impressment Paradox', *Journal of Early Modern History* 14 (2010), 33.

18 Marcus Rediker, *Between the Devil and the Deep Blue Sea: Merchant Seamen, Pirates, and the Anglo-American Maritime World, 1700–1750* (Cambridge: Cambridge University Press, 1987), 32.

population', to use Alan Bewell's term.[19] As Nicholas Rogers points out, pressed men were typically 'treated as criminals upon capture, dumped in dark holds', which 'were seething cellars of disease'.[20] In his discussion of eighteenth-century maritime culture, Marcus Rediker describes the devastating consequences of enforced service:

> During Queen Anne's reign, seaman had entered the navy like men 'dragged to execution'. And that is precisely what naval service amounted to for untold thousands, since almost half of those pressed in the seventeenth and eighteenth centuries died at sea. Those lucky enough to stay alive often went unpaid. Some commanders, in an effort to prevent desertion, held the wages of their crews in arrears for three, four, or up to six and a half years. The state's demand for labour and the seaman's refusal to be the supply produced something of a civil war over maritime muscle and skill.[21]

Comparisons between impressment and imprisonment and, indeed, slavery were thus prevalent and in many ways merited. Gillian Russell notes that 'In 1792 William Wilberforce was attacked in a caricature for championing the cause of abolitionism while ignoring the plight of the soldier and sailor',[22] and numbers of periodical articles make the case of the injustice of the similarity between slavery and impressment.[23] The sheer numbers of sailors forced into service meant that, as Brunsman observes, only enslaved Africans formed a 'larger group of forced laborers in Britain's Atlantic empire during the [long eighteenth] century'.[24] Positioned as a necessary evil, 'Standing as a bulwark against aggression and conquest', impressment,

19 Alan Bewell, *Romanticism and Colonial Disease* (Baltimore: Johns Hopkins University Press, 1999), 71.

20 Rogers, *The Press Gang: Naval Impressment and Its Opponents in Georgian Britain*, 112, 83.

21 Rediker, *Between the Devil and the Deep Blue Sea*, 33.

22 Russell, *Theatres of War*, 12–13

23 Hazel Waters notes the pervasiveness of such comparisons in her discussion of the 1835 nautical melodrama, *My Poll and My Partner Joe*. Hazel Waters, 'Jacks and Diamonds – Some Aspects of Race on the London Victorian Stage', *Race and Class* 50/3 (2008), 81.

24 Denver Brunsman, 'Men of War', 23.

according to J.R. Hutchinson, 'ground under its heel the very people it protected and made them slaves in order to keep them free'.[25]

The trials associated with impressment capture the cultural imagination throughout the early nineteenth century, where they were commemorated in verse, in adventure tales, and, of course, on the stage. Yet, over time portrayals of impressment become increasingly romanticized, a matter due in large part to the portrayal of the seaman on the stage. The British Jack Tar – that 'emblem of popular patriotism',[26] as Hazel Waters rightly terms him – that rose to prominence in the postwar era was, as many scholars observe, 'largely a creation of the [early nineteenth-century] theatre'.[27] His characterization on the nineteenth-century stage manifests a 'powerful [cultural] need [...] to conceive of the sailor as simple, good-hearted, and unthreatening'.[28] As this image comes to eclipse earlier conceptions of the sailor as inherently uncivilized and subversive, literary works recollecting the Napoleonic era, both on the stage and in adventure tales, from Captain Marryat's *Mr Midshipman Easy* (1836) to W.H.G. Kingston's *The Two Shipmates* (1875), increasingly include impressment as a mere incidental event in a romantic treatment of thrilling maritime life. As Rediker points out, over time, the 'romantic image of seafaring has tended to obscure important features of life at sea [and] has thus misrepresented or omitted vital segments of the seaman's experience'.[29]

However, later historical novels often notably revisit and revise earlier dramatic forms in order to foreground the pressed sailor's plight, exoticism, and, often, in particular, his connection to slavery. Perhaps the most prominent example is Elizabeth Gaskell's 1863 novel, *Sylvia's Lovers*, which shares

25 Hutchinson, *The Press Gang*, 15.

26 Waters, 'Jacks and Diamonds – Some Aspects of Race on the London Victorian Stage', 77.

27 Russell, *Theatres of War*, 99. See also, for instance, J.S. Bratton on the ideology of the Jack Tar, heroism, and melodrama. J.S. Bratton, 'British Heroism and the Structure of Melodrama', in J.S. Bratton, ed., *Acts of Supremacy: The British Empire and the Stage, 1790–1830* (Manchester: Manchester University Press), 18–61.

28 Russell, *Theatres of War*, 105.

29 Rediker, *Between the Devil and the Deep Blue Sea*, 4–5.

with *The Trumpet-Major* in its connection of impressment to an examination of the construction of history and, importantly, its indebtedness to earlier forms of nineteenth-century drama. In Gaskell's case it is especially nautical melodrama; the novel's plot bears the influence of Douglas Jerrold's enormously popular play, *Black-Eyed Susan* (1829), and also, as I argue elsewhere, engages in complex ways with the plot of the fugitive slave in its portrayal of the pressed man's exile and return.[30] Hardy meanwhile invokes the English pantomime and many other theatrical elements in his novel, taking aim, as he does so, at the construction of a national history of heroism and achievement that elides the personal narratives of loss and victimhood arising from the experience of war. As I shall show, Bob Loveday's connection to the black mask of the pantomime figure of Harlequin in *The Trumpet-Major* makes the application of Bewell's term – 'subaltern'– to the sailor all the more resonant. Ultimately, the text's generic hybridity, which becomes most pronounced in its press gang sequence, necessarily and emphatically links the nation's participation in war, in the theatrical, and in spectacle to literal and figurative enslavement.

An activity that was itself increasingly elided from dominant histories of a triumphant Britannia, impressment offers Hardy a metaphor for the violence and erasure of identity and experience so often attendant upon the act of historical construction. In this way, *The Trumpet-Major* can be seen to dramatize the degree to which impressment represents an act of violence against not only those men it captured and capitalized upon, but against cultural memory itself. As it assimilates the individual into abstract, triumphalist conceptions of nation and victory, impressment violates a culture's knowledge of its past and its access to history.

30 See Sara Malton, 'Vanishing Points: Elizabeth Gaskell, Impressment, and Cultural Memory', forthcoming in *Nineteenth Century Studies* 28 (2015). On the fugitive slave plot and the Victorian novel more broadly, see Julia Sun-Joo Lee, *The American Slave Narrative and the Victorian Novel* (Oxford: Oxford University Press, 2010).

II.

Hardy's portrayal of the press gang in *The Trumpet-Major* shows the degree to which his thinking about legislative authority, violence, and cultural memory informs his literary vision in the broad sense. *The Trumpet-Major* notably coincides with a significant period in Hardy's life – the 1880s – during which time he commenced a period of intensive engagement with legal issues, embarking, as William A. Davis points out, on a 'course of self-education in the law'.[31] In 1884, Hardy became a practicing magistrate, and he was 'in fact, an active magistrate longer than he was a practicing novelist'.[32] Many of Hardy's works reveal his marked interest in the law, especially, as we know from his later *Tess of the D'Urbervilles* (1891) and *Jude the Obscure* (1895), its fierce application and capacity to destroy the human spirit. Anticipating the more sustained scrutiny of the law that will emerge in such later works, in *The Trumpet-Major*, through a complex of treatment of history and genre, 'Hardy effectively puts on trial the subject of history'.[33] If in a novel such as *Sylvia's Lovers* the individual and society become disfigured by the activities of the press gang and the version of history it serves, Thomas Hardy's *The Trumpet-Major* envisions history itself as permanently disfigured.

Set on the English coast during the height of fears about Napoleon's invasion in the early years of the nineteenth century, Hardy's novel focuses on two brothers, sons of the local miller, – one wily and alluring, the other reliable and earnest – who vie for the affections of the heroine, Anne Garland.[34] Having returned to land for a time, the former, sailor Bob

31 William A. Davis, *Hardy and the Law: Legal Presences in Hardy's Life and Fiction* (Newark: University of Delaware Press, 2003), 17.

32 Davis, *Hardy and the Law*, 17.

33 Shires, introduction, xxxiv.

34 The parallels between *The Trumpet-Major* and *Sylvia's Lovers* are numerous. John Rignall explores some of these in J.M. Rignall, 'The Historical Double: *Waverly, Sylvia's Lovers, The Trumpet-Major*', *Essays in Criticism* 34/1 (Winter 1984). For more on Gaskell's novel and impressment, see Malton, 'Vanishing Points'.

Loveday, is ultimately sought after by the press-gang. While he eludes them for a time, Bob is ultimately absorbed into the fabric of a broader history of national achievement: he returns to sea of his own accord, driven in search of valour, adventure – erotic and otherwise – and victory. While much of the plot is characterized by comedic elements, the novel concludes on an intensely somber note that altogether undercuts Bob's narrative of conquest and bravery. In choosing Bob, Anne clearly chooses the wrong man; but although Bob ultimately abandons Anne for the thrill of adventure at sea, his brother, the unassuming trumpet-major, will be absorbed into a yet darker version of history, one pervaded by anonymity and death: 'Battles and skirmishes, advances and retreats, fevers and fatigues told hard on Anne's gallant friends in the coming time. Of the seven upon whom [her] wishes were bestowed, five, including the trumpet-major, were dead men within the few following years, and their bones left to moulder in the land of their campaigns'.[35] Time and again the dark side of history intrude into a narrative typically seen as a light romance.[36]

According to Julian Wolfreys, the novel's conclusion depicts 'the transmission of the experience of historical rupture and violence, through the experience of history's others, people such as Robert, Anne, and John, civilians, soldiers, and sailors who have no historical voice in conventional, broad accounts of war'.[37] The novel's spectral and dramatic figuring of voices contrasts the materiality of various other texts that pervade the novel, such as the newspapers that grant Anne the 'privilege of reading history in long columns', various letters, and public notices, which the community presumes to mark 'matters of public moment'.[38] Yet as implicated as they are in the production of lasting or 'real' reports of the past, these

35 Hardy, *The Trumpet-Major*, 300.

36 See Jane Thomas's complication of this view and Hardy's 'controversial relationship to realism' in 'Hardy's "Romances and Fantasies": *A Pair of Blue Eyes*, *The Trumpet-Major*, *Two on a Tower*, and *The Well-Beloved*: Experiments in Metafiction', *A Companion to Thomas Hardy*, ed. Keith Wilson (Oxford: Blackwell), 2013, 281.

37 Julian Wolfreys, *Dickens to Hardy 1837–1884: The Novel, The Past and Cultural Memory in the Nineteenth Century* (New York: Palgrave Macmillan, 2007), 196.

38 Hardy, *The Trumpet-Major*, 41, 98.

texts are marked by their insubstantiality: they manifest the flattening of the contours of history as it is translated into news, legal record, report, and documentation, their apparent structure and authority concealing the actual 'transitory, episodic, and heterogeneous qualities of any periodical publication, especially a newspaper.'[39] Such insubstantiality highlights what, in his discussion of the historical novel in this period, John Rignall has identified as the 'elusiveness of history', generally and 'the irrevocable pastness of the Napoleonic wars'[40] that captivated Hardy throughout his life in particular and that would reach its culmination in his epic drama of the Napoleonic era, *The Dynasts*.

As I have mentioned, *The Trumpet-Major* centres on a particularly elusive event from the Napoleonic era, one, in fact, that does not happen: the invasion of England by France. Yet Napoleon is not the only ruler who consistently fails to *materialize* in the novel. Just as 'the Bogey of Bonaparte',[41] haunts the inhabitants of coastal England, the *image* of King George looms parodically large on the landscape. Characterized by absence, deferral, and deflation, the representation of the king's visit to the area provocatively illustrates the way that icon, image and spectacle are central to the production of history. *The Trumpet-Major* is in many ways but one performance or spectacle after another, underpinned by what Robert Gittings terms a 'substructure of theatre ritual'.[42] This emphasis on the theatrical spectacle shows Hardy's sensitivity to the way that 'the majority of the population [during this period] experienced war as theatre – the performance of maneuvres and sham fights, the display, colour, and music of a parade, choreography of large scale reviews presided over by the king'.[43] Throughout the novel, the theatrical is shown to serve the nation's broader interests, both martial and imperial.

39 Nikki Hessell, *Literary Authors, Parliamentary Reporters: Johnson, Coleridge, Hazlitt, Dickens* (Cambridge: Cambridge University Press, 2012), 331.

40 J.M. Rignall, 18, 27.

41 Linda Colley, *Britons: Forging the Nation 1707–1837* (New Haven: Yale University Press, 2005), 306.

42 Robert Gittings, *Thomas Hardy's Later Years* (Boston: Little, Brown, 1978), 21.

43 Russell, *Theatres of War*, 17.

The reader's 'encounter' with the spectacle of royalty occurs while Miller Loveday, his son John (the hopeful trumpet-major), Anne, and her mother (the widow Mrs Garland) ascend a nearby hilltop in anticipation of the King's arrival: 'They lingered and lingered, but no King came to break the silence of that beautiful summer night. As half-hour after half-hour glided by, and nobody came, Anne began to get weary'.[44] In this vacuum of time, history fails to enter. When the arrival finally occurs, the fulfillment of expectation is nullified by the seeming *dis*-appearance of the monarch: 'The *cortege* passed abreast [...] Anne was told to look in the first carriage [...] for the King and Queen, and was rewarded by seeing a profile reminding her of the current coin of the realm; [...] none of the royal family looked out of the carriage windows. It was said that the two elder princesses were in the same carriage, but they remained invisible'.[45]

The King and Queen appear not as people, but as one-dimensional replicas from the mint. Their coined silhouettes point to the material iconography into which history is condensed and shaped for the purpose of legalized public circulation and consumption. An inhabitant of 'the land of romance', Anne's mother nonetheless thus duly praises this moment of divine vision, saying 'Thank God, I have seen my King!'[46] Yet for Anne, who is disappointed by the sight of what is palpably absent and 'invisible', there really is nothing to see here.

This non-event anticipates Anne's more widely discussed gaze 'into the stream of recorded history' while the King is on the Esplanade at Weymouth – the latter a scene that also emerges as but 'a gorgeous centerpiece'.[47] What Linda Colley has identified as 'apotheosis' of George III, which depended on the revival of enhanced 'ritual splendour' as well the 'marked increase in royalty's physical mobility',[48] resonates in these and other scenes involving the monarch. During George's reign, Colley observes, the achievement of a 'renovated and assertively nationalistic royal image' made it imperative

44 Hardy, *The Trumpet-Major*, 83.
45 Hardy, *The Trumpet-Major*, 86.
46 Hardy, *The Trumpet-Major*, 80, 87.
47 Hardy, *The Trumpet-Major*, 93, 92.
48 Colley, *Britons*, 230, 233.

that the monarchy 'be seen to be splendid, but above all, it must be *seen*'.[49] Hardy's attentiveness to this imperative emerges in his various other renderings of the King's 'disembodied' appearance: the farcical episode with his bathing machine (where we merely see his royal head bobbing in the water), for instance, and in one other image that most overtly emphasizes the one-dimensionality of the spectacle of monarchy—and, I would suggest, of the text of history itself. Here I have in mind the enormous 'picture of the king on horseback' being cut out – or excavated – on the down.[50] Again seeking opportunity for romance in a viewing of the King's image, the trumpet-major tells Anne enthusiastically, 'The king's head is to be as big as our mill-pond and his body as big as this garden; he and his horse will cover more than an acre'.[51] But, unfortunately,

> The equestrian figure [...] was scarcely intelligible to John and Anne [once] they were close, and after pacing from the horse's head down to his breast and his hoof, back by way of the king's bridle-arm, past the bridge of his nose, and into his cocked-hat, Anne said that she had had enough of it, and stepped out of the chalk clearing upon the grass. The trumpet-major had remained all the time in a melancholy attitude within [...] his Majesty's right spur.[52]

Hardy's frequent emphasis on the way in which history is both dramatized upon and literally inscribed in the landscape – Egdon Heath of his *The Return of the Native* (1878) being perhaps the most prominent example – is ironized here as an artificial exercise doomed to hilarity and incomprehension. Yet, as is usually the case in *The Trumpet-Major*, hilarity is tinged by looming tragedy. Again disappointed, Anne turns her back on this grossly contrived text of history. John, we might note, ominously remains embedded within it, marking a gulf between the sometime lovers that, as Anne ultimately chooses Bob, and John returns to duty, will never be crossed.

49 Colley, *Britons* 235. Italics in original.
50 Hardy, *The Trumpet-Major*, 273.
51 Ibid.
52 Hardy, *The Trumpet-Major*, 276.

III.

Hardy's figuring of human relations into the landscape, such that, in the words of Michael Irwin, 'Figures and landscapes are mutually exploratory, mutually explanatory',[53] emerges, then, with great force in *The Trumpet-Major*, and in a manner that, as I suggested above, recalls to a certain degree the primacy and force of the landscape in *The Return of the Native*. Yet many apparent contrasts exist between the two texts. Whereas, superficially, the landscape of *The Trumpet-Major* is marked by its colourful spectacles of soldiery and monarchy – the intrusion of modernity, we might say – Egdon Heath is marked by its blackness and primal foreboding. In the early stages of the novel, we witness Charley, a solitary boy, crossing the heath: 'He appeared on the dark ridge of heathland, like a fly on a Negro, bearing the articles with him, and came up breathless with his walk'.[54] The land is imagined as a great, black body, one potentially subject to colonization and enslavement by the forces of modernity. Although she does not cite this provocative passage, Jane Bownas' discussion of Hardy and imperialism offers an extensive consideration of the representation of the 'primitive' nature of Egdon Heath and draws a provocative comparison between the racialization of Eustacia Vye and Joseph Conrad's well-known African woman in his later *Heart of Darkness* (1899).[55] Associated with the blackness of the Heath and with witchcraft (which Bownas links to West Africa), Bownas sees Eustacia as 'an extension of the landscape she inhabits'.[56] She also, we might add, is notably subject to, an enforced removal to the Heath:

> Budmouth was her native place, a fashionable seaside resort at that date. She was the daughter of the bandmaster of a regiment which had been quartered there – a Corfiote by birth, and a fine musician – who met his future wife during her trip

53 Michael Irwin, *Reading Hardy's Landscapes* (London: Macmillan, 2000), 6.

54 Thomas Hardy, *The Return of the* Native, ed. Phillip Mallett (New York: Norton, 2006), 111.

55 Jane L. Bownas, *Thomas Hardy and Empire* (Farnham: Ashgate, 2012), 101–3.

56 Bownas, *Thomas Hardy and Empire*, 102.

> thither with her father the captain, a man of good family. The marriage was scarcely in accord with the old man's wishes, for the bandmaster's pockets were as light as his occupation. But the musician did his best; adopted his wife's name, made England permanently his home, took great trouble with his child's education […] and throve as the chief local musician till her mother's death, when he left off thriving, drank, and died also. […] The girl was left to the care of her grandfather. […] She hated the change; she felt like one banished; but here she was forced to abide.[57]

Rightly acknowledging that Hardy is 'not generally recognized as being an 'imperial' writer', Bownas makes many resonant claims regarding the 'imperialism' under the surface of Hardy's works',[58] which could be applied to this brief passage, what with its references to Eustacia's problematic mixed Ionian heritage and her grandfather's maritime profession, which ultimately leads to her social exclusion near the Heath.

One might usefully extend such a reading to Eustacia's covert assumption of the exoticized role of the Turkish Knight in the mummers' play later in the novel; Charley's journey across the Heath's 'negro' body, above, is in fact the occasion for his delivery of his costume to Eustacia, who intends to borrow it for her performance. Although we are told that Eustacia conceals her face beneath the Knight's 'Ribboned visor',[59] David Worrall's discussion in *Harlequin Empire* of the connection between mummery and racialized performance turns us toward the legacy of black face and the black mask, which becomes all the more poignant in *The Trumpet-Major*. Worrall notes that '[d]isguise under a black face was requisite for those mummers who thought their anarchic and highly improvised comedy was likely to result in retribution from the owners of the big houses and farmers on their circuits […] blacking up amongst mumming performers conferred safe anonymity'.[60]

The constellation of issues of racialized performance, history, and exoticism raised by the black mask indeed return us to the *The Trumpet-Major*,

57 Hardy, *Return of the Native*, 63.

58 Bownas, *Thomas Hardy and Empire*, 1.

59 Hardy, *Return of the Native*, 117.

60 David Worrall, *Harlequin Empire: Race, Ethnicity and the Drama of Enlightenment* (London: Pickering & Chatto, 2007), 137.

a novel, we do well to remember, that appeared only two years after the publication of *The Return of the Native*. *The Trumpet-Major's* engagement with blackness and enslavement emerges most poignantly in its theatrical treatment of the press gang and its invocation of the black masked Harlequin figure, here assumed by Bob Loveday, the crafty sailor. The press gang sequence acutely captures the text's preoccupation with arbitrariness, haunting, absence, and substitution, as it forcefully dramatizes what Julian Wolfreys identifies in Hardy's work as 'the intrusion of the historical as both literary mode and material reality.'[61] The press gang's intrusion serves as one yet another episode in a series – from the appearance of the royal family on the Esplanade to the emergence of King George in his bathing machine – that collectively identify history as a distant, often comedic, spectacle sharply at odds with the experience of those individual voices of history that have been so often suppressed. If, as Wolfreys suggests, Hardy's reference to figures such as Wellington and the Penninsular Wars 'marks the fiction rudely with the intrusion of historical context',[62] the press gang's arrival is literally the rudest of all, emasculating Bob, who falls and faints during his escape, and requiring the rescue of two women, Anne, and her rival, the wily actress Matilda. The gang's position as a force of invasion is literalized here to the point of farce, as Bob's pursuers crash through doors, peep through keyholes, and dive into great bins of corn in pursuit of their man. Further on, they 'arrive just in time to see Captain Bob's legs and shoe-buckles vanishing through the trap-door in the joists overhead, his person having been whirled up by the machinery like any bad of flour, and the trap falling to behind him'.[63]

This sequence, as I have mentioned, has been noted for its indebtedness to the English pantomime, which constituted, as Jim Davis notes, 'a crucial component of Victorian popular culture'.[64] The resonance of the pantomime extends throughout the novel, beyond the press gang episode,

61 Wolfreys, *Dickens to Hardy*, 194.

62 Wolfreys, *Dickens to Hardy*, 195.

63 Hardy, *The Trumpet-Major*, 229.

64 Jim Davis, introduction to ed. J. Davis, *Victorian Pantomime: A Collection of Critical* Essays (London: Palgrave Macmillan, 2010), 1.

though here it reaches its climax. Each of the novel's central characters can be linked to a typical figure of the Harlequinade. The old miser Derriman is the 'traditional Pantaloon' and Festus, his scheming nephew, who also courts the unwilling Anne, is the traditional 'Boasting Captain of the Italian masks'.[65] Anne herself serves as the typical 'demure [yet] coquettish' Columbine, and her beloved Bob, the figure of Harlequin.

Hardy's connection to the Victorian theatre has been well documented, perhaps most extensively by Keith Wilson's *Thomas Hardy on Stage*.[66] In *Thomas Hardy: A Biography Revisited*, Michael Millgate describes Hardy's enduring ambivalence regarding the theatre, observing that 'Throughout his life Hardy was to be simultaneously beguiled by the excitement of the theatre and repelled by its artifice [...] even as he adapted to his own specific purposes some of the techniques and conventions of both the serous and the popular stage'.[67] Chapter III of *The Life and Work* of *Thomas Hardy* describes Hardy's enthusiasm for the London stage, and also, as Millgate points out, notes his assumption of a walk-on part in a 1866/67 Gilbert à Beckett pantomime, *Ali-Baba and the Forty Thieves; or, Harlequin and the Genii of the Arabian Nights*.[68] In it, Hardy played a role in the final Harlequinade.[69] It was also during this time that Hardy had 'formed an ideal of writing plays in blank verse',[70] something which he would not fully realize until his composition of *The Dynasts*.

It is notably at the Theatre Royal that Bob first appears in a 'splendid suit' indeed more befitting a Harlequin than one of her majesty's servicemen: 'Pantaloons and boots of the newest make; yards and yards of muslin wound round his neck, forming a sort of asylum for the lower part of his

65 Gittings, *Thomas Hardy's Later Years*, 19.

66 Keith Wilson, *Thomas Hardy on Stage* (Houndmills: St Martin's Press, 1995).

67 Michael Millgate, *Thomas Hardy: A Biography Revisited* (Oxford: Oxford University Press, 2004), 95.

68 Millgate, *Thomas Hardy*, 55.

69 I am very grateful to Keith Wilson for directing me to this information, and for his general observations about Hardy's relationship to the theatre, which he explores at length in *Thomas Hardy on Stage*.

70 Millgate, *Thomas Hardy*, 55.

face, two fancy waistcoats, and coat-buttons like circular shaving glasses'.[71] At the theatre the King once more appears, and '"Rule Britannia" was called for and sung by the whole house';[72] Hardy here shows his attentiveness to the theatrical realm's imbrication with nineteenth-century patriotism, how, as Russell explains, 'the theatre at this time was dedicated to the commemoration of the war and the enhancement of patriotic values'.[73] It is also, notably, at the theatre where the devious Festus Derriman first sets the press gang on Bob's trail. Columbine and Harlequin are typically pursued by Pantaloon and his servant, the Clown; but here, paternal authority intervenes in the form of the state's representatives – the press gang. Bob, though, as we have seen, ultimately escapes their grasp, carrying out the 'leap' made famous in the early years of the harlequinade, his 'figure flying like a raven's across the sky'.[74]

The blackness of Bob's figure is worth dwelling on, for it points to the way that, in aligning his pressed sailor with Harlequin, Hardy's use of the pantomime invokes the cultural legacy a figure often located at 'the intersection of slave culture',[75] alongside the black minstrel, the clown, and the 'blackman' of English folk drama. The blackface performer emerges elsewhere in Victorian fiction, such as in the figure of Tom Gradgrind in Dickens's *Hard Times* (1854), who ends up as a blackface circus clown, 'a comic blackamoor' with 'seams in his black face' and 'hands which were looking like the hands of a monkey'.[76] Identifying the 'blackface clown [as] closest to the circus and the pantomime clown', Michael Pickering notes in his discussion of racial ideology and blackface performance that blackface minstrelsy was one of the most pervasive forms of popular entertainment in England and the rest of Britain during the Victorian period.

71 Hardy, *The Trumpet-Major*, 219.

72 Hardy, *The Trumpet-Major*, 221.

73 Russell, *Theatres of War*, 60.

74 Hardy, *The Trumpet-Major*, 228.

75 Eric Lott, *Love and Theft: Blackface Minstrelsy and the American Working Class* (Oxford: Oxford University Press, 1993), 22.

76 Charles Dickens, *Hard Times* (1854), eds, Fred Kaplan and Sylvère Monod (New York: Norton, 2001), 210, 212.

It was associated most of all with the minstrel show and music hall, but it was taken up in all sorts of other performance venues, from street corners to seaside piers,[77] no doubt including the likes of Weymouth, the seaside setting of *The Trumpet-Major*.[78] While Hardy's writings offer little direct comment on minstrelsy itself, given its pervasiveness as entertainment throughout the nineteenth century there can be little doubt that Hardy had encountered minstrel performance.[79]

Noting in *Harlequin Empire* the degree to which the 'black mask has been neglected by modern scholars'[80] Worrall provocatively argues that 'black mask performance was a staple of British pantomime with Harlequin's mask being just one of the ways in which performance conventions problematize issues about the role of black face minstrelizing on the contemporary stage'.[81] In considering his leap from bondage, then, we do well to note that as a result of his physical contortions, Bob ultimately

77 Michael Pickering, 'The Blackface Clown', *Black Victorians/Black Victoriana*, ed. Gretchen Holbrook Gerzina (New Brunswick, NJ: Rutgers University Press, 2003), 166, 159.

78 George Rehin focuses especially on the prevalence of longstanding tradition of the performance of blackface minstrelsy in the latter locales – 'those places of recreation to which Londoners made their excursions'. George Rehin, 'Blackface Street Minstrels in Victorian London and its Resorts: Popular Culture and its Racial Connotations as Revealed in Polite Opinion', *Journal of Popular Culture* 15/1 (Summer 1981), 20. Waters, too, discusses the 'enormously popular and enduring fashion for Blackface minstrelsy' in the nineteenth century. Waters, 'Jacks and Diamonds – Some Aspects of Race on the London Victorian Stage', 85.

79 Hardy makes reference to a minstrel song –'Listen to the Mockingbird' (1855) – in his 'Poetical Matter' Notebook. The editorial note states that '"Listen to the Mockingbird" was a perennial standard, regularly included in successive editions of *The Christy Minstrels' Song Book* [...] and Hardy very probably saw one or more of its London performances'. Thomas Hardy, *Thomas Hardy's 'Poetical Matter' Notebook*, eds Michael Millgate and Pamela Dalziel (Oxford: Oxford University Press, 2009), 81, 121. I am very grateful to Keith Wilson for directing me to this significant detail.

80 Worrall, *Harlequin Empire*, 24. Worall points the work of John O'Brien, whose *Harlequin Britain: Pantomime and Entertainment, 1690–1760* (Baltimore: Johns Hopkins University Press, 2004) serves as a notable exception.

81 Worrall, *Harlequin Empire*, 24.

avoids being pressed aboard the *Black Diamond*. The ship's name may most immediately call to mind Harlequin's traditional chequered trousers. Yet there is in fact a whole history of seaside resort and music hall minstrelsy performance that may inflect Hardy's representation here: a number of minstrel troupes went by that name, which thus signals a common reference to popular forms of black choral music and entertainment.[82] Viewed in this light, the details of Bob's Harlequin representation situates him within a broad context of enslavement and injustice.

While informed by her romantic interests, the terms of Anne's response to Bob's potential impressment nonetheless offers a telling commentary on the individual's relative insignificance in relation to both the law and the operation of the machinery of history. For her part, Anne finds the actions of the gang altogether absurd and fails to see why her beloved Bob cannot be spared, as if loving him were 'protection' enough from the gang. As she says to Bob, 'It cannot make such a vast difference to the country whether one man goes or stays!'[83] This is indeed a vast drama, in which all the players are but players assuming stock comedic roles. Later, when Bob eludes the grasp of the gang, we rightly learn that one man can easily be substituted for another: 'They have been lucky to-night; they have caught fifteen or twenty men at places farther on; so the loss of Bob was no hurt to their feelings'.[84]

Although not finally taken by force, Bob ultimately participates in his own impressment, so to speak, and obliges the demands of King and country, in part driven by the absence that he finds everywhere apparent:

> He had that practical knowledge of seamanship of which the country stood much in need, and it was humiliating to find that impressment seemed to be necessary to teach him to use it for her advantage. Many neighbouring young men, less fortunate than himself, had been pressed and taken; and their absence seemed a reproach to him. […]

82 See, for instance, Bernard L. Peterson, *The African American Theatre Directory, 1816–1960: A Comprehensive Guide to Early Black Theatre Organizations, Companies, Theatres, and Performing Groups* (Westport, CT: Greenwood, 1997), 216.

83 Hardy, *The Trumpet-Major*, 225.

84 Hardy, *The Trumpet-Major*, 235.

> 'Certainly, I am no man to lie here so long for the pleasure of sighting that young girl forty times a day and letting her sight me – bless her eyes! – till I must needs want a press-gang to teach me what I've forgot. As is it then all over with me as a British sailor? We'll see'.[85]

The press gang, then, proves itself a powerful force of memory, removing Bob from the comedic context, as it reminds him of his allegiance not to Anne, but to his nation and its service. He soon returns to sea of his own accord; when 'the family got up the next day, Bob had vanished'[86] – like a ghost. Having willingly changed costume, donning his 'old seafaring garments', in order to prevent Ann from notably '*chaining* him down'[87] Bob seeks to fulfill his patriotic ambitions, secure himself a place aboard the *Victory* with Captain Hardy. Adopting the typical rhetoric of rationalization, the latter himself acknowledges to Bob, 'There has been a severe impressment. It is of course a disagreeable necessity, but it can't be helped'.[88] In choosing to board the *Victory* of his own volition, Bob overwrites his potential alternative history aboard the *Black Diamond*, submitting himself as a willing participant in a narrative of heroic achievement rather than form part of the form of enslavement – on *The Black Diamond* – that underpinned it.

In the responses to Bob's reenlistment, Hardy makes this plain. Soon after Bob's departure, Anne suffers from the thought of the potential loss of both men who have claimed to love her. But Mrs Loveday urges her daughter not to 'trouble and vex about it. [...] They are both instruments in the hands of Providence [...] And he'll come back soon, [...] And then he'll tell us all he has seen, and the glory that he's won, and how he has helped to sweep that scourge Buonaparte off the earth'.[89] Mrs Loveday participates in the production of the same naïve discourse that absorbs Bob within the realm of history. Although he eludes the

85 Hardy, *The Trumpet-Major*, 236–7.

86 Hardy, *The Trumpet-Major*, 247.

87 Hardy, *The Trumpet-Major*, 237. Emphasis added.

88 Hardy, *The Trumpet-Major*, 243.

89 Hardy, *The Trumpet-Major*, 246.

physical coercion of the gang, Bob is nonetheless pressed into service by more subtle machinations – by patriotic sentiment, the kind elsewhere fuelled by the spectacle of the king abroad and the ongoing military operations on the surrounding downs.

While the more worthless lover thus ultimately willingly submits to the march of history, it is the worthier John who is slain by it. The ongoing moral contrast between the two brothers is reinforced both by the trumpet-major's gentler character and, importantly, in the oft-remarked pallor of his *white* face, a rendering, according to Gittings, of 'the French creation of the sad, pensive, white faced Pierrot'.[90] At the novel's 'stage-lit' conclusion, we can, with Anne, merely watch as this gentler hero 'plunged into the darkness and went off to blow his trumpet till silenced forever upon one of the bloody battle-fields of Spain'.[91]

The press gang's responsibility for likewise plunging so many 'into the darkness' becomes central to Hardy's confrontation of the challenge of historical representation and his scrutiny of the law's often highly problematic role in the construction of that history. In identifying impressment as a spectacle of enslavement and loss, Hardy marks history itself as both spectre and spectacle, something existing perpetually beyond conventional accounts of the past. Haunting the prevailing tales of heroism and imperial glory that come to dominate the historical record, Hardy's pressed man – blackened as he is – stands as a fading remembrance of the spectacular injustices carried out in service of nation, empire, and history. And so the trumpet-major dies not as one individual on the battlefield, but as one among many. This is not a close-up, but a wide-angle shot – a panorama of historical failure and of loss in the theatre of war.

90 Robert Gittings, *Thomas Hardy's Later Years*, 19.

91 Hardy, *The Trumpet-Major*, 301.

Bibliography

Armstrong, Tim, *Haunted Hardy: Poetry, History, Memory* (Houndsmills: Palgrave, 2000).

Bewell, Alan, *Romanticism and Colonial Disease* (Baltimore: Johns Hopkins University Press, 1999).

Bownas, Jane L., *Thomas Hardy and Empire* (Farnham, England: Ashgate, 2012).

Bratton, J.S., 'British Heroism and the Structure of Melodrama', in J.S. Bratton, ed., *Acts of Supremacy: The British Empire and the Stage, 1790–1830* (Manchester: Manchester University Press), 18–61.

Brunsman, Denver, *The Evil Necessity: British Naval Impressment in the Eighteenth-Century Atlantic World* (Charlottesville and London: University of Virginia Press, 2013).

——, 'Men of War: British Sailors and the Impressment Paradox', *Journal of Early Modern History* 14 (2010), 9–44.

'Characteristics of the Sailor', *The Naval and Military Magazine* (March 1827), 94–5.

Colley, Linda, *Britons: Forging the Nation 1707–1837* (New Haven: Yale University Press, 2005).

Dames, Nicholas, *Amnesiac Selves: Nostalgia, Forgetting, and British Fiction, 1810–1870* (Oxford: Oxford University Press, 2001).

Davis, Jim, Introduction to ed. J. Davis, *Victorian Pantomime: A Collection of Critical* Essays (London: Palgrave Macmillan, 2010)

Davis, William A., *Hardy and the Law: Legal Presences in Hardy's Life and Fiction* (Newark: University of Delaware Press, 2003).

Dickens, Charles, *Hard Times* (1854), eds, Fred Kaplan and Sylvère Monod (New York: Norton, 2001).

Gittings, Robert, *Thomas Hardy's Later Years* (Boston: Little, Brown, 1978).

Hardy, Thomas, *The Return of the* Native (1878), ed. Phillip Mallett (New York: Norton, 2006).

——, *Thomas Hardy's 'Poetical Matter' Notebook*, eds Michael Millgate and Pamela Dalziel (Oxford: Oxford University Press, 2009).

——, *The Trumpet-Major* (1880), ed., Linda M. Shires (London: Penguin, 1997).

Hessell, Nikki, *Literary Authors, Parliamentary Reporters: Johnson, Coleridge, Hazlitt, Dickens* (Cambridge: Cambridge University Press, 2012).

Hutchinson, J.R., *The Press Gang: Afloat and Ashore* (New York: E.P. Dutton, 1914).

Irwin, Michael, *Reading Hardy's Landscapes* (London: Macmillan, 2000).

Lincoln, Margarette, *Representing the Royal Navy: British Sea Power, 1750–1815* (Aldershot, England: Ashgate, 2003).

Lott, Eric, *Love and Theft: Blackface Minstrelsy and the American Working Class* (Oxford: Oxford University Press, 1993).

Malton, Sara, 'Vanishing Points: Elizabeth Gaskell, Impressment, and Cultural Memory', forthcoming in *Nineteenth Century Studies* 28 (2015).

Millgate, Michael, *Thomas Hardy: A Biography Revisited* (Oxford: Oxford University Press, 2004).

Neill, Edward, 'Mixed Modes in *The Trumpet-Major*', *Essays in Criticism* 56/4 (October 2006), 351–69.

O'Brien, John, *Harlequin Britain: Pantomime and Entertainment, 1690–1760* (Baltimore: Johns Hopkins University Press, 2004).

Peterson, Bernard L., *The African American Theatre Directory, 1816–1960: A Comprehensive Guide to Early Black Theatre Organizations, Companies, Theatres, and Performing Groups* (Westport, Connecticut: Greenwood, 1997).

Pickering, Michael, 'The Blackface Clown', in Gretchen Holbrook Gerzina, ed., *Black Victorians/Black Victoriana* (New Brunswick, New Jersey: Rutgers University Press, 2003), 159–71.

Rediker, Marcus, *Between the Devil and the Deep Blue Sea: Merchant Seamen, Pirates, and the Anglo-American Maritime World, 1700–1750* (Cambridge: Cambridge University Press, 1987).

Rehin, George, 'Blackface Street Minstrels in Victorian London and its Resorts: Popular Culture and its Racial Connotations as Revealed in Polite Opinion', *Journal of Popular Culture* 15/1 (Summer 1981), 19–38.

Rignall, J.M., 'The Historical Double: Waverly, Sylvia's Lovers, The Trumpet-Major', *Essays in Criticism* 34/1 (Winter 1984), 14–32.

Rodger, N.A.M., *The Wooden World: Anatomy of the Georgian* Navy (Annapolis, Maryland: Naval Institute Press, 1986).

Rogers, Nicholas, *The Press Gang: Naval Impressment and its Opponents in Georgian Britain* (London: Continuum, 2007).

Russell, Gillian, *Theatres of War: Performance, Politics, and Society 1793–1815* (Oxford: Oxford University Press, 1995).

Shires, Linda M., introduction to Thomas Hardy, *The Trumpet-Major* (1880) ed., Linda M. Shires (London: Penguin, 1997), xix–xlii.

Sun-Joo Lee, Julia, *The American Slave Narrative and the Victorian Novel* (Oxford: Oxford University Press, 2010).

Thomas, Jane, 'Hardy's "Romances and Fantasies": *A Pair of Blue Eyes*, *The Trumpet-Major*, *Two on a Tower*, and *The Well-Beloved*: Experiments in Metafiction', in Keith Wilson, ed., *A Companion to Thomas Hardy* (Oxford: Blackwell 2013), 281–98.

Waters, Hazel, 'Jacks and Diamonds – Some Aspects of Race on the London Victorian Stage', *Race and Class* 50/3 (2008), 77–89.

Wilson, Keith, *Thomas Hardy on Stage* (Houndmills: St Martin's Press, 1995).

Wolfreys, Julian, *Dickens to Hardy 1837–1884: The Novel, The Past and Cultural Memory in the Nineteenth Century* (New York: Palgrave Macmillan, 2007).

Worrall, David, *Harlequin Empire: Race, Ethnicity and the Drama of Enlightenment* (London: Pickering & Chatto, 2007).

ZARA BARLAS

Transcultural Operatics: India on the British Stage in *The Nautch Girl, or, The Rajah of Chutneypore*

ABSTRACT

Amidst the charge of British imperialism and increasing cultural flows, artistic products with 'exotic' settings grew progressively in the metropole. India, the so-called 'jewel in the crown', became the subject of many a British work, upon the page, the canvas and the stage. The performative female body was a particular highlight, with an entire genre of artworks featuring nautch girls – Indian dancing girls. The comic operetta, *The Nautch Girl, or the Rajah of Chutneypore* (1891), by Edward Solomon, George Dance and Frank Desprez, was one such product that solicits investigation, owing to its significance within the context of imperialism and its components: the anti-nautch movement, feminist imperialism and the appropriation of the 'exotic' female body within particular hegemonic frameworks. Taking debates around orientalism and transculturality into consideration, and utilizing the methodologies of new musicology, postcolonial studies and colonial discourse analysis, this essay expounds the ways that *The Nautch Girl* constructs an imagined Indian identity using the female body, through the musical, visual and literary aspects of the operetta. The essay explains how *The Nautch Girl* tended to reflect abstractions of India that resulted in imaginary and illusory generalizations and stereotypifications, which reflected colonial discourse. In general, the female characters of the opera were shown to be immoral, indecent and sexually exploitative, resonating the voices of the anti-nautch movement. However, owing to the transculturality of the operetta, the female characters also reflected many aspects of contemporary British society. Depictions of India in this operetta were by no means static polarities of India versus Britain, but rather a dynamic imagined society constructed by an ever-changing society itself. Yet, by locating a beautiful, lustful and often corrupting female body in an 'exotic' setting that remained somewhat close to Britain, the operetta could evade the controversy of eroticism onstage through spatial and cultural distance.

***

And if you ask us whence this endless joy–
This happy lot – this bliss without alloy?
We answer, 'tis the guerdon of our art,
Which few attain, for few can play the part.[1]

Amidst the zenith of British imperialism and increasing cultural flows, artistic productions with 'exotic' settings proliferated in the metropole and beyond. India, the so-called 'jewel in the crown', became the subject of many a British work, upon the page, the canvas and the stage. The performative female body was a particular highlight, with an entire genre of artworks featuring nautch girls – Indian dancing girls. The comic operetta, *The Nautch Girl, or, the Rajah of Chutneypore* (1891), by Edward Solomon, George Dance and Frank Desprez, is one such artwork that solicits particular examination, owing to its centrality on the subject of nautch girls and its significance within the context of imperialism and its components: the anti-nautch movement, feminist imperialism and the appropriation of the 'exotic' female body within particular hegemonic frameworks. In addition to contributing to the configuration and categorization of the nautch girl and the Indian in British discourses, the interactions between nautch girls and Britons in India also contributed to the reassessment of British attitudes and principles regarding gender roles in society. The operetta serves as a singular and outstanding example among many of the multi-layered representations of India, Britain, women and the public and private spheres of society within a work of art or entertainment for public consumption.

The nexus between politics and art is crucial in the cultivation of our understanding of societies and their interactions with each other. And while it is a historical theme, the legacies of colonialism and so many other historic practices resonate and have significant repercussions on societies and their

1 Holly Beebee in: George Dance and Frank Desprez, *A New Indian Comic Opera in Two Acts, Entitled The Nautch Girl Or, The Rajah of Chutneypore. Libretto by George Dance. Music by Edward Solomon. With Lyrics by George Dance and Frank Desprez* (London, 1891), 7.

interactions today. Indeed, this is not to say that all art is politicized, but rather that all art can acquire political meaning during the process of production and reception. Within the context of Britain and India's historical relationship, cultural imperialism must be taken into consideration,[2] albeit cautiously. It is useful to examine the imperialist narratives which swept through Britain during the long nineteenth century, which manifested themselves in various ways. Understandings of orientalism are undeniably endemic to this field of enquiry, making it is possible to consider 'exotically' set artworks and their insinuations within the societies they were produced and immediately received in. Admittedly, problematic terms such as 'the West', 'the East', 'the Other' and 'the exotic' are employed in this chapter for purposes of context and convenience, although they solicit further scrutiny. That India was represented as 'exotic' in *The Nautch Girl* is undeniable, given the element of difference in the operetta.[3] *The Nautch Girl* presents an unusual – if somewhat paradoxical – portrayal of these dancing girls, who are represented simultaneously as Indians and as women. Gender and sexuality are particularly important themes to consider owing to their centrality in the entire narrative and aesthetics of the work. Rather apposite for this operetta are Edward Said's remarks on the subject: 'The Orient was a place where one could look for sexual experience unobtainable in Europe'.[4] In such a context, the relationship between Britain and India must not only be perceived as a political relationship, but also a cultural one; where cultures could interact, conflict and develop in a process of transculturality, leading

2 With much owed to Michel Foucault's works on power and governmentality: Michel Foucault, 'Truth and Power', in *Essential Works of Foucault*, ed. by James D. Faubion, 1st edn (New York, 2001); Michel Foucault, 'Governmentality', in *Essential Works of Foucault*, ed. by James D. Faubion, 1st edition (New York, 2001).

3 The 'exotic' is considered here as a derivative or version of the 'Other', whereby the 'exotic' implies spatial or geographical difference to the 'Self', in addition to cultural or social difference in other manifestations of the 'Other'.

4 Edward Said, *Orientalism* (London, 2003), 190 Additionally, Meyda Yeğenoğlu's *Colonial Fantasies* warrants mention in the furthering of our understanding of sexuality, desire and fantasy and its connection to colonial discourse.

to new practices in cultural production.[5] Considering debates surrounding orientalism and transculturality, this chapter expounds on the ways that *The Nautch Girl* bilaterally constructs an imagined Indian identity as well as British one by exploiting the Indian dancing girl, through the visual, musical and narrative aspects of the operetta.

The concept of 'nautch girl'

The term 'nautch girl' is somewhat problematic,[6] coined by the British to denote an expansive category of Indian women in performative roles and loaded with generalized assumptions featuring various negative as well as positive connotations. The anglicized term was used reductively in British discourses, where it encompassed a variety of female Indian dancers, singers, musicians, prostitutes and courtesans – the latter two of which marked her as a controversial entity. Enjoying local entertainment was perceived as one of the perquisites of imperialism, and within India nautches became a particular favourite. In actuality, the various groups of women that fell under the term 'nautch girls' were often dancers or singers who tended to remain unmarried and were sometimes affiliated with a Hindu temple or Mughal court. The nautch girl would sing, dance and/or recite poetry, and in many cases was part of a historical tradition with great societal and religious importance. However, the fallacious categorization of *devadasis* from Hindu temples and *tawaifs* from Mughal courts – among various other female performers and artists – in the same group as prostitutes did a substantial amount to damage and tarnish their reputation.

5 Transculturality has been concisely defined by Nicholas Mirzoeff as 'the violent collision of an extant culture with a new or different culture that reshapes both into a hybrid transculture that is itself then subject to transculturation'. See: Nicholas Mirzoeff, *The Visual Culture Reader*, 3 edition (London: New York, 2012), 477.

6 Derived from the Hindi or Urdu word *nāch*, meaning *dance*.

Yet nautch girls continued to be a thing of marvel, even during the early decades of the British Raj. In British society, attending nautches became a common cultural activity, particularly among those in the upper echelons of society. Edward, Prince of Wales (later King Edward VII) famously attended a nautch performance in 1875 – an event that met with little dispute. However, in 1890 Albert Victor's (Edward's eldest son) attendance at a nautch was met with great outrage.[7] Within a period of 15 years, British opinions and perspectives on the nautch tradition appeared to have developed dramatically and an anti-nautch movement began to spread during the 1890s.[8] By the 1920s, the movement led to the passing of the Anti-Nautch Bill, which outlawed dancing in temples.[9] Coincidentally, the operetta *The Nautch Girl* premiered in London in 1891, just as the anti-nautch movement was beginning to gain momentum. In one anti-nautch writing, *The Wrongs of Indian Womanhood*, the author Mrs Marcus B. Fuller, wife of an English missionary in Bombay, stated: 'It is saddening to see royal and aristocratic families irretrievably ruined by these women. Many a wealthy man has had to court poverty and disgrace on this account. Even in middle class society, many fritter away their youth and money to quench the insatiable thirst of sanctified immorality'.[10] It appeared, from such writings, that nautch girls posed a threat to British society in their apparent ability to *ruin* families, which is – surprisingly – suggestive of an admission of a power asymmetry that weighed in favour of Indian women.

There was nothing comparable to the nautch girl in the West, making it difficult for the British audience to grasp a precise understanding of the roles and practices of the various entitles that they collectively referred to as nautch girls. For many anti-nautch proponents, the British patronage of nautch girls legitimized prostitution. British responses to actual nautch

7 William L. Hicks, 'Social Discourse in the Savoy Theatre's Productions of The Nautch Girl (1891) and Utopia Limited (1893): Exoticism and Victorian Self-Reflection' (unpublished M.Mus Thesis, University of North Texas, 2003), 34.

8 Hicks, 'Social Discourse in the Savoy Theatre's Productions', 34.

9 S. Muthiah, 'When the Postman Knocked', in *Madras Miscellany: A Decade of People Places and Potpourri* (2011).

10 Marcus B. Fuller, *The Wrongs of Indian Womanhood* (New York, 1900), 132–3.

performances, both in India and across Europe, were mixed and often unfavourable. For example, *The Era* reported in 1838: 'The performances of the Nautch women are generally exceedingly monotonous, consisting of a sliding, shuffling motion along the floor; the movement of hands, arms, and eyes; and the adjusting and the readjusting of the veil'.[11] Various other reviews also followed suit, with claims that the women were unattractive and their performances dull and unimpressive. Yet, nautch performances continued to be popular throughout the nineteenth century and even in the early years of the twentieth century. Artworks featuring nautch girls were phenomenally popular during the long nineteenth century, spanning across literature, music and the visual arts and coinciding with anti-nautch discourses that sought to outlaw nautch practices. Solomon's operetta *The Nautch* Girl was particularly striking, especially within the context of the emerging anti-nautch movement, and its representation of nautch girls and women in general offers a significant talking point. To what extent did Solomon's operetta correspond to or deviate from anti-nautch discourses, and to what effect?

The Nautch Girl, or, The Rajah of Chutneypore

With music by Edward Solomon and lyrics by George Dance and Frank Desprez, *The Nautch Girl, or, The Rajah of Chutneypore* was a comic operetta that premiered at the Savoy Theatre in 1891, only six years subsequent to the premiere of Gilbert and Sullivan's *The Mikado, or the Town of Titipu*. It was the first musical entertainment at the Savoy Theatre that had not been penned by Gilbert and Sullivan, running respectably for about two hundred performances but never quite establishing itself as 'part of the larger Savoy canon'.[12] At its premiere, *The Nautch Girl* received a mixture of criticism and praise among its British audiences. In its review, the *Daily News* described the operetta as being received favourably and that that the

11 Anon., 'The Bayaderes', *The Era* (14 October 1838), 29.

12 Hicks, 'Social Discourse in the Savoy Theatre's Productions', i.

artists 'were warmly cheered'[13] while the *Birmingham Daily Post* noted that '[w]hen the curtain fell there were a few dissentient voices'.[14]

While productions of *The Nautch Girl* flourished for some time, their popularity promptly dwindled. Even to this date, performances of the operetta are extremely scarce and usually confined to smaller, amateur theatre companies. The eventual rarity of the operetta may lead one to the assumption that this operetta failed to leave any real mark on Britain's musical canon although the piece generally followed the typical traits of Gilbert and Sullivan works of the preceding decades. The reasons for *The Nautch Girl*'s diminishing popularity might be found in how the operetta differed from Gilbert and Sullivan's works, whether in its artistic quality or subject matter. Additionally, that the operetta premiered at the Savoy Theatre in the 1890s is an important point of consideration, since the Savoy's successes were far fewer in number than in the previous decade and the theatre temporarily closed down twice.[15] *The Nautch Girl*'s lack of popularity may therefore have partially been reflective of a wider pattern of failings for the Savoy Theatre during this time. However, when the failings of the operetta were not felt immediately and rather after approximately two hundred performances, the causes for the operetta's decline must be sought elsewhere in the very content of the operetta itself.

Image

Musical entertainments set in 'exotic' locations often relied on visual hints and pointers to locate the work in a specific regional and cultural setting and *The Nautch Girl* was no exception. These 'exotic' signifiers existed in the form of physical objects, stage props and costumes and were reported

13 Anon., 'London, Wednesday, July 1', *Daily News* (1 July 1891).

14 Anon., 'The New Comic Opera at the Savoy', *Birmingham Daily Post* (1 July 1891).

15 Once in 1895 and a second time in 1903. Robin J. Wilson and Frederic Lloyd, *Gilbert & Sullivan: The D'Oyly Carte Years* (London, 1984), 52.

on in various reviews of the premiere production of the operetta. Many reviews insinuated that *The Nautch Girl* was an aesthetic delight, such as the *Glasgow Herald*: 'Even the mounting itself, with its wealth of real Indian dresses, would suffice to draw large audiences'.[16] Reviews revelled over the costumes and imagery of the operetta, where strong references were made to the 'Indian-ness' of the visuals. For example, a review of an 1891 production of *The Nautch Girl* in Darlington stated that the 'costumes are carefully designed on the traditional lines of the native Brahmins and Hindus',[17] which would suggest that *authenticity* was an inherent aspect of this artwork. Many reviewers similarly highlighted the presence of 'Indian-ness' in the operetta, as though it were of central importance. Indeed the operetta's own costume designer Percy Anderson remarked:

> When designing the dresses for Mr Edward Solomon's opera *The Nautch Girl*, for the Savoy Theatre, I was hunting for facts in the Indian Museum.[[18]] There I came across an Eastern dancing dress, which I copied as accurately as the conditions of comic opera and our stage would allow. The great quantity of material used, in order that the dancers might envelop themselves in billowy folds of drapery, seemed to be an obstacle, but the result was curiously graceful.[19]

These sources suggest that providing an 'authentic' representation of India and its nautch girls was a particular expectation or desire, and that this operetta succeeded in achieving it through the art of copying. Photographs from the premiere production of *The Nautch Girl*,[20] together with coloured illustrations of the premiere production by pantomime enthusiast Jonathan Cleveland Milbourne,[21] demonstrate that the costumes of the nautch girls

16 Anon., '"The Nautch Girl" at the Savoy', *Glasgow Herald* (1 July 1891).

17 Anon., 'A New Opera in Darlington', *Northern Echo*, 16 December 1891, Nineteenth Century British Newspapers.

18 Presumably the now defunct India Museum in South Kensington, rather than the Indian Museum in Calcutta.

19 Percy Anderson, 'Art in the Theatre: Costume on the Stage', in *The Magazine of Art* (London, 1894), 10.

20 Available online in the public domain.

21 John Cleveland Milbourne, 'Page 47 of Mr Milbourne's Scrapbook Showing Costumes from THE NAUTCH GIRL Produced on June 30th, 1891, at the Savoy

were indeed colourful and somewhat representative of Indian clothing. In fact, some of the nautch girls' costumes from the premiere are astonishingly similar to the clothing of actual nautch girls who were painted by British artists like William Carpenter, who had travelled to India to paint Indian subjects and landscapes first-hand. These similarities would suggest that the costumes from the operetta were intended to represent actual clothing that nautch girls would have worn and were generally received as such. In one costume, Lenore Snyder as the main nautch girl, Hollee Beebee, is dressed in a long, glowing white robe, with pink flowers in her long black hair. She wears numerous bangles on her arms, as well as various pieces of jewellery draped across her neck and on her head. The costume features great resemblance to the clothing of the nautch girls in William Carpenter's watercolour *Two Natch Girls, Kashmir*, suggesting an element of copying or borrowing between the arts.

Clearer photographs are available of a 1901 production of *The Nautch Girl* at the Royal Theatre and Opera House, Abbey Road, which reveal the intricacies of the costumes and a peculiar mixture of 'Western' and 'Eastern' styles of fashion that could barely be associated with India (see Figures 1 and 2). Nonetheless, the women are depicted effeminately and gracefully, holding themselves with an air of confidence. Interestingly, the peculiarities of the costumes are most notable in the male character of Bumbo, the Hindu idol who has come to life, who is dressed in a unique other-worldly costume in both the premiere production and the 1901 production of the operetta (see Figure 3 for the latter). The peculiarities and absurdities of the costumes in *The Nautch Girl* insinuate that ideas and understandings of India have changed since the days of imperialism. Understandably, as a comic operetta the intention of the work was to provide light entertainment, and so the idiosyncrasies may have sought to serve this purpose. Additionally, the original 1891 production may have offered a more accurate

---

Theatre, London. It Also Shows Costume Details for LITTLE BO-PEEP at the Theatre Royal, Drury Lane on December 26th, 1892, the Rest of the Entry Being Continued on Page 48' (London, 1891), Special Collections, University of Kent at Canterbury – UKC/SCRAP/MILB: F203528/P47.

Figure 1: A photograph depicting a nautch girl (most likely Holly Beebee) from *The Nautch Girl* at the Royal Theatre and Opera House, Abbey Road in 1901 demonstrates few (if any) elements of 'Indian-ness'. Photo courtesy of TOPS Musical Productions.

Figure 2: A photograph depicting a nautch girl in 'exotic' garb from the 1901 production of *The Nautch Girl*. Photo courtesy of TOPS Musical Productions.

Figure 3: A photograph of Bumbo from the 1901 production of *The Nautch Girl*. Photo courtesy of TOPS Musical Productions.

copy of nautch girl garb. However, since Gilbert and Sullivan's musical collaborations were generally known for their absurdities, it should come as no surprise that their clothing reflected elements of eccentricity. In general, the representation of nautch girls' appearances in the operetta offered a mixture of the familiar and the unfamiliar to offer an aesthetically curious though pleasant experience, with well-intended attempts to copy the real dresses of nautch girls in the premiere production.

While there is limited information about the staging and sceneries of the early productions of *The Nautch Girl*, reviews emphasized their 'oriental' nature: 'The Indian costumes, the soft draperies of the Nautch dancers, with their strings of coins, and the Oriental scenery made up a series of stage pictures the fascinating brightness and beauty of which it would be difficult to exaggerate'.[22] Photographs of the early productions of *The Nautch Girl* provide little information about the set design, except for the presence of trees (possibly palms) and a vase in an iron stand in the premiere production photographs. The *Glasgow Herald*'s review of the premiere noted that the opening scene featured the 'outskirts of Chutneypore, a beautiful scene with overhanging palm trees, while in the distance in the valley lies the city'.[23] Palm trees contributed to make the scene an 'exotic' one – as something quite different from one in Britain. In the same review, the writer notes: 'As the curtain falls in the second act we are in the courtyard of the Royal Punka's Palace, a pure Indian scene, lit up by the dull red Indian sunset'.[24] Mirroring this, a review in the *Northern Echo* states: 'The pictures of Indian native life which form a setting as it were for dancing, and the movements of the Nautch girls, are delightfully rich and effective'.[25] These comments emphasize the significance of the 'Indian' location of the operetta, and the aesthetic and performative aspects of the nautch girl characters within it. The descriptions in the operetta about the outskirts of an Indian city featuring Pariahs bowing

22 Anon., 'The New Savoy Opera', *Freeman's Journal and Daily Commercial Advertiser* (1 July 1891).

23 Anon., '"The Nautch Girl" at the Savoy'.

24 Anon., '"The Nautch Girl" at the Savoy'.

25 Anon., 'Our London Letter', *Northern Echo* (1 July 1891).

to the ground before the Rajah of Chutneypore offer a very particular representation of India as a location. Bringing this rendition of India and its nautch girls to the British stage during the period of the British Raj could certainly have impacted the way that audience-goers would *see* India, potentially feeding into imperial agency.

Sound

The original orchestral score and production promptbook for *The Nautch Girl* no longer appear to exist,[26] which limits the analysis of the operetta and has probably contributed to the rarity of productions of *The Nautch Girl* today. However, the lyrics and vocal score are available and offer somewhat of an insight into the operetta's musical and narrative journey. Generally, the musical environment of *The Nautch Girl* comprises common parlour music with exoticist nuances, generating a soundworld in which the Self and Other co-exist, albeit somewhat turbulently.

Following suit after previous musical entertainments held at the Savoy Theatre, *The Nautch Girl* featured parlour ballads and other popular styles of music that were typical of Gilbert and Sullivan operas. This comes as no surprise since the success of *The Mikado* meant that Solomon would attempt to evoke a similar response with his work. However, unique to *The Nautch Girl* was the fact that there were strong aspects of exoticism present in *The Nautch Girl* that attempted to authenticate the Indian setting. The *Times'* review stated: 'In several passages, and notably in the last number, local colour is used with happy effect and much intelligence.

26 Hicks has pointed out that according to a posting on Savoynet, it is possible that the orchestral score was destroyed in the 1965 fire at Chappell and Company, or that it was lost in the process of shifting storage space. See: Hicks, 'Social Discourse in the Savoy Theatre's Productions', 20.

Actual Hindoo melodies are apparently introduced here and there'.[27] Similarly, a review of the premiere by the *Daily Times* stated that 'the choruses and accompaniments frequently have an Eastern tinge to supply them with local colour'.[28]

While the use of authentically Indian musical excerpts in the operetta is questionable, it is certainly clear that exoticist musical devices were employed in order to colour the melodies and locate the operetta within its Indian setting. This was achieved through the employment of chromaticism (intersperses of the diatonic scales with foreign notes) and dissonance in various musical numbers as well as through the choice of instrumentation. A potent example of the use of chromaticism occurs when the character Pyjama dramatically warns the others about the dreaded awakening of the idol Bumbo – an unusual and 'exotic' unfolding of events that is mirrored effectively in the chaotic colouring of the scale. Musical dissonance – the use of a combination of notes that appear harsh or unpleasant to the ear – is prevalent in various songs in the operetta, most noticeably in the chromatic 'Melos' (No. 14) but also in the nautch girls' 'Indian Lullaby' (No. 22). Though a musical fashion of its time, in the context of 'exotic' setting, the dissonance in the operetta could be seen to convey particular sentiments about the nautch girls and Indians in general through the use of inharmonious melodies. It is worthy to note here that painter William Daniell remarked about an actual nautch performance he experienced in India that '[t]he most unpleasant part of the nautch is the dissonant music with which it is accompanied, and in which the dancers themselves every now and then join with voices as shrill and unmusical as the note of the peacock'.[29] One might deduce from this that the use of dissonance in *The Nautch Girl* could be seen to reflect the reception of actual nautch performances by British audiences. If this is indeed true, one can observe

27 Anon., '"Opening Night Review". Review of The Nautch Girl; Or, The Rajah of Chutneypore, Savoy Theater', *The Times* (1 July 1891).

28 Anon., 'The "Nautch Girl" at the Savoy', *Daily News* (1 July 1891).

29 William Daniell and Hobart Caunter, *The Oriental Annual, or, Scenes in India* (1836), 73.

mimetic practices being harnessed in British music in response to the cultural encounter with India, among other 'exotic' locations.

While the original orchestral score is no longer known to exist, reviews of the operetta indicate the use of heavy percussion, which was an oft-used tool in musical exoticism to represent the Orient. There are several references to the use of a gong – an instrument that originated in East and South East Asia, rather than in South Asia, but was generally adopted in music to generate an 'exotic' soundworld that had no specific location beyond the Other. Referring to *The Nautch Girl*, George Bernard Shaw suggested that the artists 'had better remove the bassoon, the piccolo, the cymbals, the triangle, and the drums, both *timpani* and *tamburo* from the theatre' and that Solomon had given him the worst headache that he had ever had in theatre.[30] While there was an element of percussion prevalent in many types of actual nautch, the use of percussion in the operetta seemed somewhat excessive and exaggerated, much like a caricature.

But there are also inflections in *The Nautch Girl* that bring the operetta back to a British – or at least Western – soundworld. For instance, the Rajah's introductory song, which is full of patriotism and masculine expression, appears to be framed around the rhythmic pattern of the popular British nursery rhyme 'The House that Jack Built'.[31] Additionally, there is a reference to Handel's *Messiah*, with a quotation of a strain from the 'Hallelujah' chorus awkwardly positioned within the up-tempo 'Quartette' (No. 8). Generally, it seems that Solomon combined the typical parlour and popular music of Britain with exoticist elements that sought to place the operetta within its Indian locale while maintaining an element of relatability for the British audience. In doing so (in *The Nautch Girl* as well as many other exotically set musical works), artists were changing the very fashions of musical tradition in Britain, insinuating that India and other 'exotic' places had a significant cultural impact on British culture.

30 David Trutt, ed., 'London Music by George Bernard Shaw', 1888, 26.

31 Anon., 'The New Savoy Opera'.

Narrative

The story of *The Nautch Girl* offered much of the usual dramatic spectacle of general light operas, though heavily localized with many 'Indian' and 'Hindu' elements. In the story, Indru, the son of Punka, the Rajah of Chutneypore, is of a higher caste (Brahmin) than his love interest, Holly Beebee, who is a nautch girl. To bypass the caste laws that prevent them from marrying, Indru renounces his caste, while Holly Beebee is suddenly raised to the status of Brahmin, comically reversing the situation while retaining the original conundrum. Indru's caste renouncement leads him and his father to be sentenced to death by crocodile by Bumbo, an enraged Hindu idol who awakens after one of his diamond eyes is stolen. Moments before the death sentence is executed, Bumbo is overfilled with joy when he notices his stolen eye hanging from Beebee's neck. Bumbo acquits Indru and Punka and approves the restoration of Indru's Brahmin status, presumably enabling Indru and Holly Beebee to finally marry. The synopsis shows how Indian 'colour' is used to revitalize the age-old story of a forbidden love that must be fought for, relying heavily on aspects of Indian religion and social practices. Additionally, gender and sexuality are placed as central themes in *The Nautch Girl*, where most of the events that unfold are the direct consequences of the nautch girls' and other female characters' actions.

Notably, the disrepute with which nautch girls were received by the British in India was also carried over into the operatic representation of nautch girls. The libretto is filled with implications that the nautch girls pursue sexual exploits. For instance, in an exchange between Indru and Baboo Currie (the proprietor of the nautch troupe), Currie warns that Holly Beebee is flirtatious and potentially unfaithful, and even warns: 'Of feminine beauty beware, Sir!'[32] Such descriptions about the fictitious nautch girl of the operetta resonate with the real-life discourses of the anti-nautch

32 Solomon, Dance and Desprez, *The Nautch Girl, Or, The Rajah of Chutneypore*, 15.

movement, which similarly warned about the dangers of the nautch girls and their questionable moral behaviour.[33] These alleged immoral practices of nautch girls are verified by the nautch girl characters of the operetta themselves, which would suggest that these were traits of truth rather than accusation:

> We never woo
> As others do
> With passion ardent, firm and true;
> For we would stay
> Unwed for aye,
> To love, and love, and run away.[34]

In such passages, the nautch girls proudly proclaim that they are dishonest, licentious and unwilling to settle down with a partner, reflecting real British concerns that were being raised by the anti-nautch movement.[35] The nautch girls of the operetta even admit to playing on the vulnerabilities of others:

> With merry song we trip along,
> treading through the idle throng,
> While from our eyes the fire flies
> that kindles hope in the unwise.[36]

33 The nautch girl earned a particularly bad name among the memsahibs, the British women in India, for whom the presence of this 'loose' and 'free' nautch girl seemed immoral and a threat to Victorian social values, especially those around the family. In a significant amount of literary works of this time, many of which were written by female British authors, the nautch girl characters pursued sexual relations with married British men and partook in other corrupt practices, such as thievery, espionage and other forms of malice. For examples, see: Charn Kamal Kaur Jagpal, '"I Mean to Win": The Nautch Girl and Imperial Feminism at the Fin de Siècle' (unpublished Ph.D. diss., University of Alberta, 2011).

34 Dance and Desprez, *The Nautch Girl, Or, The Rajah of Chutneypore*, 6.

35 For details, see: Pran Nevile, *Nautch Girls of India: Dancers, Singers, Playmates* (1996); Jogan Shankar, *Devadasi Cult: A Sociological Analysis* (1990).

36 Solomon, Dance and Desprez, *The Nautch Girl, Or, The Rajah of Chutneypore*, 20.

Such proclamations are even demonstrated in the operetta, when the nautch girls exploit their feminine wiles to distract Pyjama, the Grand Vizier, from his meeting with Bumbo through a provocative song and dance in 'Indian Lullaby' (No. 22). In this way, the nautch girls are presented as both powerful and corrupt, in a mixture of positive and negative aspects. Elsewhere in the libretto, Bumbo is described as being 'obviously amenable to the charms of female beauty'[37] – a phenomenon that appears to be widespread amongst the men throughout the narrative of the operetta. With such descriptions woven throughout the operetta, it is clear that a particular view of nautch girls and their characteristics is being conveyed – one that coincides with anti-nautch sentiments, albeit in a lighter and comical manner. Moreover, *The Times'* review of the premiere of *the Nautch Girl* noted that the dances of the performance 'passed through the crucible of the theatre's censorship, [coming] out as immaculate as the 'blameless dances' of Ruddygore'.[38] From this one can only assume that there were some controversies of a sexual nature regarding the dances involved in this production that necessitated toning down.

The entire unfolding of the plot of the operetta relies on the role of feminine beauty and conspiring women: it is feminine beauty that lands the Rajah and Indru into so much trouble, it is conniving women who attempt to rescue the Rajah and Indru from imprisonment and death, and it is through their feminine wiles that the nautch girls are able to distract men and achieve their ultimate goals – and all successfully so. Given the historical context, and British attempts to instil a particular discourse about India in official narratives as well as social ones, the significance of artworks like *The Nautch Girl* become very important. It appears that sexuality – and its exploitation – could be explored rather freely in a story set in an 'exotic' locale. The nautch girls of the operetta were dancing in a most 'engaging fashion'[39] with the justification that this was a 'true' representation of the nautch girls of India. However, this operetta may also

37 Dance and Desprez, *The Nautch Girl Or, The Rajah of Chutneypore*, 46.

38 Anon., 'Opening Night Review'.

39 As the Daily News noted: Anon., 'The "Nautch Girl" at the Savoy'.

have been attempting to explore sexuality and gender roles more generally allowed in the operetta, where the setting of India would permit the artists to pass comment on British societal values on gender and sexuality without stirring controversy. It is likely no coincidence that Gilbert and Sullivan dislocated their works from Britain and relocated them in 'exotic' locations in order to soften the satirical blow, such as in *The Mikado, The Gondoliers* and *Utopia, Limited*. In *The Nautch Girl* it appears that gender and sexuality could be explored much more deeply as a concept if it were done so in a comical and foreign setting, so as to displace and distance oneself from the issue at hand.

The exploration of gender and sexuality in the operetta reflect real-life concerns that emerged during the anti-nautch movement, which was linked to the extensive missionary work that took place by British and other Western Christian groups. Evangelicalism was particularly significant, with its movement to reform moral behaviour and manners within a conservative framework, which would naturally include the perceived practices of nautch girls. Mrs Marcus B. Fuller's *The Wrongs of Indian Womanhood* is just one of numerous examples of observations and criticisms of Indian women written from the perspective of a British woman, which had been based on Christian values and even sought to *rescue* these women (with true imperialist vigour). Fuller described *devadasis* as practising 'a most debasing custom'[40] and that '[t]hese girls are the common property of the priests'.[41]

Despite criticisms against the nautch girl for her alleged corrupting nature and her ability to destroy British family values, there was also much sympathy felt for her – a need for her to be rescued from the clutches of patriarchy.[42] During this period, an increasing number of British women (and men) began to raise their voices to fight for the rights of women in India, and it is interesting to note Catherine Hall's point that this occurred at a time when industrialization was causing many of women's traditional

40 Fuller, *The Wrongs of Indian Womanhood*, 119.

41 Fuller, *The Wrongs of Indian Womanhood*, 119–20.

42 See: Jagpal, 'I Mean to Win', 6.

skills to become redundant in the era of technological advancements.[43] The challenges to the role of the British woman due to the consequences of industrialization may have contributed to her increasing role as superior sister to her allegedly disadvantaged counterpart in the 'East', in an attempt to relocate the power asymmetry.

Contrarily and somewhat momentously, Mrs Fuller admits: 'It frequently happens that these dancing-girls are rich, beautiful and very attractive, besides being witty and pleasant in conversation; and they are the only women that move freely in men's society'.[44] Mrs Fuller's comment implies a strong element of admiration for the nautch girl, since she has the freedom to exist within the male public sphere, transcending beyond the traditional female private – or domestic – sphere. The centrality of the themes of gender and sexuality in British politics, as demonstrated by Catherine Hall, shed yet another light on the issue; could we perhaps see works of art like *The Nautch Girl* as a commentary not merely on India but on Britain's 'social organization of power'[45] with specific reference to gender roles? Particularly important here is Hall's distinction between the male public sphere and the female private or domestic sphere – the women in the operetta *The Nautch Girl* can be seen to transcend the boundaries at will.

It is also interesting to note, as Jagpal does, that following from the drama surrounding the immorality of nautch girls in India, British female performers discovered a 'newfound independence' at the turn of the century, through self-choreography and solo performances that could be seen to have been stimulated by the Indian nautch girl.[46] Whether this was indeed true, the fact that nautch dances were being emulated on the British stage (in works such as *The Nautch Girl*) already represented a change in British cultural practices that was a direct consequence of the entanglements between Britain and India. In productions of *The Nautch Girl*, artists had embraced exoticist embellishments, including reproductions of

43 Catherine Hall, *White, Male and Middle Class: Explorations in Feminism and History* (Hoboken: Routledge, 2013), 153.

44 Fuller, *The Wrongs of Indian Womanhood*, 130.

45 Hall, *White, Male and Middle Class: Explorations in Feminism and History*, 45.

46 Jagpal, 'I Mean to Win', 222.

Hindu gods and Indian costumes, interpretations of Indian melodies and dance, and representations of Indian social and religious practices within a narrative. Resultantly, the boundaries of cultures could be confronted and surpassed, leading to the production of transcultural art.

The theme of religion is also woven throughout the narrative of *The Nautch Girl*, presenting a significant issue that was itself a real-life imperialist concern. The fact that the characters of *The Nautch Girl* are Hindus plays an imperative role in the entire unfolding of the plot: it is owing to the caste system that Indru, a Brahmin, is unable to marry the lower-caste Beebee. Indru and his father are to be sentenced to death as punishment for caste renouncement. The death sentence is to be meted out by an awakened Hindu idol. The entire plot relies heavily on the caste system, or at least an interpretation of it, at a time when it was a huge topic of debate in law and governance. It is worth noting that the Hindu caste system had been the subject of great discussion and debate in British politics, and was often simplified and essentialized in European discourse. Under British rule, the government attempted to codify and rigidify the Hindu caste system, while in actuality the caste system was tremendously complex, with thousands of divisions and dynamically evolving features.[47] Its simplification, reduction and misrepresentation in the operetta (for example, a chorus of Hindu Pariahs say 'Salaam' in the operetta, which is a Muslim greeting) contributed to the simplification, reduction and misrepresentation of India and its religions. Similarly, the *Times'* opening night review brings up the possibility of hurting Buddhist sentiments, while the operetta makes no mention of Buddhism and therefore seems to have been rather misinformed.

The caste system is overall heavily criticized in the operetta, with Indru referring to it as 'shackles' that must be undone and the nautch girls referring to it as something that is 'hated'. The *Daily News'* review states that this operetta 'satirises the absurdities of Indian caste',[48] revealing a negative reception about the caste system among audience-goers. The misrepresentation

47 Nicholas Dirks, *Castes of Mind Colonialism and the Making of Modern India* (Princeton: Princeton University Press, 2001), 68–70.

48 Anon., 'The "Nautch Girl" at the Savoy'.

of the caste system within this operetta and its audience illustrates the misconception of other cultures, societies and belief systems – the castes are essentialized and altered in order to make them accessible and palatable to the Victorian audience.

At the same time, there are various quips in *The Nautch Girl* that also locate the operetta as a truly British one, with references to contemporary British social issues. For example, Pyjama sings: 'Nor the House of Commons person who wants feminine M.P.'s [sic]'[49] – a direct reference to the women's suffrage movement. Similarly, Hicks notes how Punka is obsessed with the shape of his skull, linking it to the rise of the British Phrenological Society only four years prior to this operetta's premiere.[50]

Other references to British society include how the women of the court – the poorer relations of the Rajah – are described as 'common fry':

> Governesses, teachers, nurses,
> Lady-helps with slender purses,
> Toiling, broiling, day by day
> In a common, humdrum way –[51]

Such a description is reflective of the Victorian image of the working-class woman, and could therefore be seen as a commentary not on Indian society but rather on one much closer to home. Similarly, Punka boasts of his 'blue-bloodedness' to Holly Beebee, which – naturally – refers to the Western concept of deriving from nobility or aristocracy.[52]

While *The Nautch Girl* contains only Indian characters and is set in the fictional region of Chutneypore in India, there are various references to the West within the operetta that are important to analyse. Holly Beebee expresses her wish to escape with Indru to Europe because it provides escape from the tragedy of the Hindu caste system – it is where the romance

49 Dance and Desprez, *The Nautch Girl Or, The Rajah of Chutneypore*, 17.

50 Hicks, 'Social Discourse in the Savoy Theatre's Productions', 36–7.

51 Dance and Desprez, *The Nautch Girl Or, The Rajah of Chutneypore*, 24.

52 Dance and Desprez, *The Nautch Girl Or, The Rajah of Chutneypore*, 13.

between Indru and Beebee can finally be realized. Similarly, at the end of Act I, the chorus of nautch girls sing:

Away, away
  Across the main,
Beyond the sway
  Of Brahma's reign,
Unto a spot
  Far o'er the sea,
Where caste is not
  And men are free.[53]

Here the Hindu caste system is presented as a tragedy that can be escaped from by travelling overseas. The women appear to be trapped in India, in need of rescuing – reflecting alleged concerns among Britons for the well-being of Indian women in the various discourses about *sati* (widow-burning) and female infanticide. These concerns have been interpreted by various scholars as a practice of feminist imperialism, which envisioned supremacy through the power of British women to emancipate their Indian 'sisters' from their ills.[54] In the operetta, the nautch girls similarly appear to need (or at least desire) rescuing from a faraway land.

Moreover, the 'exotic' caste system is directly juxtaposed with Western democracy in the operetta. When a group of Pariahs bow before the Rajah, the Rajah sings:

Bow not, good people, to the earth,
We all are men of equal worth;
For though a Brahmin such as I
By Hindu law may not come nigh
Plebeian fellows such as ye,
Yet I despise that harsh decree!
The year, the hour, the day is past,

53 Dance and Desprez, *The Nautch Girl Or, The Rajah of Chutneypore*, 23.

54 See: Antoinette Burton, *Burdens of History: British Feminists, Indian Women, and Imperial Culture, 1865–1915*, First Edition (The University of Carolina Press: Chapel Hill, 1994).

> When men should serve the Despot Caste,
> So there's a hand, and there's a hand,
> and grasp it firm and true!
> I love you much, for I am such
> a democrat Hindu.[55]

Rather clearly the operetta presents a conflict between the concept of democracy and the Hindu caste system, implying that the two are incompatible and thereby offering political commentary on the state of governance in India. Despite the Rajah's good intentions, Bumbo, who plays the role of a villain, intends to carry out 'Hindu law' by sentencing Indru (and Punka) to death for renouncing his caste. While this ultimately fails to play out, the Hindu law of the villain is seen to override the democratic principles of one of the protagonists of the operetta. Evidently, negative and positive connotations are respectively applied to different systems of governance and belief, seemingly contributing to imperialist assertions.

Conclusion

While considering *The Nautch Girl* within the context of imperialism, it is important not to reduce the main subjects of the operetta to victims. Indian women have arguably been rendered mute and helpless, with judgements placed upon them, but it is important not to forget the power that they have also exercised. The portrayal of nautch girls in the operetta as beautiful and powerful women who could achieve whatever they wanted outside any jurisdiction seems to reflect an admirable view of the nautch girls and their freedom. Moreover, the fact that actual nautch girls' costumes and performances were emulated for the purpose of a musical artwork – which was incorporated into the folds of Western practices – was

55 Solomon, Dance and Desprez, *The Nautch Girl, Or, The Rajah of Chutneypore*, 5–7.

testament to the acceptance of Indian nautch girls as a cultural product. The representation of nautch girls on the British stage deviated significantly from the original *devadasis*, *tawaifs* and other female performers reductively categorized as nautch girls, but there was a strong connection between the two nonetheless.

The Nautch Girl tended to reflect abstractions of India that resulted in imaginary and illusory generalizations and stereotypes, which reflected imperialist discourse. In general, the female characters of the operetta are shown to be immoral, indecent and sexually exploitative, resonating the voices of the anti-nautch movement. But there is also a deeper layer of social commentary in the operetta that is intended to apply to British society itself. Through art, laden with political implications, artistic discourse about nautch girls could simultaneously contribute towards the broader imperial vision and open up a debate about gender and sexuality in British society.

Depictions of India in this operetta were therefore by no means intended purely as static polarizations of India versus Britain, but rather as dynamic imagined society constructed by an ever-changing society itself. Most significantly, *The Nautch Girl* was an operetta about the Self just as much as it was about the Other. It is a mere example of the kinds of artistic production that were to cultivate as a result of cultural entanglements as well as to their significance within a historical context.

Bibliography

Anderson, Percy, 'Art in the Theatre: Costume on the Stage', *The Magazine of Art* (London, 1894), 7–12.

'The Bayaderes', *The Era* (14 October 1838), 29.

Burton, Antoinette, *Burdens of History: British Feminists, Indian Women, and Imperial Culture, 1865–1915*, 1st edition (Chapel Hill, 1994).

Daniell, William, and Hobart Caunter, *The Oriental Annual, Or, Scenes in India* (1836).

Dirks, Nicholas, *Castes of Mind Colonialism and the Making of Modern India* (Princeton, 2001).

Foucault, Michel, 'Governmentality', in *Essential Works of Foucault*, ed. by James D. Faubion, 1st edition (New York, 2001).

——, 'Truth and Power', in *Essential Works of Foucault*, ed. by James D. Faubion, 1st edition (New York, 2001).

Fuller, Marcus B., *The Wrongs of Indian Womanhood* (New York, 1900).

Hall, Catherine, *White, Male and Middle Class: Explorations in Feminism and History* (Hoboken, 2013).

Hicks, William L., 'Social Discourse in the Savoy Theatre's Productions of The Nautch Girl (1891) and *Utopia Limited* (1893): Exoticism and Victorian Self-Reflection' (unpublished M.Mus Thesis, University of North Texas, 2003).

Jagpal, Charn Kamal Kaur, '"I Mean to Win": The Nautch Girl and Imperial Feminism at the Fin de Siècle' (unpublished Ph.D. diss., University of Alberta, 2011).

'London, Wednesday, July 1', *Daily News* (1 July 1891).

Milbourne, John Cleveland, 'Page 47 of Mr Milbourne's Scrapbook Showing Costumes from THE NAUTCH GIRL Produced on June 30th, 1891, at the Savoy Theatre, London. It Also Shows Costume Details for LITTLE BO-PEEP at the Theatre Royal, Drury Lane on December 26th, 1892, the Rest of the Entry Being Continued on Page 48' (London, 1891), Special Collections, University of Kent at Canterbury – UKC/SCRAP/MILB: F203528/P47.

Mirzoeff, Nicholas, *The Visual Culture Reader*, 3rd edition (London-New York, 2012).

Muthiah, S., 'When the Postman Knocked', in *Madras Miscellany: A Decade of People Places and Potpourri* (2011).

'"The Nautch Girl" at the Savoy', *Glasgow Herald* (1 July 1891).

'The "Nautch Girl" at the Savoy', *Daily News* (1 July 1891).

Nevile, Pran, *Nautch Girls of India: Dancers, Singers, Playmates* (1996).

'The New Comic Opera at the Savoy', *Birmingham Daily Post* (1 July 1891).

'A New Opera in Darlington', *Northern Echo*, 16 December 1891, Nineteenth Century British Newspapers.

'The New Savoy Opera', *Freeman's Journal and Daily Commercial Advertiser* (1 July 1891).

'"Opening Night Review". Review of The Nautch Girl; Or, The Rajah of Chutneypore, Savoy Theater', *The Times* (1 July 1891).

'Our London Letter', *Northern Echo* (1 July 1891).

Said, Edward, *Orientalism* (London, 2003).

Shankar, Jogan, *Devadasi Cult: A Sociological Analysis* (1990).

Solomon, Edward, George Dance, and Frank Desprez, *A Comic Opera, in Two Acts, Entitled The Nautch Girl, Or, The Rajah of Chutneypore* (London, 1891).

Trutt, David, ed., *London Music by George Bernard Shaw* (1888).

Wilson, Robin J, and Frederic Lloyd, *Gilbert & Sullivan: The D'Oyly Carte Years* (London, 1984).

SERENA GUARRACINO

Singing the Exotic Body across the Atlantic: From *The Mikado* to the *Swing Mikado* and Beyond

ABSTRACT

While Western opera has been traditionally devoted to the staging of the exotic Other on show for the pleasure of European ears and eyes – as first argued by Edward Said in *Culture and Imperialism* – the politics of such representation have scarcely been explored in relation to British comic opera. Considered a minor genre both in relation to Western *grand opera* and British stage drama, Victorian comic opera enacts the deep contradiction between the purportedly 'authentic' representation of an exotic setting and the paradigmatically non-naturalistic conventions of musical theatre. The travelling of these works to different Anglophone locations further complicates this paradox: in the (former) colonies, performers who were themselves considered exotic came to inhabit a fictional exotic body, thus staging a different claim to whiteness.

This essay will explore these issues by reviewing the stage history of Gilbert and Sullivan's opera *The Mikado* (1885), with particular reference to its 1939 Chicago all-black restaging, the *Swing Mikado*. William S. Gilbert's obsession with making this opera 'authentically Japanese' offers some of the most telling anecdotes of London stage history, as well as an opportunity to investigate how the purported whiteness of the singer under the make-up of the exotic character works within the context of comic opera. It may be argued that *The Mikado* stages fictional Japanese bodies over British bodies for British audiences, which are subsequently identified as hegemonic against the subaltern, exotic, and fictional Other. However, this fictional exotic body opens a performative space where previously subaltern, non-white bodies can access a claim to whiteness and normativity: across the Atlantic, *The Mikado* was staged by an all-black company, re-set in the South Pacific and renamed *Swing Mikado*. A performance that was met with huge success, it left white audiences disappointed by the lack of stereotypical blackness, and opened the operatic stage to African American performers in a time when opera (comic and otherwise) was still inaccessible to black singers.

***

There is little doubt that the 'gentlemen of Japan' opening William S. Gilbert and Arthur Sullivan's *The Mikado* may have seemed, to their first audiences, as 'queer and quaint' as their opening lines suggest:[1] Gilbert's notorious attention to detail in terms of staging and costume assured that his British singers and dancers would look as exotic as possible, and move accordingly in what was at the time an already recognizable Japanese fashion. Yet while this peculiar type of theatrical exoticism – the impersonation of racial Others by European performers for entertainment – stands at the core of this particular work, my intention here, aside exploring its historical context, is rather to follow the diverse incarnations of the *Mikado*'s own exotic body through time. Gilbert and Sullivan's piece has had a rich theatrical life that carries on to the present day; as a consequence, the pseudo-Japanese bodies staged in *The Mikado* have in their turn experienced many an incarnation, some of which definitely unforeseeable by their creators. Moreover, with the passing of time and of theatrical conventions, Gilbert and Sullivan's own corpus has itself become exotic, representative as it is of a Victorian England as 'queer and quaint' as their Japanese-esque creation appeared to their contemporaries.

This contribution aims at focusing on *The Mikado* not as a vehicle for staging the Other but as an exotic body *per se*, whose permanence in contemporary theatres allows for a continuous redefinition of what stands as Other in a given context. In every re-enactment of the Gilbert and Sullivan classic, performers negotiate the original exotic paradigm of Japan on their own bodies, be these British, African American, or white Australian, and in doing so they at the same time recall the original concept of exoticism embedded in the opera while elaborating one of their own. My attempt to read the performance history of *The Mikado* in this light is inspired by contemporary performance studies paradigms, 'stress[ing] the extent to which signification is constructed through the act of performance, and generally through acts of negotiation either between performers, or between them and the audience'.[2]

1 William Schwenk Gilbert, 'The Mikado or The Town of Titipu', in Ian Bradley, ed., *The Complete Annotated Gilbert and Sullivan* (Oxford: Oxford University Press, 2001), 559. Further reference to the libretto and notes are from this edition, with page number in brackets.

2 Nicholas Cook, 'Music as Performance', in Martin Clayton, Trevor Herbert and Richard Middleton, eds, *The Cultural Study of Music: a Critical Introduction* (New York and London: Routledge, 2002), 205.

Looking at and listening to the exotic body of *The Mikado* from the vantage point of the present, a complex layering of representational codes emerges, dismantling the apparent consistency of the original's Japanese fantasy. Starting from the authorial investment in the authenticity of the first production, my investigation will then move to the African American *Swing Mikado* produced in Chicago in 1939, and then to the 2011 DVD of the production of *The Mikado* by the Opera Australia Company, whose aesthetics places itself at the temporary end of the long and intricate performance history of Gilbert and Sullivan's opera.[3] All these very different instances are still productions of a single work, Gilbert and Sullivan's *The Mikado*, which in turn becomes an exotic body used to negotiate different identity politics; my intention is not to offer a comprehensive analysis of these productions or of the performance history of *The Mikado* as a whole, but to take them as examples of the complex and sometimes contradictory ways in which late nineteenth-century exoticism in musical theatre persists, but is also dramatically altered as the time and place of production change.

Inserting the *Swing Mikado* between two productions of the original work is also meant to avoid any developmental framework; indeed, being a staging of Gilbert and Sullivan's original work, the Australian *Mikado* represents both the source and a result of the African American *Mikados* of the 1930s. These were the first productions to create a close circuit in the accumulation and imperfect overlapping of different codifications for the exoticism embedded in the original text, and represent themselves a fundamental precedent for contemporary productions of *The Mikado*. In both the African American and the Australian productions, the specific type of Japanese exotic created by *The Mikado* is not eschewed altogether, but reshaped to embody different paradigms in the relationship between cultural identity and the exotic.

3 *The Mikado*, directed by Stuart Maunder, conducted by Brian Castles-Onion; recorded live on 24 and 25 May 2011 (Opera Australia, 2011).

'The whole of Japan is a pure invention'

'The whole of Japan is a pure invention': thus famously wrote Oscar Wilde in 1891,[4] commenting on the Japanese fashion that had been all the rage in London for some years, a fashion that *The Mikado*, first staged in 1885, certainly capitalized on. It is not by chance, then, that Josephine Lee reworks Wilde's assertion in the title of her 2010 *The Japan of Pure Invention*, where she probes deep into the orientalism that is at the roots of Gilbert and Sullivan's Japanese fantasy throughout its performance history.[5] Yet, while Edward Said's foundational statement that 'the Orient was Orientalized, not only because it was discovered to be "Oriental" in all those ways considered commonplace by an average nineteenth-century European, but also because it *could be* – that is, submitted to being – *made* Oriental'[6] surely applies to *The Mikado*, the self-reflexive humour typical of the Gilbert and Sullivan canon sets their production apart from the operatic exoticism that can be found in the European musical theatre of the same years.

In her seminal essay on Giacomo Puccini's 1903 opera *Madama Butterfly*, arguably the most long-lasting example of the Japanese exotic in European musical theatre, Teresa de Lauretis underlines how at the end of the nineteenth century Japan was the object of both a private and public fantasy first emerging in travel literature and then spreading virally through prints, narratives and imports.[7] De Lauretis identifies the inception of this fantasy in Pierre Loti's *Mme Chrysanthème*, published in 1887, although earlier versions of the same story such as Alphonse Daudet's (1873)

4 See Oscar Wilde, 'The Decay of Lying', in *The Decay of Lying and Other Essays* (London: Penguin, 2010), 31.

5 Josephine Lee, *The Japan of Pure Invention: Gilbert and Sullivan's* The Mikado (Minneapolis and London: University of Minnesota Press, 2010).

6 Edward W. Said, *Orientalism* (London: Penguin [1978] 1985), 5–6 (italics in the text).

7 Teresa de Lauretis, 'Popular Culture, Public and Private Fantasies: Femininity and Fetishism in David Cronenberg's *M. Butterfly*', *Signs: Journal of Women in Culture and Society* 24/2 (1999), 303–34.

may also be worth mentioning.[8] All these narratives feature the *geisha* as central stereotypical character, who appears as a veritable impersonation of Japan as seen through Western eyes: submissive in the face of the West and devoted to an exotically constructed self-sacrificial ethics culminating in the ceremony of *séppuku* (ritual suicide), one of the elements that guarantee *Madama Butterfly*'s ongoing fascination for the Western world.[9]

As Gilbert and Sullivan were working on their own Japanese opera neither *Madama Butterfly* nor its lesser-known antecedent, Pietro Mascagni's 1898 *Iris* – also featuring a suicidal *geisha* – had of course been performed yet. Nevertheless, European *grand opera* already teemed with tragic, often dark-skinned heroines, from Verdi's 1871 *Aida* to Bizet's 1875 *Carmen* and Léo Delibes's 1883 *Lakhmé*, illustrating 'not only a fascination with racial otherness but also […] a connection between racial and gender otherness'.[10] *The Mikado* is both indebted and critical of this tradition. The definition 'comic opera' for their production[11] – often used in alternative with 'Savoy opera', which more narrowly identifies the works written and produced for the Savoy theatre – was explicitly meant to associate Gilbert and Sullivan's work with European *grand opera* and its renown for 'respectable

8 See Jan van Rij, *Madame Butterfly: Japonisme, Puccini, and the Search for the Real Cho-Cho-San* (Berkeley: Stone Bridge Press, 2001), 50ff.

9 For the role of *seppuku* in *Madama Butterfly* and more generally in the Western imaginary on Japan see Joshua S. Mostow, 'Iron Butterfly: Cio-cio-san and Japanese Imperialism', in Jonathan Wisenthal, Sherrill E. Grace, e Melinda Boyd, eds, *A Vision of the Orient: Texts, Intertexts, and Contexts of Madame Butterfly* (Toronto: University of Toronto Press, 2006).

10 Herbert Lindenberger, *Opera in History: From Monteverdi to Cage* (Stanford: Stanford University Press, 1998), 187.

11 'Comic opera' is actually the general English definition for light opera, and includes Italian *opera buffa* as well as French *operetta*; Gilbert and Sullivan borrowed heavily from both traditions and enabled the entrepreneur Richard D'Oyly Carte to almost singlehandedly establish the tradition of comic opera in English in his Savoy Theatre; see Carolyn Williams, *Gilbert and Sullivan: Gender, Genre, Parody* (New York and Chirchester: Columbia University Press, 2011), 77–80.

and high-class entertainment',[12] musical as well as theatrical sophistication. On the other hand, their work often mock the melodrama of continental opera by capitalizing on the British tradition of satirical theatre, dating back to 1728 and John Gay's *The Beggar's Opera*. Gilbert and Sullivan looked to continental Europe for respectable entertainment and art music, but also parodied it and thus claimed a distinctive British identity for their work.

While sharing with continental theatre the allure of outlandish settings and characters, *The Mikado* intertwined exoticism with its peculiar topsy-turvydom, which had already become a typical element of the Savoy repertoire. Hence the work shows a contradictory coexistence of the authentic and the absurd, the supposedly realistic and the explicitly illogical. The setting itself, the imaginary town of Titipu, is more a tongue-twister than a reference to any actual Japanese city or town; and this happens twenty-five years after 1860, when Japan opened its borders to Europe and the US, so audiences would know they were not expected to refer the location to any actual place.

The plot itself eschews the tropes of exotic travel narratives to target many elements of Victorian Britain as object of humour and ridicule. There are no *geishas* in *The Mikado*: Ko-Ko, the comical male character typically at the centre of the plot, has three wards and is going to marry one of them, Yum-Yum, as the opera starts. Ko-Ko, formerly a tailor, is now Lord High Executioner of Titipu, the highest position in the town's administration, which he achieved thanks to the rather peculiar law under which flirting is illegal, and anyone who is caught in the act is condemned to be beheaded: an extreme, paradoxical situation where a fancy and sexualized Orient works as a rather thin veil for a mockery of Victorian society's repressive attitude towards sexuality, and especially towards the temperance movement that had already been the humorous object of Gilbert and Sullivan's previous hit *The Sorcerer*.[13]

12 Milllie Taylor, *Musical Theatre, Realism and Entertainment* (Farnham: Ashgate 2012), 17.

13 For the arguments supporting the reading of Titipu exclusively as proxy for Victorian Britain see Michael Beckerman, 'The Sword on the Wall: Japanese Elements and Their Significance in *The Mikado*', *The Musical Quarterly* 73/3 (1989), 306.

The Japanese element seems rather negligible in reference to the opera's plot; and indeed it is in the elements more related to the performing body, i.e. staging and music, that the exotic becomes more of a structural component of *The Mikado*. It would be in fact quite useless to try and identify significant elements of European musical exoticism in Sullivan's score, with the notable exception of 'Miya Sama' (619), the chorus introducing the Mikado in Act II. This tune, originally a 1868 Japanese military march, though still recognizable, was heavily manipulated by Sullivan in order to function as non-European music generally does in opera, that is, to offer European audiences an easily recognizable musical language for a commodifiable, exotic difference: as Susan McClary convincingly argues about *Carmen*, '[t]he actually signifying practices of ethnic music matter little here, for what the European ear expected to hear in exotic music was its own image of difference: this music reinscribes not so much its ostensible musical model as European notions of what the Other is like'.[14]

This is indeed what happens with the 'Miya Sama' tune, a single exotic piece of music used to create a contrasting feeling of both familiarity and unfamiliarity, allowing the composer to shift quite easily 'between the pseudo-Oriental style and his "normal" mode'.[15]

But it is especially in the material elements of production, in the setting up and clothing up of the performing bodies on stage that *The Mikado* emerges undoubtedly as a racial fantasy based on the imperial appropriation of the Japanese. The opera's first production has a rich anecdotic tradition that proves how much Gilbert especially was keen to have *The Mikado* look (if not sound) as Japanese as possible: the company even hired two Japanese performers to show supposedly authentic Japanese moves to the Savoy Opera singers.[16] The performers were hired from a Japanese exhibition which had been all the rage in Knightsbridge in the same year, as it offered 'a complete village with all its shops, tea house, theatre, and place

14 Susan McClary, *Georges Bizet: Carmen* (Cambridge: Cambridge University Press, 1992), 54.

15 Beckerman, 'The Sword on the Wall', 308.

16 See Lee, *The Japan of Pure Invention*, 44–7.

of worship, as well as their inhabitants', as the description of the attraction in the *Illustrated London News* reads.[17] In addition, costumes for the production strictly followed Japanese models, forbidding corsets for both men and women, and providing one of the female leads with a kimono that was a two-hundred-year-old original especially shipped from Japan.[18]

There was, then, a massive investment, economic as well as symbolic, in the opera's authentic representation of Japan, which expanded and capitalized on the contemporary craze for Japanese imported goods. *Japonaiserie* was in its turn part and parcel of what Anne McClintock has defined 'commodity racism', where 'commodity kitsch made possible, as never before, the mass marketing of empire as an organized system of images and attitudes'.[19] Yet, while McClintock's definition applies especially to the use of racial stereotyping in commodity culture to define a norm of whiteness, here I partially follow Lee's appropriation of the term to define 'how the understanding of racial difference can be shaped by the interaction of consumers and goods rather than by experiences of body contact'.[20] Indeed, the first lines of the libretto support Lee's reading of the overlapping between characters and objects of consumption in the opera: the chorus of Japanese notables introduces itself as the both exotic and familiar figurines appearing 'on many a vase and jar/on many a screen and fan',[21] hence more as objects to be consumed than as exotic bodies in performance.

Yet Lee's very convincing argument abstains from a confrontation with the specific semiotics of musical theatre, and in particular with issues of anti-realism in relation to racial impersonation. I will be focusing on the question of impersonating the exotic Other in a short while; but first it is necessary to foreground the anti-verisimilitude of musical theatre as the counterpart of Gilbert's obsession with making his *Mikado* accurately

17 Quot. in Beckerman, 'The Sword on the Wall', 305.

18 Lee, *The Japan of Pure Invention*, 77.

19 Anne McClintock, 'Soft-Soaping the Empire: Commodity Racism and Imperial Advertising', in *Imperial Leather: Race, Gender, and Sexuality in the Colonial Contest* (London: Routledge, 1995), 507.

20 Lee, *The Japan of Pure Invention*, xv.

21 Lee, *The Japan of Pure Invention*, 559.

Japanese. As Raymond Knapp argues, adding music to a scene that could work perfectly in regular prose underlines its artificiality by breaking the illusion of naturalistic representation.[22] In *The Mikado*, this is heightened by the use of a distinctly European musical language – including its own type of exoticism, as mentioned above – which inevitably exposes the British singing body under the yellowface and kimono-looking costume. This explicit anti-realistic aesthetics underlines the artificiality and self-awareness of even pseudo-authentic representations of the exotic in musical theatre, which is inevitably exposed as a travesty.

What happened to the 'nigger serenader'?

The Mikado actually hints at the complex layers of theatrical conventions in racial impersonation through a reference to another, very common practice. During what is arguably the most famous song of the opera, Ko-Ko's 'little list' of people who could be executed in case of necessity, one of the social stereotypes that 'never would be missed' is 'the banjo serenader, and the others of his race'.[23] This is how the line reads today, yet it was permanently altered only in 1948: the original 'nigger serenader' was much objected by 'coloured persons', as D'Oyly Carte himself states.[24] Yet the reference was probably targeted, more than to black performers, to the ubiquitous black-face 'Ethiopian minstrels', who were very popular in Victorian *vaudeville*. Their popularity may explain their mentioning here among the 'people who eat peppermint and puff it in your face'[25] and the 'apologetic statesmen of

22 Raymond Knapp, *The American Musical and the Formation of National Identity* (Princeton, NJ: Princeton University Press, 2005), 12.

23 William Schwenk Gilbert, 'The Mikado or The Town of Titipu', in Ian Bradley, ed., *The Complete Annotated Gilbert and Sullivan* (Oxford: Oxford University Press, 2001), 573.

24 Gilbert, 'The Mikado', 572.

25 Gilbert, 'The Mikado', 571.

a compromising kind'[26] that are also the target of Ko-Ko's invective: their success made them contenders to the Savoy in the market of London's theatrical performances, and their type of popular entertainment was in many senses the antithesis to Gilbert and Sullivan's efforts for a respectable British musical theatre.

All the differences between minstrelsy and Savoy actor-singers notwithstanding, the animosity emerging from this short reference also beckons to the similarities between their respective strategies of performing the exotic body. Quite to the point here is Lee's argument that 'in a broader sense, the style of playing Japanese in *The Mikado* is put in place not only by British orientalism but also by blackface minstrelsy',[27] as both practices guarantee the privilege of whiteness as 'the unmarked category against which difference is constructed, [which] never has to speak its name, never has to acknowledge its role as an organizing principle in social and cultural relations'.[28] The same invisibility is not accorded to black skin in performance, and the superimposition of the Japanese exotic body over the already racialized bodies of African American performers in early twentieth century United States does lead to very different shores. The *Swing Mikado* and its imitators are indeed the first to perform the exotic body of *The Mikado* as a polymorphous cultural entity which complicates the opera's racial impersonation by intersecting comic opera with black vaudeville.

The first *Swing Mikado*, advertised as an 'all-Negro' version of Gilbert and Sullivan's opera, was conceived and directed by Harry Minturn, a white actor and assistant director whose background in vaudeville shaped many of the Negro unit productions for the Federal Theatre Project, whose members were also mostly vaudevillians.[29] It opened in Chicago in 1939 and featured a cast of seventy-five African American performers, with a chorus of 50 elements. Its first six-month run was an unprecedented success, and

26 Gilbert, 'The Mikado', 573.

27 Lee, *The Japan of Pure Invention*, 89.

28 George Lipsitz, *The Possessive Investment in Whiteness: How White People Profit from Identity Politics* (Philadelphia: Temple University Press, 1998), 1.

29 See Rena Fraden, *Blueprints for a Black Federal Theatre* (Cambridge: Cambridge University Press, 1996), 189.

after closing in Chicago the show moved to Detroit and Los Angeles as well as New York, just a week before Michael Todd's *Hot Mikado* opening in the same city on March 8, 1939.

There is little left, in terms of sheet music and audiovisual recordings, of these and subsequent African American versions of *The Mikado*. What is left is the impressive coverage the original Chicago enterprise and subsequent productions had in the press, including – quite obviously for a FTP enterprise – the *Chicago Defender*, a newspaper especially targeting African American readers which closely chronicled the *Swing Mikado*'s success, its tour, its appearance on the national radio broadcast, and the influence of these productions on fashion and style.[30]

All early twentieth-century 'swing' productions of the *Mikado* share an element that highlights the issues brought up by an exotic East Asian body being performed by another exotic, though very differently so, African American body. These *Mikados* are not set in Japan, but in what was defined as 'a cellophane South Sea Island': 'the settings [...] are refreshingly at variance with the rules laid down by the Savoy theatre [...]. There are no Japanese lanterns, no screens, no pagodas – coconut palms, bamboo and totem poles instead. Sarongs replace the ladies' kimonas [sic], turbans and loin cloths outfit the men and the Mikado wears a tophat and makes his entrance [...] to the lapping of waves in a South Sea war canoe!'.[31]

The choice was probably influenced by the criticism targeting previous productions of *The Mikado*, such as one staged by the Washington Conservatory of Music, which had been harshly disparaged for the inadequacy of its racial make-up.[32] Black performers could not claim the same neutrality and invisibility as their British counterparts; Minturn's solution to the conspicuousness of black skin in racial impersonation was to eliminate or at least reduce it by darkening the exotic bodies portrayed on stage accordingly. Moreover, the Pacific setting capitalized on an imperial fantasy

30 All following quotes from the *Chicago Defender* are from the ProQuest Historical Newspapers Archive available at the Centre for Black Music Research in Chicago; I am deeply thankful to Gianpaolo Chiriacò for granting me access to this material.

31 'WPA Swing "Mikado" to Open Here July 4', *Chicago Defender* (1 July 1939).

32 See Lee, *The Japan of Pure Invention*, 100.

specific to the USA, who had already for decades pursued an aggressive policy in the Philippines and Samoa; yet it is not clear how much the *Swing Mikado* can be read as an African American attempt at partaking of this imperial effort. Stephanie Leigh Batiste, who actually supports this claim, must indeed acknowledge that 'little evidence exists of a specifically African American interest in a political and social imperial relationship to the identities performed in the production'.[33] It could be presumed that there was no authoritative investment in the authenticity of the exotic setting in the *Swing Mikado* as there was for the Gilbert and Sullivan original: on the contrary, what can be found here is a mash-up between two specifically USA types of exoticism, black American swing and the South Sea which stood for a vaguely orientalized landscape.

From accounts of the time it is evident that, although costumes and staging included canoes and sarongs, both the score and the stage action were shaped not to mimic South Pacific ethnicities or cultural practices, but to accommodate staple black performance tropes in the otherwise respectable entertainment offered by British comic opera. This emerges for example from the praise received by Herman Greene's 'hilarious, *Harlemesque* portrait of the Lord High Executioner',[34] who played Ko-Ko 'as Bert Williams might have'.[35] Bert Williams had been the first interpreter and producer of an all-black musical on Broadway, the 1903 hit *In Dahomey*, and this reference clearly motions to this crucial artist's project for a respectable black theatre, of which the *Swing Mikado* was perceived as an epigone.[36]

The aspiration to respectable, high-class entertainment that was embedded in Gilbert and Sullivan's operas can be found here intact, and was recognized by the official representatives of the artistic duo, the Gilbert

33 Stephanie Leigh Batiste, *Darkening Mirrors: Imperial Representation in Depression-Era African American Performance* (Durham, NC: Duke University Press, 2011), 117.

34 'WPA Swing 'Mikado' to Open Here July 4', *Chicago Defender* (1 July 1939); my italics.

35 Geoffrey Parsons, Jr., 'Six Times Eyewitness of *The Mikado*', *New York Herald Tribune* (27 February 1939); quoted in Lee, *The Japan of Pure Invention*, 111.

36 See Camille F. Forbes, *Introducing Bert Williams: Burnt Cork, Broadway, and the Story of America's First Black Star* (New York: Basic Civitas, 2008), 100ff.

and Sullivan Society of the USA, who formally endorsed the production in April 1939 with the motivation that 'the Federal Theatre project did not destroy the beauty and spirit of *The Mikado* by over-emphasizing the swing aspects of its production'.[37] On a different note, when a second swing Mikado opened in March 1939, worries were voiced as of its being up to the standards of its predecessor, and especially as to whether the singers would manage to meet the requirement of the operatic score. Criticism on this second show implicitly underlines what were considered the assets of the Federal Theatre production: the two main interpreters, Billy Mitchell (Ko-Ko) and Leroy 'Sparkplug' George (the Mikado) 'are of the old school of comedians [...] [j]ust whether they will be able to learn the script and speak the parts is problematical', while the voice of Mable Sanford Lewis (Katisha) 'does not appear to meet the requirement of the operatic score'.[38] Reviews after the opening were even harsher, defining the show 'in Georgia minstrel fashion', which 'turned the opera into slapstick comedy'.[39]

The question was not whether the performers could offer an authentic representation of the 'cellophane' South Sea locale, but whether they were able to perform operatic music – even when swingin' it. The dismissive mention of the 'Georgia minstrel fashion' highlights how the *Swing Mikado* was conceived by the African American community as a showcase for black talents and one step up the ladder of social and artistic respectability. In an article aptly titled 'Swing Mikado: an Opportunity' a *Chicago Defender* commentator stated: 'America, you have an opportunity to wake up, open your eyes and realize that black people are efficient in scores of fields, commercial, professional and otherwise, and if men can be discovered with guts to stand by the ideals of equal opportunity for all, there will be a new baptism of prosperity unlike anything ever known in the land. The time is now'.[40] While the British production was based on presenting an authentic

37 'The "Swing Mikado" Production Witnessed by over $39,000 patrons', *Chicago Defender* (15 April 1939).

38 'New "Swing Mikado" Comic Opera Will Make Debut in Chicago, Then Travel', *Chicago Defender* (18 March 1039).

39 'Comedians Spoil "Mikado in Swing"', *Chicago Defender* (8 April 1939).

40 '"Swing Mikado": An Opportunity', *Chicago Defender* (4 March 1939).

vision of Japan, these African American *Mikados* relinquish any attempt at claiming the authenticity of their racial performances as symbolic and cultural capital. There is no authoritative investment in the exotic setting here as there was in the Gilbert and Sullivan original: on the contrary, the South Sea locale features here as a safe space for black skins to inhabit what the *Defender* still defines 'an operatic score'. Through the exotic body of *The Mikado*, African American performers could perform that specifically USA type of exoticism that was black minstrelsy and intersect it with the respectable entertainment of opera.

Exotic Victoriana in Australia

The re-elaboration of the original work by the African American troupes of the *Swing Mikado* was made possible by the United States' own anti-imperialistic policy *vis-à-vis* the former motherland. In what can be easily read as a revanchist move against Britain's supposed cultural superiority, USA federal law refused to recognize British copyright laws, which granted the D'Oyly Carte company exclusive rights over any production of the Savoy operas. Production rights did not only limit to royalties in case of staging, and the company also expected the original staging was reproduced in every respect, i.e., that the exotic body of *The Mikado* was presented as Gilbert had originally intended it: 'for nearly one hundred years of performing *The Mikado*, the D'Oyly Carte style defined an authoritative Japaneseness whose appearance was defined by elaborate latex headpieces and wigs, heavy eye make-up, and spectacular costumes, and whose gestural vocabulary included mincing steps, fluttering fans, and exaggerated bowing'.[41]

Of course there were plenty of bootleg productions which sometimes even rewrote the original material to some extent, as the *Swing Mikado* and its followers show; yet it was only in 1982, after the company was disbanded,

41 Lee, *The Japan of Pure Invention*, 67.

that *The Mikado* was open to new stagings on British territory. The relevance of this work to twentieth-century Britain is witnessed by the fact that it took less than a year for a new, updated version of the Gilbert and Sullivan classic to appear on stage; in 1983, a new production directed by Christopher Renshaw, with sets and costumes by Tim Goodchild, created a new standard to which the 2004 Australian staging is clearly indebted, as shown by the recurrence of Goodchild as designer. Other versions proliferated, among which a *Hot Mikado* opening in Washington in 1986, with new lyrics by David Bell and arrangements by Rob Bowman. This production, preceded by a 1975 British *Black Mikado*, represented an explicit homage to its early twentieth-century forefathers, with the setting moved to 1940s American nightclub and the characters clothed in zoot suits.[42]

The *Hot Mikado* choice sees the emergence of another element in this polymorphous exotic body – the past, a 'foreign country', as L.P. Hartley famously had it, where things are done differently. And Victorian Britain, more than a timeless and stereotyped Japan, is the 'queer and quaint' Other of contemporary productions, as happens for example in the 1987 TV movie directed by John Michael Phillips, where all reference to Japan disappears and characters move in an three-dimensional European *fin de siècle* setting.[43] The Victorians also become the epitome of the exotic in current productions of *The Mikado* which take the cue from Renshaw's seminal attempt to confront Gilbert and Sullivan's problematic permanence in contemporary repertoires. The most recent among them, the Opera Australia production, has been filmed for a 2011 DVD, and this new form guarantees for its virality. Part of a series of Gilbert and Sullivan's operas made available on DVD – among which a *Pirates of Penzance* whose staging echoes the notorious Disney's *Pirates of the Caribbean* franchise, with the Pirate King becoming a Jack Sparrow lookalike – this production represents the

42 Ian C. Bradley, *Oh Joy! Oh Rapture! The Enduring Phenomenon of Gilbert and Sullivan* (Oxford: Oxford University Press, 2005), 169. A follow-up of this production is available on record: *Hot Mikado: Original Cast Recording* (Exallshow Ltd, 1995).

43 *The Mikado*, directed by John Michael Phillips, with Eric Idle and Richard Angas (Thames Television, 1987).

impermanent end of the many incarnations of *The Mikado*'s exotic body, emerging in yet another former British colonial context.

In this production, the Japanese exotic is not dispensed with, but reshaped to signifying a temporal more than a spatial otherness. The scene still is packed with Japanese paraphernalia, often oversized or misused; indeed, the production quite literally summons the aforementioned market of imported objects from Japan such as fans, pots, lacquered vases, screens and the like, the very market *The Mikado* both sustained and fed upon. What makes this production intriguing, however, is its displacement of the codes of exoticism, as Japanese objects also feature as British Victoriana: not only the two coexist, but the Victorian and Japanese exotic are so intertwined as to become practically indistinguishable. For example, the oversized teapot Pitti-Sing handles at the end of Act I works both as a reference to Japanese pottery – a typical element of *japonaiserie* – and to the British tradition of tea time; in the opening scene, Japanese courtiers in bowler hats read *The Times* off Japanese fans, use ties as belts for their kimonos, and their faces sport Victorian sideburns on the white make-up that traditionally represents East Asian ethnicity in Western theatre. The same make-up is used for the Mikado, yet the stripes of colour shaping his facial features are oddly remindful of another British imperial icon – the Union Jack, with diminished crown and ermine-lined, kimono-shaped royal cape to match.

Seen from the distant shores of an Australia still dealing with its colonial past (and present), the Victorian body, with its pseudo-Japanese costumes, becomes the exotic spectacle; against this backdrop humour can be directed to local and contemporary public figures and stereotypes, much as in the original piece. This happens in the rendition of the 'little list' number, in which Mitchell Butel, who plays Ko-Ko, has taken up the recent tradition of rewriting the list for contemporary audiences.[44] This practice has an important antecedent in Thomas Allan singing a partially

44 This version, including the updated lyrics, is available on the Opera Australia Youtube channel at <https://www.youtube.com/watch?v=1NLV24qTnlg> accessed 8 May 2015;

amended version of the list at the 2004 Night at the Proms.[45] Butel reprises some of the lines from Allan's version, such as 'purists who insist piano music stops at Brahms', but rewrites most of the lyrics to focus on topical references to Australian public personas such as 'the politician prancing round in speedos tightly packed' (Tony Abbot, who would be elected President in 2013), or 'Canberra's leading red-head who's afraid of sticky beaks' (Julia Gillard, elected in 2010 the first woman Prime Minister of the country and still in office at the time of the performance). The original 'banjo serenader', Gilbert and Sullivan's competitors on the Victorian entertainment market, disappears to give way to another lowly esteemed form of musical entertainment, 'Australian Idol singers who pathetically persist' – with appropriate melismas on the last syllable.

Here a familiar body – Butel's, himself a well-known cabaret artist – surfaces under the British-Japanese patchwork that makes up the exotic body of this Australian *Mikado*. In this explicitly anti-realistic take, where a pseudo-Japanese Victorian complains about 'the merchant banker wankers and the bonuses they flout', exoticism comes back devoid of its power as a cultural device for the orientalization of foreign peoples and cultures, to be implemented as a self-reflective tool to elaborate – and, to an extent, disavow – the relationship between the rhetoric of imperial Britain and the controversial identity-making process of Australia as a Commonwealth nation.[46] This shift in the location of the exotic body exposes its impermanence and subjection to the specific temporal conditions of performance, but also its permanence in the English-speaking imaginary as a place of negotiation for cultural identities.

45 See 'Thomas Allen Sings "I've got a little list" from *The Mikado* – Last Night of the Proms 2004' <https://www.youtube.com/watch?v=WlOboXMxt84> accessed 7 May 2015.

46 For an in-depth discussion of Australian cultural politics and racial constructions see Katherine E. Russo, *Practices of Proximity: The Appropriation of English in Australian Indigenous Literature* (Newcastle: Cambridge Scholars Publishing, 2010).

Bibliography

Batiste, Stephanie Leigh, *Darkening Mirrors: Imperial Representation in Depression-Era African American Performance* (Durham, NC: Duke University Press, 2011).

Beckerman, Michael, 'The Sword on the Wall: Japanese Elements and Their Significance in *The Mikado*', *The Musical Quarterly* 73/3 (1989), 303–19.

Bradley, Ian C., *Oh Joy! Oh Rapture! The Enduring Phenomenon of Gilbert and Sullivan* (Oxford: Oxford University Press, 2005).

'Comedians Spoil "Mikado in Swing"', *Chicago Defender* (8 April 1939).

Cook, Nicholas, 'Music as Performance', in Martin Clayton, Trevor Herbert and Richard Middleton, eds, *The Cultural Study of Music: A Critical Introduction* (New York and London: Routledge, 2002), 204–14.

Forbes, Camille F., *Introducing Bert Williams: Burnt Cork, Broadway, and the Story of America's First Black Star* (New York: Basic Civitas, 2008).

Fraden, Rena, *Blueprints for a Black Federal Theatre* (Cambridge: Cambridge University Press, 1996).

Gilbert, William Schwenk, 'The Mikado or The Town of Titipu', in Ian Bradley, ed., *The Complete Annotated Gilbert and Sullivan* (Oxford: Oxford University Press, 2001).

Hot Mikado: Original Cast Recording (Exallshow Ltd, 1995).

Knapp, Raymond, *The American Musical and the Formation of National Identity* (Princeton, N.J.: Princeton University Press, 2005).

de Lauretis, Teresa, 'Popular Culture, Public and Private Fantasies: Femininity and Fetishism in David Cronenberg's *M. Butterfly*', *Signs: Journal of Women in Culture and Society* 24/2 (1999), 303–34.

Lee, Josephine, *The Japan of Pure Invention: Gilbert and Sullivan's* The Mikado (Minneapolis and London: University of Minnesota Press, 2010).

Lindenberger, Herbert, *Opera in History: From Monteverdi to Cage* (Stanford, California: Stanford University Press, 1998).

Lipsitz, George, *The Possessive Investment in Whiteness: How White People Profit from Identity Politics* (Philadelphia: Temple University Press).

McClary, Susan, *Georges Bizet: Carmen* (Cambridge: Cambridge University Press, 1992)

McClintock, Anne, 'Soft-Soaping the Empire: Commodity Racism and Imperial Advertising', in *Imperial Leather: Race, Gender, and Sexuality in the Colonial Contest* (London: Routledge, 1995), 506–17.

The Mikado (dir. John Michael Phillips, Thames Television 1987).

The Mikado (dir. Stuart Maunder, Opera Australia 2011).

Mostow, Joshua S., 'Iron Butterfly: Cio-cio-san and Japanese Imperialism', in Jonathan Wisenthal, Sherrill E. Grace, e Melinda Boyd, eds, *A Vision of the Orient: Texts, Intertexts, and Contexts of Madame Butterfly* (Toronto: University of Toronto Press, 2006), 181–95.

'New "Swing Mikado" Comic Opera Will Make Debut in Chicago, Then Travel', *Chicago Defender* (18 March 1039).

van Rij, Jan *Madame Butterfly: Japonisme, Puccini, and the Search for the Real Cho-Cho-San* (Berkeley: Stone Bridge Press, 2001).

Russo, Katherine E., *Practices of Proximity: The Appropriation of English in Australian Indigenous Literature* (Cambridge Scholars Publishing, 2010).

Said, Edward W., *Orientalism* (London: Penguin [1978] 1985).

'"Swing Mikado": an Opportunity', *Chicago Defender* (4 March 1939).

'The "Swing Mikado" Production Witnessed by over $39,000 patrons', *Chicago Defender* (15 April 1939).

Taylor, Millie, *Musical Theatre, Realism and Entertainment* (Farnham: Ashgate 2012).

Wilde, Oscar, 'The Decay of Lying', in *The Decay of Lying and Other Essays* (London: Penguin, 2010), 1–38.

Williams, Carolyn, *Gilbert and Sullivan: Gender, Genre, Parody* (New York and Chirchester: Columbia University Press, 2011).

'WPA Swing 'Mikado' to Open Here July 4', *Chicago Defender* (1 July 1939).

SOPHIE DUNCAN

A Progressive *Othello*: Modern Blackness in Chakrabarti's *Red Velvet* (2012)

ABSTRACT

This essay examines Lolita Chakrabarti's *Red Velvet* (2012), a theatrical biopic of Ira Aldridge (1807–1867), centring on his 1833 *Othello*. Combining close reading with reviews and evidence from the rehearsal room, I argue that Chakrabarti's speculative restaging of Aldridge's *Othello* associates nineteenth-century blackness not merely with the 'exotic', but also emphatically with the modern and progressive. This appears most clearly through *Red Velvet*'s metatheatrical exploration of embodied performance and the evolution of acting. Potentially ahistorically, Aldridge is presented as both Victorian (and thus stylistically 'exotic' and distant from today's audiences) and as innovatively modern. It also manifests in the cognitive consequences of Adrian Lester's casting as Aldridge. In 2012, Lester was simultaneously a celebrity and classical actor: an alumnus of the RSC, Peter Brook and Cheek by Jowl, he remained best-known for seven series of primetime BBC drama *Hustle*. Lester was also poised to play *Othello* in a high-profile, overtly modern National Theatre production, resituated in a contemporary overseas military operation (suggestive of Afghanistan). Finally, *Red Velvet* aligns Aldridge with multiple progressive figures marginalized by their radical identities and networks: racial, sexual, republican and international. The essay also considers Chakrabarti's selection of historical material. The historical Aldridge was simultaneously self-exoticizing and assimilative, his self-promotional strategies including the stage name 'Keene' (homonymic for 'Kean'), the creation of a highly sexualized, fetishistic aesthetic of skin colour in later *Othellos*, whiteface, and an extensive 'Jim Crow' repertory. Chakrabarti's deployment of source material on Aldridge's career de-emphasizes the racially uncomfortable aspects of his self-fashioning, emphasizing instead a binary of London racism vs. continental European acclaim. The result is a progressive history of Aldridge, enabling twenty-first-century theatre to comfortably revisit exoticized, and self-exoticizing nineteenth-century bodies.

***

On 25 March 1833, the white actor Edmund Kean collapsed on stage at Covent Garden, while playing Othello to his son Charles's Iago. Historical lore records Kean's final words as 'I am dying – speak to them for me', described by Richard W. Schoch as 'the theatrical equivalent of the rule of primogeniture'.[1] Nevertheless, French theatre manager Pierre Laporte took an apparently colossal risk. Edmund Kean's replacement was African-American Ira Aldridge, the first black actor to play Othello in London. The production reopened on 10 April 1833, as Parliament debated abolishing slavery in the British colonies.[2] Aldridge gave two performances, the second on 12 April. Then the production closed.[3]

On 11 October 2012, Lolita Chakrabarti's play *Red Velvet* opened at the Tricycle Theatre, London, with the British Adrian Lester as Aldridge.[4] The play illuminates the racist backlash against Aldridge's Covent Garden Othello, recalled in flashback by an acclaimed, embittered Ira, touring Poland.[5] Halina, a young journalist, asks Ira why he only appeared once at Covent Garden and once at London's Lyceum. Ira emphasizes his successes in 'Cologne, Vienna, Dresden, Leipzig, St Petersberg, Moscow, Berlin, Prague', describing London as 'a limited pocket of work'. Halina, meanwhile, calls London as 'the peak' for actors.[6] The play establishes a binary of early London censure vs. European acclaim. Works before *Red Velvet* had sought to counter Aldridge's obscurity: in 1958, Herbert Marshall and Mildred Stock's landmark biography attacked the 'systematic exclusion of Ira Aldridge from the works of theatre historians'.[7] In 2012, *Red Velvet*'s director identified Aldridge as a 'role model', hoping 'young people [would] see the play and go, "Wow, if he can do it [...]"'.[8] Subsequently, it

1 Barry Cornwall, *The Life of Edmund Kean* (London: E. Moxon, 1835), II.241. Richard W. Schoch, *Performing History in the Theatre of Charles Kean* (Cambridge: 1996), 23.

2 Hazel Waters, *Racism on the Victorian Stage* (Cambridge: Cambridge University Press, 2007), 72.

3 Waters, *Racism on the Victorian Stage*, 75.

4 Lolita Chakrabarti, *Red Velvet* (London: Bloomsbury, 2014), vi.

5 In this article, I distinguish between the historical Ira Aldridge as 'Aldridge', and Chakrabarti's character as 'Ira'.

6 Chakrabarti, *Red Velvet*, 18–20.

7 Herbert Marshall and Mildred Stock, *Ira Aldridge: The Negro Tragedian* (Washington, DC: Howard University Press, 1958), 7.

8 Kate Kellaway, 'Adrian Lester on Ira Aldridge', *Observer* (7 October 2012) <http://www.theguardian.com/stage/2012/oct/07/red-velvet-tricycle-lester-chakrabarti-rubasingham-interview> accessed 12 March 2015.

was reported that Aldridge would be included on the curricula of drama schools including the Central School of Speech and Drama.[9] The 2012 production of *Red Velvet* received extensive press coverage and multiple awards. It was revived in 2014 before a well-received transfer to the St Ann's Warehouse in Brooklyn.[10]

Chakrabarti's dramatization of the critical backlash against Ira's *Othello* presents three central objections: an aversion to Ira's physical contact with Ellen Tree, the young white actress cast as Desdemona; the cultural belief that a black man lacked the intelligence to personate such a noble, complex character as Shakespeare's Othello; and Ira's perceived inability to speaks the lines, rooted in a predictably reductive, racist view of African physiognomy. A scene set on the morning of 11 April 1833 depicts the cast reading newspaper reviews that Laporte attempts to conceal from them. Publication titles are spoken aloud or given in stage directions.[11] Ira is described scornfully as 'Mr Henry Wallack's black servant', mockingly as 'Othello forsooth!!!' and accused of subjecting 'an interesting actress and a decent girl like Miss Ellen Tree to the indignity of being pawed about'.[12] Finally, most appallingly for theatre audiences, the *Times*'s review calls Ira a 'genuine nigger', claiming 'owing to the shape of his lips it is utterly impossible for him to pronounce English in a manner to satisfy even the unfastidious ears of the gallery'.[13]

Red Velvet's reviewers most frequently reproduced this last quotation, conveniently and viscerally conveying Aldridge's reception's

9 Geoff Colman, speaking at 'Red Velvet Salon', *Bloomsbury Institute* (28 January 2013).

10 Awards included Best Actor for Adrian Lester (Critics' Circle, 2012); Most Promising Playwright for Lolita Chakrabarti (Evening Standard Award *and* Critics' Circle, 2012). Further nominations included the Olivier Awards (2013) and Whatsonstage London Newcomer of the Year and Best New Play (2012). Samuel French, '*Red Velvet* Lolita Chakrabarti', *SamuelFrench.com* (2015) <http://www.samuelfrench.com/p/44465/red-velvet> accessed 12 March 2015.

11 Chakrabarti, *Red Velvet*, 75–7.

12 Chakrabarti, *Red Velvet*, 76.

13 Chakrabarti, *Red Velvet*, 79.

nastiest aspects.[14] It was also included in the Tricycle's online resource pack, as an unattributed quotation beneath the heading 'Reviews of Ira's first performance'.[15] Nevertheless, uniquely among the reviews read aloud in *Red Velvet*, this quotation is not an authentic review of Aldridge's *Othello*. It comes from the *Times*'s 1825 review of Aldridge's Oroonoko in *The Revolt of Surinam* at the Coburg.[16] Bernth Lindfors discusses the *Times's* review of Oroonoko in his 2011 biography, noting that although it was *Surinam*'s 'only overtly negative' review, syndication in the *Evening Mail* and *Evening Chronicle* magnified its impact.[17] Texts before *Red Velvet* also transposed the *Times*'s attack from *Oronooko* to *Othello*. In 2003, the *Guardian* described how 'the pro-slavery lobby had closed [Aldridge's] production, and the *Times*'s critic had written: 'Owing to the shape of his lips it is utterly impossible for him to pronounce English'. This article also dated *Othello* to 1825, the year of *Surinam*.[18]

14 Major print publications reprinted the quotation explicitly as a review of Aldridge's *Othello*, including the *Financial Times*, the *Spectator*, the *Telegraph* (for the revival). Others reprinted the comment but were vague about when it had been applied to Aldrige. See: Griselda Murray Brown, 'Dramatic Differences', *Financial Times* (12 October 2012) <http://www.ft.com/cms/s/2/d68e51cc-11fa-11e2-b9fd-00144feabdc0.html> accessed 12 March 2015. Lloyd Evans, 'Racial Tensions', *Spectator* (27 October 2012) <http://www.spectator.co.uk/arts/theatre/8707341/racial-tensions/> accessed 12 March 2015. Tim Walker, 'Red Velvet, Tricycle Theatre, review', *Telegraph* (1 February 2014) <http://www.telegraph.co.uk/culture/theatre/theatre-reviews/10609578/Red-Velvet-Tricycle-Theatre-review.html> accessed 12 March 2015.

15 Anna Myers, '*Red Velvet* Resource Pack' (Powerpoint presentation) Tricycle Theatre (2 October 2012) <http://www.tricycle.co.uk/wp-content/uploads/2012/10/Red-Velvet-Resources.pptx> accessed 12 March 2015.

16 Anon., 'The Coburg Theatre', *Times* (11 October 1825), 2. Newspaper articles are anonymous, unless otherwise stated.

17 Bernth Lindfors, *Ira Aldridge: The Early Years 1807–1833* (Rochester, NY: University of Rochester Press, 2011), 83.

18 Samantha Ellis, 'Paul Robeson in Othello, Savoy Theatre, 1930', *Guardian* (3 September 2003), <http://www.theguardian.com/stage/2003/sep/03/theatre> accessed 12 March 2015.

As an act of imaginative and theatrical life-writing, Chakrabarti's decision to transpose the *Times*'s review is legitimate: it is, after all, a genuine and deeply racist *Times* review, attacking Aldridge as tragedian. Thomas Southerne's 1695 adaptation of Aphra Behn's *Oronooko* (1688) had been the most popular British play throughout the eighteenth century. *The Revolt of Surinam* was a melodramatic adaptation from Southerne, starring – like *Othello* – a noble black hero whose love for a white woman leads to her murder and his suicide. Although the *Times* review in *Red Velvet* is not authentic to 1833, *Figaro in London* was equally vicious, calling Aldridge 'that miserable nigger' who 'dishonoured' the stage.[19] This article is not concerned with the validity of Chakrabarti's authorial action, but with examining the effect of critical readings of the moment as factually accurate, even verbatim historical theatre.[20] Chakrabarti's selective, dexterous redeployment of historical material supports an imaginative project of restaging Ira Aldridge for a twenty-first century audience. Placing one review's transposition in the context of wider documentary evidence for Aldridge's 1833 reception illuminates Chakrabarti's depiction of Ira's exoticism, racial oppression and modernity on the nineteenth-century London stage. Chakrabarti's adaptation and speculative restaging of Aldridge's *Othello* associates nineteenth-century blackness not merely with the 'exotic' but also emphatically with the modern, progressive and intersectional. Reassessing Aldridge's simultaneously assimilationist and self-exoticizing performance strategies has consequences for *Red Velvet*'s revisionist text. Notably, Chakrabarti's deployment of source material on Ira's career beyond *Othello* de-emphasizes the racially uncomfortable aspects of his self-fashioning, including roles as Mungo in Isaac Bickerstaffe's *The Padlock*, and an extensive 'Jim Crow' repertory.

19 *Figaro in London* (6 April 1833), 56.

20 The production's venue reinforced this association. From 1994–2007, under artistic director Nicholas Kent, the Tricycle specialized in 'tribunal plays', verbatim theatre depicting real-life public inquiries. These documentary plays included *The Stephen Lawrence Inquiry – The Colour of Justice* (1999), *Guantanamo: Honor Bound to Defend Freedom* (2004) and *Bloody Sunday: Scenes from the Saville Inquiry* (2005).

Scene Five of *Red Velvet* includes only extremely negative *Othello* reviews. Bernth Lindfors similarly delineates massed opposition: the *Times*, *Sun*, *Bell's Weekly Messenger* (syndicated by the *Morning Herald*), *Weekly Dispatch*, *Old England*, *New Court Journal* and *Athenaeum* agreed with *Figaro in London* that Aldridge's performance was both specifically bad and culturally unacceptable.[21] Their complaints included the 'pawing' *Red Velvet* quotes, and racialized objections to Aldridge's physiognomy: his 'feet and hands disproportionately large [...] lips protruding, and chin underhung.'[22] His emotional legibility was condemned. The *English Chronicle*'s review, syndicated in *Morning Herald* and *Bell's Weekly Messenger* (giving their critic disproportionate impact) noted that the 'conformation of the lower portion of the negro face [...] prevents all Africans from [...] delineating, at least to an European audience, the changes produced on the countenance by the different transitions of feeling and passion.'[23]

The *Red Velvet* verdict echoes Bernth Lindfors, who despite acknowledging that a handful of publications identified innovative new effects, or were mixed or at least not overtly racist in their criticism, still concludes that 'the critics savaged him.'[24] However, the fuller range of reviews made available through electronic archives indicate considerable support for Aldridge's performance, and the production. The *Age* praised 'a very clever piece of acting [...] he put forth some beauties [...] his reception was of the most flattering description', and asserted that the management should let him continue.[25] *The Ladies' Cabinet*, an upper-middle-class and relatively conservative journal, syndicated the *Literary Gazette*'s review, which identified 'a great deal of merit' in Aldridge, whose only fault was 'tameness.'[26] The *Theatrical Observer* similarly thought Aldridge's professional achievement 'highly to his credit.'[27] The *Guardian* identified 'parts of the performance

21 Lindfors, *Ira Aldridge*, 154–6.
22 *Town Journal* (14 April 1833), 118.
23 *Bell's Weekly Messenger* (14 April 1833), 116.
24 Lindfors, *Ira Aldridge*, 5.
25 'Theatres', *Age* (14 April 1833), 118.
26 'Covent Garden', *Literary Gazette* (13 April 1833), 236.
27 'Covent Garden Theatre', *Theatrical Observer* (13 April 1833), 1.

[...] in which he was not exceeded by any actor [...] with the single exception of Kean'.[28] The initially wary *Standard* expressed 'unqualified delight' in Aldridge's second performance, noting audience reactions akin to 'awe'.[29] The *Morning Chronicle*, initially deeming Aldridge a mere novelty, cast and applauded solely because of his race, ultimately commended his achievement in gaining the role, his 'absence of rant and violence', said he 'deserved much praise', wished him every success, and identified 'improved effect' in his second performance.[30] One controversy surrounded Aldridge's behaviour at the curtain call. By the *fin-de-siecle*, 'coming forward' was customary, but in the 1830s, it was strictly provincial behaviour.[31] The *Morning Chronicle* called Aldridge's curtain address 'a flummery got-by-heart speech', the evening's 'worst' aspect, but by 13 April, both the *Chronicle* and *Globe and Traveller* noted approvingly that Aldridge had adapted sufficiently to 'declin[e] coming forward'.[32] This wasn't a racialized criticism of a black performer entering white theatre, but of a successful provincial performer inappropriately repeating a popular regional performance strategy in the metropolis.

History and *Red Velvet* diverge most dramatically regarding Aldridge's violence. Aldridge's later Othellos were brutal. Madge Kendal, Aldridge's Desdemona at his final London *Othello* (1865) recalled being dragged round the stage by her hair in the murder scene, to the audience's 'vociferous' hissing.[33] In *Red Velvet*, Ira's performance style, 'simmering with impending violence', leaves Ellen Tree 'winc[ing]', in a sequence Bernard Warde describe as 'awfully rough'.[34] Ira's 'very real' anger and aggression prompt

28 'Theatrical Chit-Chat', *Guardian and the Observer* (14 April 1833), 4.

29 *Standard* (14 April 1833), quoted in Anon., *Memoir and Theatrical Career of Ira Aldridge*, 12.

30 Ibid; 'Covent Garden Theatre', *Morning Chronicle* (13 April 1833), 3.

31 Lindfors, *Ira Aldridge*, I.159.

32 'Covent-Garden Theatre', *Morning Chronicle* (11 April 1833), 2; 'Covent Garden Theatre', *Morning Chronicle* (13 April 1833), 3.

33 Madge Kendal, *By Herself*, 87.

34 Chakrabarti, *Red Velvet*, 58; 67; 76.

a jealous Charles Kean to call a doctor to examine Ellen's bruised arm.[35] Ira recognizes that racist stereotypes of black men as savage and violent underscore his dismissal by the theatre board: 'when Kean plays the Moor, we're amazed at how skilfully he descends into this base African tragedy but with me it seems I'm revealin' my true nature'.[36] Pierre confirms this, describing how 'your true nature surfaced and you descended –' and then, after Ira attacks him, saying, 'distraught', 'This is who you really are'.[37] In fact, Aldridge was twice criticized for passionless tameness: the *English Chronicle* missed Othello's 'sublime madness [...] that tornado of the breast' with 'destruction equally terrible and sudden', as did the *Theatrical Observer* which sought a 'deep and accumulating tide of passion'.[38]

I began this article by saying how Chakrabarti aligns Ira, through his blackness, with the modern and progressive. That alignment is manifested by Ira's distinctively intersectional attitudes to marginalized identities. An intersectional re-reading of Aldridge's 1833 reception is also useful along national, not merely racial lines.

Aversion to Aldridge wasn't based solely on his blackness, but on wider xenophobia about international performers in British theatre. One criticism of Aldridge's pronunciations reflects this: not because he was black, but because he was (according to misapprehension) Canadian! *Bell's Weekly Messenger* decided authoritatively that he had been 'born in Upper Canada, as may be distinctly gathered from his pronunciation of the letter *a*, to which he gives the broad French sound of *ar*'.[39] Another problem was the perception that Aldridge was Frenchman Pierre Laporte's protégé. Chakrabarti exaggerates their bond – *Red Velvet*'s Ira and Pierre have been 'Brothers in arms' for 'nine years' – but the association was unhelpful.[40] *Figaro in London* despised Laporte, decrying the 'disgrace' that a 'grasping foreigner'

35 Chakrabarti, *Red Velvet*, 72; 88.
36 Chakrabarti, *Red Velvet*, 90.
37 Chakrabarti, *Red Velvet*, 93.
38 *English Chronicle* (11 April 1833), 4; *Theatrical Observer* (11 April 1833), 1, quoted Lindfors, *Ira Aldridge*, 154.
39 Untitled item, *Bell's Weekly Messenger* (14 April 1833), 116.
40 Chakrabarti, *Red Velvet*, 92; 55.

was lessee of a national theatre previously run by the Kembles.[41] Laporte didn't long survive Aldridge at Covent Garden, resuming management of the Haymarket until his 1841 death.[42]

Classism also contributed. *Athenaeum*'s claim, quoted in *Red Velvet*, that Aldridge was 'Mr Henry Wallack's black servant' was indicative.[43] Aldridge's performance was criticized along class as well as racial lines, with *Morning Chronicle* attributing pronunciations 'unknown in good society' to Aldridge's 'humble station'.[44] However, supporters rejected this, with the *National Standard* demanding the origins of Kemble, 'the fiery and genius-gifted Kean' or 'half the performers on the stage'.[45] *Atlas* also noted that '*Othello* was a lower man than Mr Aldridge, seeing that he was "sold to slavery"'.[46] This classism was the element of Aldridge's reception to which he publicly responded, emphasizing to the *National Omnibus* that despite having 'the pleasure of Mr Wallack's friendship', he 'never was his servant, – *nor the servant of any man*', his 'respected father's circumstances' having been 'at all times too good to admit that any of his family should be placed in a state of servitude'.[47] The 1848 memoir also stressed that the boy Aldridge 'derived no pecuniary profit' from his work at the African Grove Theater, his sole, gentlemanly motivation being 'delight'.[48] Classist criticism would characterize condemnation of all nineteenth-century 'interlopers' into the acting profession: fifty years later, Lillie Langtry was condemned for lacking either theatrical antecedents or family equal to 'the old and stable nobility', unlike actresses from theatrical families.[49] Langtry was

41 'Theatricals', *Figaro in London* (11 August 1832), 144.

42 Jennifer Hall-Witt, *Fashionable Acts: Opera and Elite Culture in London, 1780–1880* (Lebanon, NH: UPNE, 2007), 294.

43 'Covent Garden', *Athenaeum* (13 April 1833), 235–6.

44 'Covent-Garden Theatre', *Morning Chronicle* (11 April 1833), 3.

45 *National Standard* (20 April 1833), 248.

46 *Atlas* (11 April 1833), 226, quoted Lindfors, *Ira Aldridge*, 158.

47 Letter from Ira Aldridge to the Editor, *National Omnibus* (17 May 1833), 60.

48 Anon. [James McCure Smith and Ira Aldridge], *Memoir* (London: Ohnwyn, 1850), 12.

49 'Who is Mrs Langtry?' *Town Talk* (30 August 1879), quoted in Laura Beatty, *Manners, Masks and Morals* (London: Chatto and Windus, 1999), 156.

subject to a 'professional determination to crush her if possible', against which *Theatre* argued that she had 'as much right as anyone' to act, no matter 'from what class they spring'.[50]

Critical response to Aldridge was heterogeneous, inflected by concerns beyond skin colour. In *Red Velvet*, Covent Garden's Board prefers to 'close the theatre rather than have [Ira] perform'.[51] In fact, the April 1833 influenza pandemic closed several major theatres. The supportive *National Omnibus* declared that 'it might as well be said that in consequence of Mr Aldridge's acting, that the Haymarket closed [...] and Drury Lane closed under similar circumstances'.[52] The 1833 pandemic 'swept Europe from East to West', proving 'much more lethal than its predecessor' in 1830–1.[53] 'Elsinore [...] Berlin and Constantinople' fell in March: England in April.[54] Morbidity in London was 80%, with 4,000 more deaths than normal.[55] Contemporary publications estimated a million cases: on the morning of 13 April (the day after Aldridge's second performance), Laporte received twelve sick notes from company members.[56] In fact, Covent Garden gave 'indisposition of several of the principal performers' as their reason for closing.[57]

Critics have asserted Covent Garden's supposedly disastrous impact on Aldridge's career. But a day after *Othello*'s cancellation, Aldridge was onstage in the same role at the Surrey Theatre, playing eleven nights over four weeks, including a benefit.[58] Manager Davidge included Aldridge's popular success at Covent Garden in the Surrey publicity materials (as Aldridge would for the rest of his life): hardly a famous disaster.[59] The

50 'Our Omnibus-Box', *Theatre* (November 1882), 307–14, 314.
51 Chakrabarti, *Red Velvet*, 92.
52 *National Omnibus* (26 April 1833), 138.
53 K. David Paterson, 'Pandemic and Epidemic Influenza, 1830–1848', *Social Science and Medicine* 21.5 (1985), 571–80; 574.
54 Ibid.
55 Paterson, 'Pandemic and Epidemic Influenza, 1830–1848', 574–5.
56 *National Omnibus* (26 April 1833), 37'; Lindfors, *Ira Aldridge*, 270.
57 'Covent Garden', *Times* (16 April 1833), 4.
58 Bernth Lindfors, *Ira Aldridge*, 274; 281.
59 Ibid.

Surrey was a minor theatre, but this was inevitable: Covent Garden and Drury Lane were shut. During the same period, Aldridge played *Othello* twice at the Pavilion, on 17 and 18 May, although Lindfors terms this a 'step down'.[60] From 11 June, Aldridge performed at the New City Theatre, which Lindfors calls 'as low as a London performer could sink'.[61] This wildly misrepresents its status. William Kidd's *New Guide to the 'Lions' of London*, published in 1832, noted the New City's high standards: 'it can boast of a very excellent company of performers; indeed, there is not any Theatre in London where the public is better catered for'. Kidd similarly identifies the Pavilion as 'very well attended' with 'very respectable' offerings.[62] Allardyce Nicoll identifies the New City Theatre as 'among the more respectable of the "minors"', with prestigious performers including 'Kean, Mrs Stirling and Webster' from 1831–6.[63] Far from exiled, Aldridge was thus in a tradition of celebrated guest stars. Crucially, the New City and the Surrey were both managed by George Bolwell Davidge, whom Kidd called 'a gentleman of a very enterprising spirit' (not unlike Laporte): enterprising enough to have given Aldridge his breakthrough role at the Coburg, while manager in 1826.[64] Like many performers, Aldridge's fortunes depended on those of supportive managers: if Davidge had still been at the Coburg in April 1833 (unfortunately he was supplanted too soon), presumably Aldridge would have followed him there. 1833 was a general time of uncertainty for managers, as well as actors. The Kemble family's three decades at Covent Garden had ended the previous autumn.[65] After Davidge failed at the Coburg in March 1833, Laporte was replaced by Alfred Bunn at Covent Garden in

60 Lindfors, *Ira Aldridge*, 281.

61 Lindfors, *Ira Aldridge*, 283.

62 William Kidd, *New Guide to the 'Lions' of London* (London: William Kidd, 1832), 22–3.

63 Allardyce Nicoll, *A History of Early Nineteenth Century Drama 1800–1850* (Cambridge: Cambridge University Press, 1930), 222.

64 Kidd, *Guide*, 22.

65 George Rowell, *The Old Vic Theatre* (Cambridge: Cambridge University Press 1993), 26.

May. Laporte then deposed Thomas Monck Mason at the Haymarket.[66] Bunn only lasted until 1835 at Covent Garden, and until 1839 at Drury Lane, losing his co-lessee Frederick Polhill in 1834: Drury Lane had six lessees between 1826 and 1833, most of whom left as bankrupts or in severe debt to the theatre's committee.[67] Aldridge's movements typify a general metropolitan upheaval. History complicates Kujawinska Courtney's statement that Aldridge 'was not recognized by the theatre establishment of the capital'.[68] Official recognition was belated: an Actors' Supper commemorating the Shakespearean tercentenary honoured Aldridge on 22 April 1864. Aldridge next performed a West End *Othello* in 1858 at the Lyceum, but received good reviews in other London theatres whenever he returned.[69] Soon after Covent Garden, Aldridge was a mourner at Edmund Kean's funeral, included in the thespians' procession following the coffin, perhaps in the group headed 'Members of Theatre-Royal, Covent-Garden'.[70] The impression in 1833 was not one of exile.

Chakrabarti's Ira is a modern exile, his blackness aligned with the progressive through his intersectional alliances. First defined by Kimberlé Crenshaw in 1989, intersectionality recognizes the interrelation of, and vertices between, different forms of social oppression, as individuals face prejudice and (perhaps) exert power on different fronts. For example,

66 Rowell, *The Old Vic Theatre*, 22.

67 Richard Elliston went bankrupt and Thomas Bish withdrew as lessee after a fortnight, both in 1826; Stephen Price was declared bankrupt in 1830; the 'broken down' Alexander Lee dissolved his partnership with Polthill in 1831; Polthill left in 1834 having lost £50,000 and owing £2,500 to the committee. F.H.W. Sheppard, ed., 'The Theatre Royal: Management', *Survey of London: Volume 35* (London: London County Council, 1970), 9–29 <http://www.british-history.ac.uk/survey-london/vol35/pp9-29> accessed 15 March 2015.

68 Krystyna Kujawinska Courtney, 'Mislike Me Not For My Complexion', Bożenna Chylińska, *Ideology and Rhetoric* (Cambridge: Cambridge Scholars, 2009), 53–70, 55.

69 'Theatres &c', *Era* (26 April 1857), 10.

70 'Edmund Kean', *Morning Chronicle* (27 April 1833), 3; 'Funeral of Mr Kean', *Morning Post* (27 May 1833), 3.

intersectional feminism demands white women attend also to racism.[71] *Red Velvet*'s Ira emerges as innately modern and intersectional: most obviously, through his egalitarian, 'avant-garde' and 'shocking' acting opposite Ellen, which she finds 'thrilling', recalling her 'exhilarating' experience as Fanny Kemble's cross-cast Romeo.[72] Ellen is one of a triumvirate of working, marginalized women with whom Ira is aligned. At the end of *Red Velvet*, Ira achieves rapport with Halina, the Polish reporter harassed and professionally sidelined as her office's 'only woman', confirming 'Yes, I know' when she describes her marginalization. In 1833, Ellen explicitly compares Ira's struggle to appear on white stages with the professional prejudice against Restoration actresses, declaring 'They said the same about women'.[73] Charles's answering injunction not to 'make this a crusade for every fringe cause' underscores the intersectionality of Ellen and Ira's alliance, versus Charles's blanket prejudice. Similarly, Ira is the only character to share significant dialogue with the African Caribbean maid Connie, asking after her 'people' and complimenting 'That Reverend Sharpe [...] extraordinary. My papa's a baptist preacher too'.[74] Both Halina and Connie are associated with anti-imperialist insubordination. The 'Prussian King and Russians' deny Halina's Polish identity, while Connie reveals her Jamaican origins only to Ira, after the white characters unthinkingly discuss a boycott of Jamaican sugar in front of her, without eliciting her contribution.[75] Equally, both women offer analogues for Ira: pursuing livelihoods in oppressive and racist marketplaces.

Ira is also the closest character to Pierre. Ira recalls a shared, politicized past of shouting 'Mutiny! Mutiny! Down with the old order!' with Pierre as 'the radical red cap son of the revolution'.[76] For Ira, Pierre's failure to support his acting constitutes 'helpin' the anti-abolitionists'; by implication,

71 See: Kimberlé Crenshaw, 'Demarginalizing the Intersection of Race and Sex', *University of Chicago Legal Forum* (1989), 137–64; Vivian M. May, *Pursuing Intersectionality* (New York: Routledge, 2015), 1–17.

72 Chakrabarti, *Red Velvet*, 62; 67; 71; 62.

73 Chakrabarti, *Red Velvet*, 69.

74 Chakrabarti, *Red Velvet*, 81.

75 Chakrabarti, *Red Velvet*, 16; 81.

76 Chakrabarti, *Red Velvet*, 90.

Pierre's reluctance to match Ira's artistic and political innovation reflects Pierre's inability to accept his own homosexuality.[77] The script strongly implies this. Ira compares contemporary rumours about himself and Ellen with an unmentionable scandal in the 'very dapper' Pierre's past, concerning another man: 'Everything looks bad from a certain angle, Pierre. [...] Paris looks real bad [...] It's your word against his'.[78] Pierre speaks indignantly of having had to 'work twice as hard because of what? – gossip, accusations', and rejects Ira's pseudo-flirtatious banter, answering 'Don't, not now', to Ira's joking, 'You've met someone else?'.[79] The 'now' implies such innuendo has been customary: something Charles further implies by accusing Laporte of 'indulging his old ways' through casting Ira.[80] The historical Laporte was married, his wife dying weeks before Aldridge's *Othello*.[81]

Crucially, Chakrabarti's language aligns the gay Frenchman's struggle with that of the African American. In their final confrontation, Ira asserts 'I've given everything to get here. I have pushed and fought and played my way in'. Pierre's final substantial speech echoes this: 'I've earned my place. It's taken me years to get here. I won this role and then I invited you in'. The men's styles overlap, in the repetition of 'get here', and in the conflicting theatrical claims: 'I [...] played my way in' vs. 'I won this role'.[82] Neither achieves victory – Pierre's theatre goes dark, and Ira is unemployed. Pierre's statement reflects solidarity's necessity across different axes of oppression in *Red Velvet*: Ira can only play *Othello* with Pierre's support, when he is 'invited [...] in'. The alternative is isolation in Lodz. Through Halina, Ellen, Connie and Pierre, *Red Velvet* aligns Ira with characters marginalized by their radical identities: racial, sexual, gendered, professional, republican and international. Accordingly, it upholds Kujawinska Courtney's 2009 assertion that British and American historians too readily view Aldridge as a perfect example of 'the Strange [...] the Other', emphasizing how at odds

77 Chakrabarti, *Red Velvet*, 92.

78 Chakrabarti, *Red Velvet*, 91.

79 Chakrabarti, *Red Velvet*, 93; 85.

80 Chakrabarti, *Red Velvet*, 53.

81 'Deaths: London and its Vicinity', *Gentleman's Magazine* (March 1833), 283–4, 284.

82 Chakrabarti, *Red Velvet*, 90; 93.

he is with the nineteenth century's socio-political landscape.[83] Theatrically, however, thus historicizing Ira makes him familiar, 'one of us': ahead of his time, recognizably modern.

Red Velvet's 2012 casting of Adrian Lester as Ira reinforces the character's alignment with progressive modernity. In 2012, Lester's best known theatre work was a ground-breaking Rosalind for Cheek by Jowl (now a queer Shakespearean icon) and a dreadlocked, modern-dress Hamlet for Peter Brook. Dwarfing even those innovative performances was his TV and film work: most notably as Mickey Stone in the glossy contemporary heist series *Hustle*. The Tricycle announced Lester's casting in *Red Velvet* in June 2012.[84] Six months earlier, the National Theatre had announced that Lester would play Othello for them in spring 2013.[85] *Red Velvet*'s first audiences thus knew Lester would play the role Ira Aldridge played. Journalists frequently included anticipatory discussions of Lester's National Othello in their reviews of his performance of Ira's version of the part. Marvin Carlson calls this process 'ghosting': an actor's performance in a role, especially a canonical role, is haunted or 'ghosted' by the accrued meanings and memories of his past roles and celebrity persona, of past interpretations of a canonical character.[86] Lester's restaging of Aldridge's Othello was necessarily ghosted by a future performance of Othello: the anticipated modernity and effectiveness of Lester's own. Audiences for *Red Velvet*'s 2013 revival would potentially have experienced an additional ghosting: Nicholas Hytner directed Lester in an ultra-modern production set in a Middle Eastern warzone. Lester insisted that their *Othello*

83 Krystyna Kujawinska Courtney, '"Mislike Me Not For My Complexion"', 54n.

84 Theo Bosanquet, 'Adrian Lester Stars in Rubasingham's First Tricycle Season', *Whatsonstage.com* (18 June 2012) <http://www.whatsonstage.com/west-end-theatre/news/06-2012/adrian-lester-stars-in-rubasinghams-first-tricycle_3815.html> accessed 12 March 2015.

85 Daisy Bowie-Sell, 'National Theatre Season', *Telegraph* (25 January 2012) <http://www.telegraph.co.uk/culture/theatre/theatre-news/9038892/National-Theatre-season-Hustle-star-Adrian-Lester-to-play-Othello.html> accessed 12 March 2015.

86 Marvin Carlson, *The Haunted Stage* (Ann Arbor, MI: University of Michigan Press, 2003) 6–7.

was 'not just about [Othello's] colour'.[87] This twenty-first-century setting rendered Iago's racism shockingly archaic. The ghosting of an environment in which, according to Hytner, 'very few people are vocally racist' might also have refocused audience perceptions of *Red Velvet*'s supporting cast.[88] Although racism dominates *Red Velvet*, Charles and Bernard are the only wholehearted racists onstage. Ira, Margaret, Ellen, Pierre and Henry are variously racially progressive, while the 1860s triumvirate of Halina, Casimir and Terence have no discernible issue with Ira's colour. Continuing the identification with Lester's own political valence as an advocate for racial equality and leading black British actor, the progressive characters in *Red Velvet* see Ira's presence and acting style as essential to the theatre becoming, in Pierre's words, 'a political act, a debate of our times'; in Ellen's vocabulary, 'more current'.[89] Their vocabulary recalls twenty-first century advocates for inclusive, radical artistic engagement. Ira's rehearsal behaviour confirms him as a modern actor. He rejects numerous theatrical conventions, facing Desdemona rather than the audience; increased physical intimacy with his leading lady, and taking Ellen's advice.[90] Rather than dominating the stage space, Ira allows Bernard, a supporting actor, to be 'front and centre', an experience Bernard has 'never' had.[91] Ira teaches Ellen new techniques for stage combat, and rejects formal verse-speaking, preferring to 'cheat' the meter.[92] Chakrabarti heightens this modernity further when Ellen identifies Ira's adherence to the 'domestic school': a deliberate anachronism, symbolizing how avant-garde he is.[93] Nevertheless, contemporaries identified the historical Aldridge as essentially melodramatic. Some found him

87 Jasper Rees, 'Adrian Lester Interview' *Telegraph* (16 April 2013) <http://www.telegraph.co.uk/culture/theatre/theatre-features/9998331/Adrian-Lester-interview-Othello-Its-not-just-about-his-colour.html> accessed 12 March 2015.

88 Jennifer Lipman, 'Hytner: Othello's Race "Not a Big Deal" to the Venetians', *Jewish Chronicle Online* (14 May 2013) <http://www.thejc.com/news/uk-news/107483/hytner-othellos-race-not-a-big-deal-venetians> accessed 12 March 2015.

89 Chakrabarti, *Red Velvet*, 48; 50.

90 Chakrabarti, *Red Velvet*, 42–3

91 Chakrabarti, *Red Velvet*, 75.

92 Chakrabarti, *Red Velvet*, 67–8; 40.

93 Chakrabarti, *Red Velvet*, 40.

unoriginal, rather than innovative.[94] When Aldridge was seen as modern, decades later, it was for eschewing violence and 'rant', rather than adopting the 'brutal, more shocking' style Ira advocates in *Red Velvet*.[95]

Ira is also strictly African American, proudly describing his New York training at the African Grove Theater, whose founders were 'burning up with talent [...] we were rough but we had passion', and ascribing its destruction through fire to white arsonists.[96] This clarifies Aldridge's racial identity as uncomplicatedly proud: in fact, Aldridge racially self-fashioned in far more complex and (retrospectively) uncomfortable ways. Although at least third-generation American, Aldridge co-wrote an 1848 *Memoir* asserting that his Baltimore-born father Daniel returned to Senegal as an exiled Fulah prince, fathering Ira there.[97] As late as 1851, Aldridge gave his birthplace as 'Africa' on the British census.[98] Aldridge's elder brother Joshua, meanwhile, identified as American-born.[99]

Lindfors describes a cohesive, loving, extended African-American family financed by Ira Aldridge, but his only enduring link to his American family is nomenclature. A nephew, David, visited England in 1857, then 'neglected' to write. He however named his son Ira Frederick in 1866, and signed himself David I. Aldridge in 1890.[100] The economic outcomes of Joshua Aldridge's family imply financial neglect. Ira didn't have Joshua's address in 1860, and omitted him from his will. Joshua remained a white washer; David was a cook; Ira's little namesake (Joshua's grandson) and his sister didn't attend high school.[101] When Aldridge needed to send his

94 *Guardian and Public Ledger* (11 April 1833), 3 and *London Weekly Journal* (13 April 1833), 3, quoted in Lindfors, *Ira Aldridge*, 155.

95 'Theatres &c.', *Era* (26 April 1857), 10.

96 Chakrabarti, *Red Velvet*, 89.

97 Lindfors, *Ira Aldridge*, 6–7.

98 *1851 England Census*.

99 *1870 United States Census*.

100 Letter from Ira Aldridge (4 June 1860), reprinted Marshall and Stock, *Ira Aldridge*, 250; *United States Census* (1870) [as above]; by 1880, 'Ira Fr Aldridge' was known simply as 'Frederick Aldridge'. *1880 United States Census*.

101 *1880 United States Census*.

son Ira Daniel abroad at nineteen, he chose Australia, not America.[102] The legacy Aldridge bestowed was his name: his sons were Ira Daniel and Frederick Ira, and two of his Australian-born grandsons were Ira Frederick and James Ira.[103] Aldridge certainly varied other aspects of his professional identity based on expediency: he initially adopted the stage-name Keene, a homonym implying his status as Edmund's analogue or successor.[104] This was especially audacious given Charles Kean's existence: instead of biological inheritance, Aldridge thus used cross-racial, artistic genealogies of succession.

Ira Aldridge's self-staging as an exotic African prince was shared by other African-American writers and performers across three centuries. Vincent Carretta notes that the supposedly African-born writer Olaudah Equiano's baptismal record describes him as born in 'Carolina', despite Equiano citing his godmother as someone who supposedly knew him as an African speaking only the language 'of Africa'; a 1773 muster book corroborates his American birth.[105] The magician Benjamin Rucker, better known as 'Black Herman', was born in Virginia in 1892, but claimed to be an African-born Zulu.[106] Blues singer 'Doctor' Clayton claimed to have been born in Africa and raised by 'an American doctor who worked there and adopted him'.[107] Documentary evidence, including his Illinois death

102 Bernth Lindfors, 'The Lost Life of Ira Daniel Aldridge (Part 1)', *Text Matters* 2.2 (2012), 195–208, 196.

103 'Public Member Trees', database, *Ancestry.com* (2015), 'Aldridge' family tree by S.V. Duncan, profiles for Ira Frederick Aldridge (1870–1894, d. Melbourne, Australia) and James Ira Aldridge (1872–1873, d. Melbourne, Australia), accessed 24 March 2015.

104 Errol G. Hill, James V. Hatch, *A History of African American Theatre* (Cambridge: 2003), 42.

105 Vincent Caretta, 'Olaudah Equiano or Gustavus Vassa?', *Slavery and Abolition* 20.3 (1999), 96–105, 102.

106 Frank Cullen, Florence Hackman and Donald McNeilly, 'Black Herman', *Vaudeville Old & New* (London: Taylor & Francis, 2004), I.114–15.

107 David Evans, 'Nicknames of Blues Singers', David Evans, ed., *Ramblin' On My Mind* (Champaign, IL: U of Illinois P, 2008), 179–221, 197.

record, indicates Peter Joe Clayton was born in Georgia, to South African parents, on 19 April 1898.[108]

There are several potential reasons for Aldridge's strategizing. Aldridge may have sought to own his heritage, identifying with Africa rather than the continent which enslaved his forebears. Self-staging as African-born royalty might have been intended to establish his authenticity and legitimacy in roles including princely Oroonoko or the general Othello: high-born Africans, formerly enslaved. Such parallel origins offered semiotic clarity extremely attractive to nineteenth-century audiences, and recalls Carretta's comment on Equiano's incentive to self-fashion as African-born: his 'rhetorical ethos – his authority to speak as a victim and eye-witness of slavery [...] was dependent on the African nativity he claimed'.[109] Aldridge, by assuming an identity perceived as exotic, could have sought to increase his commercial value as a performer. Madge Kendal recalled Aldridge's self-exoticizing performance: as the 1865 Othello, he created a highly fetishistic aesthetic of skin colour, stressing his racial difference from Kendal through 'points' that emphasized the contrast between the colour of their hands. He also reputedly sought the blondest possible Desdemonas.[110] In *Red Velvet*, two similar moments occur, when Ira kisses Ellen's hand in rehearsal, and then in performance.[111] For Ira, both moments are spontaneous and necessary to authentic, intimate performance. Crucially, this commentary on the aesthetic of skin difference is re-ascribed to Henry. His gaucherie that 'you really see the contrast then' becomes a crass moment of fetishization, misunderstanding Ira's instinctive performance, rather than the historical Aldridge's deliberate titillation of an audience with the aesthetics of interracial desire.

108 Jeff Harris, 'Clayton, Peter Joe "Doctor"', Edward Komara, ed., *Encyclopedia of the Blues* (New York: Routledge, 2006), I.213. *Illinois Deaths and Stillbirths, 1916–1947*, database, *Ancestry.com* (2011), entry for Peter Clayton (1898–1947, d. Chicago, Illinois), accessed 27 March 2015.

109 Vincent Caretta, 'Olaudah Equiano or Gustavus Vassa?', 97.

110 Madge Kendal, *Dramatic Opinions* (London: John Murray, 1890), 11 and *By Herself* (London: John Murray, 1933), 86–7.

111 Chakrabarti, *Red Velvet*, 44; 72.

In fact, Kujawinska Courtney's accusation that British and American histories of Aldridge posit him too simplistically as 'the Strange [...] the Other' downplays, like Chakrabarti's insistence on Ira's modernity, how 'strange and other' Aldridge inevitably and deliberately was.[112] Chakrabarti's Ira is personally obstreperous and, by 1867, bitter, but as the result of life-long adversity and opposition to the prevailing racist hegemony, without any possibility of collusion. Nevertheless, Aldridge's self-promotional strategies included an extensive repertory of 'Mungo' and 'Jim Crow' roles. Although he also played nuanced Caribbean folk heroes of melodramas including *Dred* and *Three-Fingered Jack*, the cancelled third performance at Covent Garden was *The Padlock*, not *Othello*. As Mungo, the comic West Indian servant originally written for blackface, Aldridge spoke and sang in a stereotypical slave dialect. Virginia Mason Vaughan notes that critics identified Aldridge's portrayal as depicting a 'veritable nigger': the role was an 'Uncle Tom-like house slave', the 'harbinger of future taste in entertainment'.[113]

Nicholas M. Evans argues that Aldridge's subsequent double bills of Othello and *The Padlock* subverted expectations of Mungo's with Othello's gravity, 'productively confus[ing]' audiences and 'invited [...] interrogation'.[114] Aldridge's reception doesn't suggest this: moreover, Evans's argument only works if *The Padlock* was a curtain-raiser, moving audiences from stereotypical Mungo to Othello's complex subjectivity. But this didn't happen: *The Padlock* is an 'afterpiece'.[115] Visually, Aldridge's Mungo was rooted in minstrelsy stereotypes: he wore a striped suit like Charles Dibdin, Mungo's white creator.[116] Aldridge later replicated T.D. Rice (of 'Jump Jim

112 Kujawinska Courtney, 'Mislike Me Not', 54n.

113 Virginia Mason Vaughan, *Performing Blackness on English Stages, 1500–1800* (Cambridge: Cambridge University Press, 2005), 169.

114 Nicholas M. Evans, 'Ira Aldridge: Shakespeare and Minstrelsy', *ATQ* 16.3 (September 2002), 165–87, 180.

115 Vanessa L. Rogers, 'Bickerstaff, Isaac', Jack Lynch and Gary Day, eds, *Encyclopedia of British Literature 1660–1789* (Oxford: Wiley-Blackwell, 2015), 111–17, 114.

116 Monica L. Miller, *Slaves to Fashion: Black Dandyism and the Styling of Black Diasporic Identity* (Durham, NC: Duke University Press: 2010), 72–3.

Crow' fame)'s originally blackface routines.[117] As Vaughan argues, Aldridge's performance 'pointed the way to [...] the humorous, singing 'nigger' of the minstrel shows'.[118] If Aldridge had played Mungo at Covent Garden, it is fascinating to consider how reappraisals of Aldridge since 2012 would have been affected, given Mungo's omission from *Red Velvet* and the obvious conflict between Aldridge's minstrelsy and Chakrabarti's imaginative project.

In 2012, *Red Velvet*'s performance context reified the play's status as progressive history. It was director Indhu Rubasingham's debut production as the Tricycle's Artistic Director. Rubasingham, the first British South Asian woman to run a major British theatre, strongly countered suggestions that – as the *Guardian* claimed – being 'female and of Asian origin made her the perfect candidate for the Tricycle'.[119] Nevertheless, *Red Velvet*'s diverse creative team and strong revisionist historical agenda were perceived as upholding the Tricycle's 'crowd-pleasing' cultural agenda of attracting more diverse audiences.[120]

Red Velvet's historical elisions, necessary to sustain Chakrabarti's artistic agenda, also reflect a scholarly tendency towards binary oppositions on Aldridge. European acclaim highlights London censure; provincial tolerance shames metropolitan attack. The Covent Garden *Othello* of 1833 has become a critical and theatrical case study. The popular rediscovery of Aldridge, Europe's first successful African American actor, in media, education and actor training is a consummation devoutly to be wished. But Aldridge's presence in popular and scholarly discourse should include awareness of the self-exoticizing, even disturbing strategies which nineteenth-century cultural agendas and economic imperatives made expedient.

117 Waters, *Racism on the Victorian Stage*, 165; Herbert Marshall and Mildred Stock, *Ira Aldridge* (London: Rockliff, 1958), 150–1.

118 Vaughan, *Performing Blackness*, 169.

119 Stephen Moss, 'Tricycle theatre's new director aims for more diverse audience', *Guardian* (19 June 2012) <http://www.theguardian.com/stage/2012/jun/19/tricycle-theatre-director-diverse-audience> accessed 13 March 2015.

120 Ibid. In addition Adrian Lester and Indhu Rubasingham, the original creative team included playwright Lolita Chakrabarti and assistant director Titas Halder, both of whom are British South Asian.

Equally, re-reading and resituating Aldridge's 1833 reception reveals a more complex, intersectional significance for Aldridge, inflected by both class and nationality as well as colour, than has been acknowledged hitherto. The omission and elision of both Aldridge's 'Jim Crow' career and the planned presence of Mungo alongside *Othello* in 1833 reflect our cultural diffidence when restaging the disconcerting nineteenth-century racial other. Twenty-first-century British culture is intensely anxious about the degree to which theatrical reappraisals of racism should graphically recreate said racism. Since *Red Velvet*, the controversy and closure of *Exhibit B* has reflected this. Brett Bailey's 2014 performance project at London's Barbican featured caged, manacled and sometimes topless black performers, symbolizing those exhibited in Victorian 'human zoos'.[121]

It is easy to imagine the controversy if, in 2012, Adrian Lester had moved from depicting Ira as Othello – a physical performance so compelling that Lester found himself tempted to 'strike the legs wide and [cover] his brow' when rehearsing at the National – to Ira preparing Mungo, perhaps singing 'Oppossum up a gumtree' with its lyrics about the 'Nigger in de hollow', or Mungo's aria concluding, 'Poor blacky must run'.[122] Lester is an award-winning musical theatre performer. His standout turn in Kenneth Branagh's 2000 *Love's Labour's Lost* film musical sparked critical concern about 'the visible effort [Lester] puts into "dancing down" to the level of the others', compromising his performance, like a long tradition of black screen performers, to avoid outshining inferior white co-stars.[123]

121 Hugh Muir, 'Slavery Exhibition Featuring Black Actors Chained in Cages Shut Down', *Guardian* (24 September 2014) <http://www.theguardian.com/culture/2014/sep/24/slavery-exhibition-black-actors-cages-shut-down> accessed 30 March 2015.

122 Stephen Moss, 'Adrian Lester and Rory Kinnear', *Guardian* (10 April 2013) <http://www.theguardian.com/stage/2013/apr/10/adrian-lester-rory-kinnear-othello, accessed 29 March 2015>. Kathleena Lucille Roark, *Acting American in the Age of Abolition: Transatlantic Black Celebrity and the Rise of Yankee Theatre, 1787–1827*, PhD thesis at the University of Illinois (Ann Arbor, MI: Proquest, 2007), 121; quoted in Dale Cockrell, *Demons of Disorder* (Cambridge: Cambridge University Press, 1997), 20.

123 Courtney Lehmann, 'Faux Show: Falling into History in Kenneth Branagh's *Love's Labour's Lost*' in Ayanna Thompson, ed., *Colorblind Shakespeare* (London: Routledge, 2006), 69–87, 82.

Simultaneously, Courtney Lehman argued, the film forced Lester into the role of minstrelsy as a 'specialty number' performer, segregated from the mostly white cast.[124] More controversial still in *Red Velvet* would have been a scene where Ira described his excellent remuneration as Mungo, without either racial anguish or the audience-diconcerting subversion Lindfors and Evans hypothesize.

If twenty-first-century society is uncomfortable with historical racism graphically restaged, we are even more uncomfortable with black collusion in it. Excellent writing and performances allow *Red Velvet* to begin Aldridge's popular rehabilitation desirable from any progressive viewpoint. Creative history retains no imperative to total historical fidelity, however likely it is to be co-opted by socio-political agendas. But the juxtaposition of Chakrabarti's creative project of aligning blackness with modernity, with *Red Velvet*'s rapturous reception reveals British society's criteria for making marginal black artists canonical figures. These criteria rest on how this 'modern' black Victorian allows twenty-first-century audiences to see themselves, and on the kinds of black historical identities that can be safely brought forward as role models. *Red Velvet* allows twenty-first-century audiences to comfortably identify with an admirable, modernized and modernizing Aldridge. Ira is as uncomplicatedly staunch in his refusal of racist ideology as *Red Velvet*'s audiences believe themselves to be.

Bibliography

1851 England Census, Parish of All Saints, Borough of Derby. Piece: 2142; Folio: 446; Page: 30.

1880 United States Census, New York City, Roll: 894; Page: 247A; Image: 0488.

'The African Actor', *Spectator* (13 April 1833), 328.

Aldridge, Ira, 'Letter to the Editor', *National Omnibus* (17 May 1833), 60.

124 Ibid.

——, [Anon., with James McCure Smith], *Memoir and Theatrical Career of Ira Aldridge* (London: Ohnwyn, 1850).

Allardyce Nicoll, *A History of Early Nineteenth Century Drama 1800–1850* (Cambridge: Cambridge University Press 1930).

Beatty, Laura, *Manners, Masks and Morals* (London: Chatto and Windus, 1999).

Bosanquet, Theo, 'Adrian Lester Stars in Rubasingham's First Tricycle Season', *Whatsonstage.com* (18 June 2012) <http://www.whatsonstage.com/west-end-theatre/news/06-2012/adrian-lester-stars-in-rubasinghams-first-tricycle_3815.html> accessed 12 March 2015.

Bowie-Sell, Daisy, 'National Theatre Season', *Telegraph* (25 Jan 2012) <http://www.telegraph.co.uk/culture/theatre/theatre-news/9038892/National-Theatre-season-Hustle-star-Adrian-Lester-to-play-Othello.html> accessed 12 March 2015.

Britton, John, and Augustus Welby Pugin, *Illustrations of the Public Buildings of London* (London: J. Taylor, 1825).

Caretta, Vincent, 'Olaudah Equiano or Gustavus Vassa?', *Slavery and Abolition* 20.3 (1999), 96–105.

Carlson, Marvin, *The Haunted Stage* (Ann Arbor, MI: University of Michigan Press, 2003).

Chakrabarti, Lolita, *Red Velvet* (London: Bloomsbury, 2012).

'The Coburg Theatre', *Times* (11 October 1825), 2.

Cockrell, Dale, *Demons of Disorder: Early Blackface Minstrels and Their World* (Cambridge: 1997).

Cornwall, Barry, *The Life of Edmund Kean* (London: E. Moxon, 1835).

'Covent Garden', *Athenaeum* (13 April 1833), 235–6.

'Covent Garden', *Bell's Weekly Messenger* (14 April 1833), 116.

'Covent Garden', *Literary Gazette* (13 April 1833), 236.

'Covent Garden', *National Standard* (20 April 1833), 248.

'Covent Garden', *Times* (16 April 1833), 4.

'Covent Garden Theatre', *Theatrical Observer* (13 April 1833), 1.

'Covent Garden Theatre', *Morning Chronicle* (13 April 1833), 3.

'Covent-Garden Theatre', *Morning Chronicle* (11 April 1833), 2.

Crenshaw, Kimberle, 'Demarginalizing the Intersection of Race and Sex', *University of Chicago Legal Forum* (1989), 137–64.

Cullen, Frank, Florence Hackman and Donald McNeilly, eds, 'Black Herman', *Vaudeville Old & New* (London: Taylor & Francis, 2004), I.114–15.

'Deaths: London and Its Vicinity', *Gentleman's Magazine* (March 1833), 283–4.

'Edmund Kean', *Morning Chronicle* (27 April 1833), 3.

Ellis, Samantha, 'Paul Robeson in Othello, Savoy Theatre, 1930', *Guardian* (3 September 2003) <http://www.theguardian.com/stage/2003/sep/03/theatre> accessed 12 March 2015.

Evans, David, 'Nicknames of Blues Singers', in David Evans ed, *Ramblin' On My Mind: New Perspectives on the Blues* (Champaign, IL: University of Illinois Press, 2008), 179–221.

Evans, Lloyd, 'Racial Tensions', *Spectator* (27 October 2012) <http://www.spectator.co.uk/arts/theatre/8707341/racial-tensions/> accessed 12 March 2015.

Evans, Nicholas M., 'Ira Aldridge: Shakespeare and minstrelsy', *ATQ* 16.3 (September 2002), 165–87.

'Funeral of Mr Kean', *Morning Post* (27 May 1833), 3.

Hall-Witt, Jennifer, *Fashionable Acts: Opera and Elite Culture in London, 1780–1880* (Lebanon, NH: UPNE, 2007).

Harris, Jeff, 'Clayton, Peter Joe "Doctor"', in Edward Komara ed., *Encyclopedia of the Blues* (New York: Routledge, 2006), I.213.

Hill, Errol G. and James V. Hatch, *A History of African American Theatre* (Cambridge: 2003).

Illinois Deaths and Stillbirths, 1916–1947, database, *Ancestry.com* (2011), entry for Peter Clayton (1898–1947, d. Chicago, Illinois), accessed 27 March 2015.

Kellaway, Kate, 'Adrian Lester on Ira Aldridge: "He Was a Pioneer for Black Actors"', *Observer* (7 October 2012) <http://www.theguardian.com/stage/2012/oct/07/red-velvet-tricycle-lester-chakrabarti-rubasingham-interview> accessed 12 March 2015.

Kendal, Madge, *Dramatic Opinions* (London: John Murray, 1890).

——, *Dame Madge Kendal by Herself* (London: John Murray, 1933).

Kidd, William, *Guide to the 'Lions' of London* (London: William Kidd, 1832).

Kujawinska Courtney, Krystyna, '"Mislike Me Not for My Complexion": The First Biography of Ira Aldridge, The First African-American Tragedian (1807–1867)', Bożenna Chylińska, *Ideology and Rhetoric: Constructing America* (Cambridge: Cambridge Scholars, 2009), 53–70.

Lehmann, Courtney, 'Faux Show: Falling into History in Kenneth Branagh's *Love's Labour's Lost*' in Ayanna Thompson, ed., *Colorblind Shakespeare: New Perspectives on Race and Performance* (London: Routledge, 2006), 69–87.

Lindfors, Bernth, *Ira Aldridge: The Early Years 1807–1833* (Rochester NY: University of Rochester Press, 2011).

——. 'The Lost Life of Ira Daniel Aldridge (Part 1)', *Text Matters* 2.2 (2012), 195–208.

Lipman, Jennifer, 'Hytner: Othello's Race "Not a Big Deal" to the Venetians', *Jewish Chronicle Online* (14 May 2013) <http://www.thejc.com/news/uk-news/107483/hytner-othellos-race-not-a-big-deal-venetians> accessed 12 March 2015.

Marshall, Herbert and Mildred Stock, *Ira Aldridge: The Negro Tragedian* (Washington, DC: Howard University Press, 1958).

Mason Vaughan, Virginia, *Performing Blackness on English Stages, 1500–1800* (Cambridge: 2005).

May, Vivian M., *Pursuing Intersectionality* (New York: Routledge, 2015), 1–17.

Miller, Monica L., *Slaves to Fashion: Black Dandyism and the Styling of Black Diasporic Identity* (Duke University Press: 2010).

Moss, Stephen, 'Tricycle Theatre's New Director Aims for More Diverse Audience', *Guardian* (19 June 2012) <http://www.theguardian.com/stage/2012/jun/19/tricycle-theatre-director-diverse-audience> accessed 13 March 2015.

——. 'Adrian Lester and Rory Kinnear: "Othello and Iago Are a Bit Cracked"', *Guardian* (10 April 2013) <http://www.theguardian.com/stage/2013/apr/10/adrian-lester-rory-kinnear-othello> accessed 29 March 2015.

Muir, Hugh, 'Slavery Exhibition Featuring Black Actors Chained in Cages Shut Down', *Guardian* (24 September 2014) <http://www.theguardian.com/culture/2014/sep/24/slavery-exhibition-black-actors-cages-shut-down> accessed 30 March 2015.

Murray Brown, Griselda, 'Dramatic Differences', *Financial Times* (12 October 2012) <http://www.ft.com/cms/s/2/d68e51cc-11fa-11e2-b9fd-00144feabdc0.html> accessed 12 March 2015.

Myers, Anna, '*Red Velvet* Resource Pack' (Powerpoint presentation) Tricycle Theatre (2 October 2012) <http://www.tricycle.co.uk/wp-content/uploads/2012/10/Red-Velvet-Resources.pptx> accessed 12 March 2015.

'Our Omnibus-Box', *Theatre* (November 1882), 307–14.

Paterson, K. David, 'Pandemic and epidemic influenza, 1830–1848', *Social Science and Medicine* 21.5 (1985), 571–80.

'Public Member Trees', database, *Ancestry.com* (2015), 'Aldridge' family tree by S.V. Duncan, profiles for Ira Frederick Aldridge (1870–1894, d. Melbourne, Australia) and James Ira Aldridge (1872–1873, d. Melbourne, Australia), accessed 24 March 2015.

Rees, Jasper, 'Adrian Lester Interview: "It's Not Just about His Colour"' *Telegraph* (16 April 2013), <http://www.telegraph.co.uk/culture/theatre/theatre-features/9998331/Adrian-Lester-interview-Othello-Its-not-just-about-his-colour.html> accessed 12 March 2015.

Roark, Kathleena Lucille, *Acting American in the Age of Abolition: Transatlantic Black Celebrity and the Rise of Yankee Theatre, 1787–1827*, PhD thesis at the University of Illinois (Ann Arbor, MI: Proquest, 2007).

Rogers, Vanessa L., 'Bickerstaff, Isaac', in Jack Lynch and Gary Day eds, *Encyclopedia of British Literature 1660–1789* (Oxford: Wiley-Blackwell, 2015), 111–17.

Rowell, George, *The Old Vic Theatre* (Cambridge: 1993).

Samuel French Ltd., '*Red Velvet* Lolita Chakrabarti', *SamuelFrench.com* (2015) <http://www.samuelfrench.com/p/44465/red-velvet> accessed 12 March 2015.

Schoch, Richard, *Performing History in the Theatre of Charles Kean* (Cambridge: 1996).

Sheppard, F.H.W., 'The Theatre Royal: Management', *Survey of London: Volume 35* (London: London County Council, 1970), 9–29 <http://www.british-history.ac.uk/survey-london/vol35/pp9-29> accessed 15 March 2015.

'Theatres', *Age* (14 April 1833), 118.

'Theatres &c', *Era* (26 April 1857), 10.

'Theatres', *Town Journal* (14 April 1833), 118.

'Theatrical Chit-Chat', *Guardian and the Observer* (14 April 1833), 4.

'Theatricals', *Figaro in London* (11 August 1832), 144.

United States Census (1870), *New York Ward 16, District 8*. Roll: M593_995; Page: 337B; Image: 532.

Walker, Tim, 'Red Velvet, Tricycle Theatre, review', *Telegraph* (1 February 2014) <http://www.telegraph.co.uk/culture/theatre/theatre-reviews/10609578/Red-Velvet-Tricycle-Theatre-review.html> accessed 12 March 2015.

Waters, Hazel, *Racism on the Victorian Stage: Representation of Slavery and the Black Character* (Cambridge: Cambridge University Press, 2007).

Notes on Contributors

ZARA BARLAS, MA, is a PhD candidate and Lecturer at the University of Heidelberg, Germany (Ruprecht-Karls-Universität Heidelberg) as a member of the 'Cluster of Excellence: Asia and Europe in a Global Context'. She specializes in Cultural History, with a particular focus on representations of the 'Other' and cultural exchanges between Britain and pre-partition India.

ARTHUR W. BLOOM is former Dean of Visual and Performing Arts, Kutztown University of Pennsylvania and holds an AB in English from Dartmouth College and a PhD in Theatre History from Yale University. He is the author of *Joseph Jefferson: Dean of the American Theatre* and *Edwin Booth: A Biography and Performance History* and is currently working on a biography of the early nineteenth-century actor Edwin Forrest. After forty years as a teacher and administrator in the arts, he is now retired and devotes himself to mentoring economically disadvantaged students who wish to go to college and for whom he has collected over a million dollars in addition to federal and state scholarships and loans.

MICHAEL BRADSHAW is a specialist in late Romantic poetry and drama, and has published on authors and themes including Thomas Lovell Beddoes, George Darley, Thomas Hood, John Keats, Alan Moore, Walter Savage Landor, Mary and Percy Shelley, *The London Magazine* and the Romantic fragment poem. He is currently working on Romantic-era representations of disability and on the comic poetry of Thomas Hood. He is Head of the Department of English & History at Edge Hill University.

SOPHIE DUNCAN is a Calleva Postdoctoral Researcher at Magdalen College, University of Oxford. Previously she was Supernumerary Fellow in English at Harris Manchester College, Oxford. She researches Shakespeare and Victorian theatre history, and works regularly in professional theatre as a dramaturge and historical advisor.

SERENA GUARRACINO has research interests in performance studies and postcolonial literature, gender and cultural studies, with a particular focus on the relationship between literature and performativity. She received her PhD in Literatures, Cultures, and Histories of Anglophone Countries from the Università di Napoli 'L'Orientale'. She recently authored *La Primadonna all'opera: Scrittura e performance nel mondo anglofono* (2010), and *Donne di passioni: Personagge della lirica tra differenza sessuale, classe e razza* (2011), the latter on contemporary rewritings of *Carmen* and *Madama Butterfly* from a postcolonial perspective. She also co-edited (with Marina Vitale) a double issue for the journal *AION Anglistica* titled *Voicings: Musica across Borders* (13.1–2, 2009). She currently teaches eighteenth- and nineteenth-century English Literature at the Università di Napoli 'L'Orientale'. She is member of the scientific board of the Società italiana delle letterate (Italian Society of Women Scholars of Literature).

SARA MALTON is Associate Professor of English at Saint Mary's University in Halifax, Canada, where she specializes in nineteenth-century literature, especially the intersection of fiction, finance and law. After receiving her PhD from the University of Toronto, she went onto a Postdoctoral Fellowship at Cornell University and thereafter joined Saint Mary's in 2005. Her book, *Forgery in Nineteenth-Century Literature and Culture: Fictions of Finance from Dickens to Wilde*, was published by Palgrave-Macmillan in 2009. Her work has also appeared in such journals as *Studies in the Novel, Victorian Literature and Culture* and the *European Romantic Review*. She is currently serving as a Trustee of the Dickens Society, and will host the 2015 Annual Dickens Society Symposium in Halifax.

TIZIANA MOROSETTI teaches at the African Studies Centre of the University of Oxford. She studied in Rome and Bologna before moving to Oxford on a Marie Curie Research Fellowship with a project on the representation of the 'exotic' body in nineteenth-century British drama. Her publications have appeared in *Research in African Literatures, West Africa Review, West African Theatre and Performing Arts Journal* and the Oxford Dictionary of African Biography. She is deputy director of the journal *Quaderni del '900*, for which she edited numbers IV (*Postcolonial*

Literature in Italian, 2005) and VII (*Italy in Anglophone Literatures*, 2008). Since 2014 she has been membership secretary of the African Theatre Association (AfTA).

MARIANNE SCHULTZ has an MA in Performing Arts from Middlesex University, London, and an MLitt in History from the University of Auckland, where she also completed her PhD in History with a thesis entitled *'A Harmony of Frenzy': New Zealand performed on the Stage, Screen and Airwaves, 1862 to 1940.* She is currently the Auckland Advisor for Dance Aotearoa New Zealand (DANZ) and Honorary Teaching Fellow, History, University of Auckland. Amongst her publications: 'Tracing the Steps of Modern and Contemporary Dance in Twentieth-Century New Zealand' (in Ralph Buck and Nicholas Rowe, eds, *Moving Oceans: Celebrating Dance in the South Pacific*, Oxford, 2013); '"Sons of the Empire": Dance and the New Zealand Male' (*Dance Research*, 29, 1, 2011); 'Phantom Limbs: Concert Dance in New Zealand from the 1930s to the 1980s' (New Zealand Journal of History, 45, 2, 2011), and '"The Best Entertainment of Its Kind Ever Witnessed in New Zealand": The Rev. Frederick Augustus Bennett, the Rotorua Maori Entertainers and the story of Hinemoa and Tutanekai' (*Melbourne Historical Journal*, 39, 2011), which was awarded the Greg Dening Memorial Prize of the *Melbourne Historical Journal*. She held the Keith Sinclair Memorial Scholarship in New Zealand History and was awarded Best Research, New Zealand Documentary, at the Documentary Edge Film Festival. Her monograph *Performing Indigenous Culture on Stage and Screen* will be published by Palgrave Macmillan in 2016.

TONI WEIN (California State University at Fresno) studied with some of the twentieth century's finest acting teachers, such as Sanford Meisner, Uta Hagen and Stella Adler, and later carried that training onto a smaller academic stage. She obtained her PhD as a Romanticist from UC Berkeley, and has taught at a variety of American institutions, including Princeton and Gettysburg College. Her work today comes from a larger project entitled 'Monstrous Fellowship: "Pagan, Turk and Jew" in Romantic England' that studies intersecting representations of the Irish, the Turks and the Jews in a range of popular culture fora.

PETER YEANDLE is Lecturer in Modern History at the University of Loughborough. He was Research Associate on the AHRC-funded 'Cultural History of English Pantomime, 1837–1901' directed by Professor Katherine Newey and Professor Jeffrey Richards. His research interests include the interrelationships of popular imperialism and popular culture in particular and the cultural history of nineteenth- and twentieth-century Britain in general. He is the author of several essays on the teaching of history, and his monograph *Citizenship, Nation, Empire: The Politics of History Teaching in England, c. 1870–1930* was published by Manchester University Press in 2015. He is co-editor of a special issue of the *Journal of Imperial and Commonwealth History* 42/5 (2014) on the imperial hero in an age of decolonization. His current project focuses on Victorian performance and exhibition culture, and includes the study of theatre, zoos, circuses and museums. He is also lead editor on *Politics, Performance and Popular Culture: Theatre and Society in Nineteenth-Century Britain*, forthcoming with Manchester University Press.

Index

Writing and Culture in the Long Nineteenth Century

Edited by J.B. Bullen and Isobel Armstrong

The long nineteenth century, extending from the Napoleonic Wars to the First World War, is a rich and complex period of cultural interaction. This series aims to publish the work of scholars and critics whose interests lie within this period. Some of the volumes will deal with issues in literature, art, the sciences, philosophy or economics; others will address the intersection between the written word, the visual and decorative arts, architecture, and music. Many scholars are now working on the cultural matrix out of which these forms emerge, and recent critical thinking has shown the importance of the prevailing economic, political, scientific and philosophical climate in creating the appropriate conditions for artistic production. Some of the series volumes will focus on specific writers and texts; others will deal with the connection between writing and the broader cultural horizon. All will contribute significantly to the widening sphere of nineteenth-century literary studies.

Proposals are welcome for monographs or edited collections. Those interested in contributing to the series should send a detailed project outline either to one of the series editors or to oxford@peterlang.com.

Published Volumes

Simon Gatrell: Thomas Hardy Writing Dress
2011. ISBN 978-3-0343-0739-0.

Anthony Patterson: Mrs Grundy's Enemies: Censorship, Realist Fiction and the Politics of Sexual Representation
2013. ISBN 978-3-0343-0887-8.

Ingrid Hanson, Wilfred Jack Rhoden and E. E. Snyder (eds): Poetry, Politics and Pictures: Culture and Identity in Europe, 1840–1914
2013. ISBN 978-3-0343-0981-3.

Phillippa Bennett: Wonderlands: The Last Romances of William Morris
2015. ISBN 978-3-0343-0930-1.

Tiziana Morosetti (ed.): Staging the Other in Nineteenth-Century British Drama
2015. ISBN 978-3-0343-1928-7.